SPIRITUALITY AND THE

This book presents a broad philosophical study of the nature of spirituality and its relationship to human well-being, addressing an area of contemporary philosophy that has been largely underexplored. David McPherson brings together a team of scholars to examine the importance of specific spiritual practices (including prayer, contemplation, and ritual observance) and spiritually informed virtues (such as piety, humility, and existential gratitude) for "the good life." This volume also considers and exemplifies how philosophy itself, when undertaken as a humanistic rather than scientistic enterprise, can be a spiritual exercise and part of a spiritual way of life. Clarifying key concepts, and engaging with major religious traditions such as Judaism, Christianity, Islam, Buddhism, and Confucianism, this book will appeal to students and scholars from various disciplines, including theology, sociology, and psychology, as well as to philosophers, ethicists, and other readers who are interested in modern spiritual life.

DAVID MCPHERSON is an assistant professor of philosophy at Creighton University. His research focuses on ethics and philosophy of religion, and has appeared in philosophical journals including *Philosophy, Religious Studies: An International Journal for the Philosophy of Religion*, and *American Catholic Philosophical Quarterly*.

SPIRITUALITY AND THE GOOD LIFE

Philosophical Approaches

EDITED BY

DAVID MCPHERSON

Creighton University

CAMBRIDGE
UNIVERSITY PRESS

CAMBRIDGE
UNIVERSITY PRESS

University Printing House, Cambridge CB2 8BS, United Kingdom

One Liberty Plaza, 20th Floor, New York, NY 10006, USA

477 Williamstown Road, Port Melbourne, VIC 3207, Australia

314-321, 3rd Floor, Plot 3, Splendor Forum, Jasola District Centre, New Delhi - 110025, India

79 Anson Road, #06-04/06, Singapore 079906

Cambridge University Press is part of the University of Cambridge.

It furthers the University's mission by disseminating knowledge in the pursuit of education, learning and research at the highest international levels of excellence.

www.cambridge.org
Information on this title: www.cambridge.org/9781107589681
DOI: 10.1017/9781316459461

First published 2017
First paperback edition 2019

A catalogue record for this publication is available from the British Library

Library of Congress Cataloging in Publication data
NAMES: McPherson, David (Assistant Professor of Philosophy), editor.
TITLE: Spirituality and the good life : philosophical approaches / edited by David McPherson, Creighton University
DESCRIPTION: New York : Cambridge University Press, 2017. | Includes bibliographical references and index.
IDENTIFIERS: LCCN 2017026032 | ISBN 9781107133006
SUBJECTS: LCSH: Spiritual life. | Religious life. | Conduct of life. | Spirituality. | Philosophy and religion.
CLASSIFICATION: LCC BL624 .S6925 2017 | DDC 204.01–dc23
LC record available at https://lccn.loc.gov/2017026032

ISBN 978-1-107-13300-6 Hardback
ISBN 978-1-107-58968-1 Paperback

For Stan Harrison, teacher and friend

Contents

Contributors

MUKHTAR H. ALI, Visiting Assistant Professor of Arabic, Claremont McKenna College

JOHN COTTINGHAM, Professor Emeritus of Philosophy, University of Reading; Professor of Philosophy of Religion, University of Roehampton

CORA DIAMOND, Professor Emerita of Philosophy, University of Virginia

FIONA ELLIS, Professor of Philosophy, University of Roehampton

SAMUEL FLEISCHACKER, Professor of Philosophy and Director of Jewish Studies, University of Illinois at Chicago

JOHN HOUSTON, Assistant Professor of Philosophy, College of Saint Benedict and Saint John's University

DAVID MCPHERSON, Assistant Professor of Philosophy, Creighton University

ROBERT C. ROBERTS, Professor Emeritus of Philosophy, Baylor University; Chair of Ethics and Emotion Theory, Jubilee Centre for Character and Virtues, University of Birmingham

MAY SIM, Professor of Philosophy, College of the Holy Cross

KAREN STOHR, Associate Professor of Philosophy and Senior Research Scholar of the Kennedy Institute of Ethics, Georgetown University

RICHARD WHITE, Professor of Philosophy, Creighton University

MARK R. WYNN, Professor of Philosophy and Religion, University of Leeds

Acknowledgments

I would like to acknowledge with gratitude the generosity of Creighton University's Kripke Center for the Study of Religion and Society for a summer research grant that enabled me to work on this edited collection. Additionally, I thank the contributors for their excellent contributions, and for all the enriching exchanges in the process. I would like especially to express my gratitude to John Cottingham for his early support and encouragement with regard to this project, which helped to get it off the ground. Special thanks are due as well to Hilary Gaskin, my editor at Cambridge University Press, for all her support and good advice along the way. I wish also to express my deep love and gratitude to my wife, Kirstin, and our children, Clare and John, for all their love and support. Finally, I dedicate this volume to my teacher and friend Stan Harrison, who helped to foster and encourage in me a philosophical way of life that was also a spiritual way of life.

Introduction

David McPherson

In contemporary secular societies, many people would acknowledge a concern for something called "spirituality," even if they are not "religious" in any conventional sense. There is a recognition that human beings have what might be called "spiritual needs," in addition to their "material needs," and that fulfilling these needs is important for living well as human beings.[1] This is perhaps most dramatically illustrated in the common phenomenon of someone having a "midlife crisis," i.e., the person who may be successful in material terms but nevertheless feels a sense of existential malaise: there is an experience here of a lack of a deeper sense of meaning in life. But this experience and the questions it involves can arise for anyone provided he or she has reached a certain level of reflectiveness and self-awareness.

This collection of essays will examine the nature of spirituality and how it can contribute to "the good life" for human beings.[2] The editor's own general working definition of spirituality is that it is *a practical life-orientation that is shaped by what is taken to be a self-transcending source of meaning, which involves strong normative demands, including demands of the sacred or the reverence-worthy*. To unpack this definition some here (it is filled out more in Chapter 4): spirituality involves *spiritual practices* – e.g., practices of prayer, meditation, self-examination, repentance, mindfulness, study, contemplation, worship, thanksgiving, communal living, charity, fasting, keeping the Sabbath, ritual observance, going on retreats or pilgrimages, imitating saints, habituation in virtue, etc. – that aim to *direct and transform one's life as a whole* toward increasing spiritual fulfillment, i.e., toward a more meaningful life. The meaning that makes for a meaningful life here is "strong evaluative meaning," i.e., meaning or value with which we *ought*

[1] See J. Cottingham, *The Spiritual Dimension: Religion, Philosophy and Human Value* (Cambridge University Press, 2005), 3.

[2] In speaking of how spirituality *can* contribute to the good life, I acknowledge that there may be forms of spirituality that do not so contribute and may even be harmful. I take up this concern in my contribution.

to be concerned and toward which we ought to orient our lives (which can and often does connect up with a concern for *the* meaning of life; i.e., there is a concern here with how our lives fit into the grand scheme of things and whether there is a cosmic or "ultimate" source of meaning to which we must align our lives). Hence, spirituality is a practical life-orientation that is shaped by what is taken to be a *self-transcending source of meaning*, which involves *strong normative demands*. Especially important among these demands are those of *the sacred* or *the reverence-worthy* (used equivalently), which are "set apart" in that they place the strongest demands on us and play a central guiding role in our practical life-orientations.

This definition of spirituality, I believe, captures well the "spiritual" concerns of the different contributors, even though they might emphasize different aspects or state things in somewhat different terms. The dominant concerns here have to do with discovering a deeper sense of meaning in life, the place of the sacred or the reverence-worthy in human life, the quality and orientation of one's interior life, and the importance of specific spiritual practices and oft-neglected and sometimes contested virtues such as piety, humility, and existential gratitude.

This collection will also explore questions about the relationship between spirituality and religion: Are they distinct, and if so how? Even if they are distinct, does spirituality, at its best, lead to religion? How might specific religious traditions help to foster and enhance the spiritual life? As suggested previously, many people today would describe themselves as "spiritual but not religious," and one might take this to be a feature of our living in a secular age, where religion is often thought to have less significance. However, in *A Secular Age*, Charles Taylor argues that we should not understand secularity simply as the decline of traditional religious belief and practice and their perceived significance or as the removal of religion from public life (though both of these may be true in many cases). Rather, it should be understood primarily as a situation in which a religious life is seen as "one option among others, and frequently not the easiest to embrace." Taylor goes on to remark: "An age or society [is] secular or not, in virtue of the conditions of experience of and search for the spiritual."[3] He also describes this as the experience of and search for "fullness": "We all see our lives, and/or the space wherein we live our lives, as having a certain moral/spiritual shape. Somewhere, in some activity, or condition, lies a fullness, a richness; that is, in that place (activity or condition), life is fuller, richer, deeper, more worth while, more admirable,

[3] C. Taylor, *A Secular Age* (Cambridge, MA: The Belknap Press of Harvard University Press, 2007), 3.

more what it should be."[4] Living in a secular age thus means that many of us will be "spiritual seekers" and with this comes the possibility that the search might fail and we can experience "exile," in which "we lose a sense of where the place of fullness is, even of what fullness could consist in; we feel we've forgotten what it would look like, or cannot believe in it any more. But the misery of absence, of loss, is still there."[5] This leaves open the possibility that the "experience of and search for the spiritual" may require completion in religious terms.

This contested issue and others explored in this collection will be approached *philosophically*, and hence the subtitle: "philosophical approaches." Although the topic of spirituality has been explored extensively in empirical psychology, it is noteworthy that it has suffered neglect within the academic discipline of philosophy, and most glaringly within specializations such as philosophy of religion and virtue ethics, where one might expect to find an interest in spirituality, whether with respect to its relationship to religion (in the case of philosophy of religion) or to the good life (in the case of virtue ethics).[6] This neglect is somewhat surprising given the prevalence and importance of spirituality in human life throughout recorded history up to the present, and given that spirituality connects up with concerns about meaning in life that are often what draw people to philosophy in the first place.[7] However, the neglect is not entirely surprising. Many philosophers are likely to be suspicious of the idea of "spirituality," which can seem overly

[4] Taylor, *A Secular Age*, 5.

[5] Taylor, *A Secular Age*, 6; cf. 302–20; cf. C. Taylor, *Sources of the Self: The Making of Modern Identity* (Cambridge, MA: Harvard University Press, 1989), 17–18.

[6] In regard to empirical psychology and spirituality, see, e.g., L. J. Miller (ed.), *The Oxford Handbook of Psychology and Spirituality* (Oxford University Press, 2012). By contrast, in W. J. Wainwright (ed.), *The Oxford Handbook of Philosophy of Religion* (Oxford University Press, 2005), there is no chapter on spirituality (the closest is one on "Mysticism and Religious Experience") and not even an entry for it in the index. I take up the issue of the neglect of spirituality in contemporary virtue ethics in my contribution. The same neglect is not there in empirical psychology accounts of character and virtues: see C. Peterson and M. E. P. Seligman, *Character Strengths and Virtues: A Handbook and Classification* (Oxford University Press, 2004), where the last "character strength" discussed is "transcendence" (chs. 23–7; ch. 27 is specifically entitled "Spirituality"). The topic of spirituality of course has not been completely neglected by philosophers (as can be seen by consulting the bibliography), but it has been very much a marginal focus in the discipline, including in philosophy of religion and virtue ethics.

[7] There has been some growth in the philosophical literature on meaning in life: see, e.g., J. Cottingham, *On the Meaning of Life* (New York: Routledge, 2003); S. Wolf, *Meaning in Life and Why It Matters* (Princeton University Press, 2010); D. Benatar (ed.), *Life, Death, and Meaning*, 2nd ed. (Lanham, MD: Rowman & Littlefield, 2010); J. Seachris, *Exploring the Meaning of Life: An Anthology and Guide* (Malden, MA: Wiley-Blackwell, 2013); and T. Metz, *Meaning* in *Life* (Oxford University Press, 2013). However, with the exception of the first of these, there has been very little explicit discussion of the connection between spirituality and meaning in life.

vague (though this just calls for philosophical clarification), too focused on inward life (in a way that is not easily amenable to the abstract or "disengaged" modes of discourse that are common in the discipline), "mystical" or "new-agey," and problematically dualistic (or "spooky") in referring to matters of "the spirit." The latter concern also points to the prominence of certain forms of "naturalism" within contemporary academic philosophy that can be resistant to "spiritual matters." Naturalism is typically (though not always) seen as opposed to "the supernatural." It can also have a scientistic aspect that privileges a "disengaged" (or third-personal or observational) standpoint that prescinds from our "engaged" (or first-personal) experiences of the meaning of things for us. "Scientific naturalism" can go so far as to try to circumscribe reality within the bounds of what the natural sciences can validate, and it may also seek to offer reductive explanations of first-personal experiences of meaning or value (e.g., in terms of our brain "wiring," or a stimulus-response mechanism, or something else of the sort).[8] This collection challenges scientistic outlooks (especially with regard to their ability to make sense of our lives) and seeks to get past the aforementioned concerns and to put the topic of spirituality firmly on the contemporary philosophical agenda by showing the extent to which it connects with central questions about the good life for human beings.

This volume can be seen as heeding the call for a more "humane" mode of philosophy (as opposed to scientistic modes), where it is regarded, as Bernard Williams puts it, "as part of a wider humanistic enterprise of making sense of ourselves and of our activities," and where this takes place "in the situation in which we find ourselves."[9] Relatedly, this collection can also be seen as seeking to recover an ancient conception of philosophy

[8] There are forms of "expansive naturalism" that seek to account for our first-personal experiences of meaning or value and show their validity. On "scientific naturalism" vs. "expansive naturalism," see F. Ellis, *God, Value, and Nature* (Oxford University Press, 2014), which argues for a type of expansive naturalism that is compatible with theism. This distinction has also been described in terms of "strict naturalism" vs. "liberal naturalism" or "broad naturalism"; see S. Goetz and C. Taliaferro, *Naturalism* (Grand Rapids, MI: Eerdmans, 2008); M. De Caro and D. Macarthur (eds.), *Naturalism in Question* (Cambridge, MA: Harvard University Press, 2004); M. De Caro and D. Macarthur (eds.), *Naturalism and Normativity* (New York: Columbia University Press, 2010). De Caro and Macarthur distinguish between an *ontological scientific naturalist*, who "holds that the entities posited by acceptable scientific explanations are the *only* genuine entities that there are," and a *methodological (or epistemological) scientific naturalist*, who "holds that it is *only* by following the methods of the natural sciences – or, at a minimum, the empirical methods of a posteriori inquiry – that one arrives at genuine knowledge" (*Naturalism in Question*, 7). Of course, these types of scientific naturalism can also be combined.

[9] B. Williams, *Philosophy as a Humanistic Discipline* (Princeton University Press, 2006), 197, 182; see also J. Cottingham, "What Is Humane Philosophy and Why Is It At Risk?," *Royal Institute of*

as itself a "spiritual exercise" and part of a "way of life." Regarding this conception, Pierre Hadot writes:

> The [ancient] philosophical school . . . corresponds, above all, to the choice of a certain way of life and existential option which demands from the individual a total change of lifestyle, a conversion of one's entire being, and ultimately a certain desire to be and to live in a certain way. This existential option, in turn, implies a certain vision of the world, and the task of philosophical discourse will therefore be to reveal and rationally justify this existential option, as well as this representation of the world.[10]

Elsewhere he writes:

> Under normal circumstances, the only state accessible to [human beings] is *philo-sophia*: the love of, and progress toward, wisdom. For this reason, spiritual exercises must be taken up again and again, in an ever-renewed effort. . . . To the same extent that the philosophical life is equivalent to the practice of spiritual exercises, it is also a tearing away from everyday life. It is a conversion, a total transformation of one's vision, life-style, and behavior.[11]

In the first essay, "Philosophy, Religion, and Spirituality," John Cottingham explores this conception of philosophy in more detail. He distinguishes between philosophy as a specialized academic discipline, which is often concerned with a careful examination of our concepts, and philosophy as a way of life, which is concerned with an examination of the overall meaning and purpose of our lives and with the "care of the soul," i.e., cultivating a life of integrity and virtue. Cottingham sees the latter conception of philosophy as clearly connected with "spiritual" concerns, and he explores this connection in the essay, first by seeking to get clear on what is meant by "spiritual" and "spirituality" (thus employing the first kind of examination in service of the second). He also explores how these spiritual concerns connect up with a religious outlook of a traditional theistic sort. Cottingham argues that when we examine common spiritual experiences, they often involve cosmic and moral dimensions that are not easily accounted for by a purely secular (i.e., non-religious) framework, but rather seem to point toward a religious framework, especially a theistic one, as what may be needed for sense-making.

Philosophy Supplement, 65 (2009), 233–55; J. Cottingham, *Philosophy of Religion: Towards a More Humane Approach* (Cambridge University Press, 2014).

[10] P. Hadot, *What Is Ancient Philosophy?*, trans. M. Case (Cambridge, MA: The Belknap Press of Harvard University Press, 2004), 3.

[11] P. Hadot, *Philosophy as a Way of Life: Spiritual Exercises from Socrates to Foucault*, ed. A. Davidson, trans. M. Chase (Malden, MA: Blackwell Publishing, 1995), 103.

In "The Problem of Impiety," Cora Diamond discusses Hume's critique of the absolute prohibition of suicide among religious people of his day, which he regarded as mere superstition. Diamond uses this to highlight what she calls "the problem of impiety": can any way of acting be ruled out as impious without appealing to divine prohibition? In other words, can human reason identify certain domains as being set apart as sacred or reverence-worthy and so as being absolutely inviolable? Diamond discusses different responses to this problem and how it pertains not just to the issue of suicide, but also to our treatment of the dead and to a host of controversial issues in biomedical, sexual, and environmental ethics. Moreover, she contends that it illustrates the difference between the sort of objectivity proper to science and that which is proper to ethics. Drawing on Iris Murdoch's work, Diamond suggests that our moral concepts are deep moral configurations of the world, rather than merely different ways of judging the facts of a common world. She also draws on the work of Elizabeth Anscombe and others to explore how our moral concepts, such as the pious and the impious, can capture important truths about the world.

Whereas Diamond explores the possibility of a non-religious understanding of piety, in "The Virtue of Piety," Robert C. Roberts discusses piety as a religious virtue. Drawing on Plato's *Euthyphro*, Roberts discusses filial piety as a prelude to thinking about piety toward God. Filial piety, he argues, involves a reverence toward one's parents simply *as* one's parents, as the source of one's existence. This is an analogue for piety toward God, who is the *fundamental* source of all existence. But there is a crucial difference: whereas filial piety is directed toward one's parents in the *role* of parents, even if they are not good parents, piety toward God, properly construed, involves an affirmation of God's perfect goodness or "glory." Piety as a virtue is thus "a developed and temporally stable disposition to appreciate the glory of God and his creation and thus to feel inhibited from actions that violate its order, including, importantly, the glory of parenthood and inhibition from actions and thoughts that violate it." Roberts argues that this theistic account of the "glory of creation" (rather than mere divine command) can help make sense of the sort of examples of impiety that Diamond discusses.

In "*Homo Religiosus*: Does Spirituality Have a Place in Neo-Aristotelian Virtue Ethics?," I explore the place of spirituality within a neo-Aristotelian account of the good life. First, I lay out my understanding of spirituality. Second, I discuss why neo-Aristotelians have often ignored or explicitly excluded from consideration the issue of the place of spirituality in the good life. I suggest that a lot turns on how one understands the "ethical naturalism" to which neo-Aristotelians are committed. Third, I argue that through a deeper exploration of the evaluative standpoint from within our human form of life as "meaning-seeking animals" we can come to appreciate better the importance of spirituality for human beings throughout recorded history up to the present and why we can be described as *homo religiosus*. I also discuss the draw to theistic spirituality in particular. Finally, I consider and respond to three important objections to giving spirituality, especially theistic spirituality, a central place within the good life: viz., (1) the wholeness objection; (2) the autonomy objection; and (3) the social peace objection.

In "Desire and the Spiritual Life," Fiona Ellis notes a common objection, articulated by Nietzsche and others, against traditional religious forms of spirituality: it supposes that religious outlooks, such as Christianity and Buddhism, deny a place for desire in the spiritual life by regarding desire as *undesirable* and so as something to be transcended. The charge then is that these views denigrate our this-worldly existence (a version of "the wholeness objection"). Ellis questions the fairness of this objection and seeks to give an account of the proper place of desire in the spiritual life that avoids both a problematic otherworldliness that rejects all desire and an equally problematic blank acceptance of desire. Some desires are desirable; some are not. To make sense of this, Ellis suggests that we need to move beyond a focus on appetitive desire to recognize non-appetitive desires that are responsive to objective values. It is such desires that are proper to the spiritual life. Ellis argues that this concession to "Platonism" (of a sort common to theistic religion) need not involve any problematic otherworldliness, and she further argues that Schopenhauer's work (representative of a Buddhist-type outlook) can be read in this light.

In "Between Heaven and Earth: Sensory Experience and the Goods of the Spiritual Life," Mark R. Wynn draws on Aquinas's account of infused moral virtue to explore a kind of good of the spiritual life that is "between heaven and earth" in that it concerns our relationship to created things as properly ordered to our relationship with God and so is a "hybrid good." Wynn also draws on William James's discussion of conversion experience to explore how the senses can contribute to the realization of such goods. The important point is that religious converts "enjoy not only a new relationship to God, but also a newly enlivened appreciation of the everyday sensory world," a "transfiguration" in light of "divine glory." There can be two key forms of perceptual change here: (1) "a deepened sense of the significance of the sensory order considered as a whole," i.e., a general change in "hue"; and (2) "a deepened sense of the differentiated significance of objects," i.e., specific changes in "salience." Wynn thus seeks to show how achieving the goods of the spiritual life not only involves the proper ordering of our thoughts, feelings, attitudes, and behavior, but also a heightened quality of sensory experience.

In "The Jewish Sabbath as a Spiritual Practice," Samuel Fleischacker explores the nature and significance of keeping Shabbat, which is central to Jewish life. Fleischacker discusses how Shabbat as a spiritual practice is first of all about *not* doing certain things, thereby relieving us of concern for material needs and work (even ideal work) and making room for other important activities: viz., spending time with family and friends, sharing meals, singing, reading, praying, worshipping, attending religious services, and otherwise living out and contemplating the "telos of creation." The restraints of Shabbat also shape our lives as a whole through cultivating and enacting a "Shabbat-consciousness," which includes cultivating a humility that frees us from various forms of idolatry. Shabbat provides a "frame" with which to appreciate our work and the goodness of creation; it also helps us to perceive the world and human life in a particularly Jewish way (cf. Wynn on perceptual change resulting from religious conversion). Additionally, Fleischacker shows how the structure of Shabbat connects up with central aspects of Jewish theology, such as negative theology and the avoidance of idolatry. He ends with some reflections on what keeping Shabbat has to teach us about spiritual practices and spirituality in general.

In "The Power of the Spoken Word: Prayer, Invocation, and Supplication in Islam," Mukhtar H. Ali examines the role of the spoken word in Islamic spirituality. He begins by discussing "the Word" in Creation and in the Qurʾān and how they along with the human soul are seen as mirrors of one another, as knowledge of each can lead to a better understanding of the others, and in the case of the human soul, it is perfected by actualizing the realities of the Qurʾānic verses within itself. Here the Islamic spiritual practices of prayer, invocation, and supplication have great importance, as Ali goes on to explore. These practices help to cultivate attitudes of worship, gratitude, and humility, as well as the remembrance of God as central to Islamic spiritual life. Ali's discussion here can be seen as providing a response to a common charge against theism as undermining human well-being in making us submissive to God (a version of "the autonomy objection"): for Ali, humble submissiveness to God in prayer, invocation, and supplication is in fact most truly liberating as it contributes to our human perfection and spiritual awakening.

In "Aristotelian Friendship and Ignatian Companionship," Karen Stohr draws on Aristotle's account of friendship and St. Ignatius of Loyola's account of companionship to consider how we can be a good friend or companion to others during their times of despair, grief, suffering, and isolation that are occasioned by serious illness, trauma, or death. The key issue here is how we can cultivate and practice a way of being fully present (or "coming close") to others during such times. Stohr argues that this requires that we accompany them on a difficult journey along an uncertain path and become aware of and then avoid our tendencies to make others' suffering into something more palatable for ourselves (in order to cope with our own fears and insecurities) and thereby fail to be fully present to others in their suffering and so to be a genuine source of consolation. Drawing inspiration from St. Ignatius's *Spiritual Exercises*, she writes: "Ignatian consolation requires that we *be* the presence of God for another, but it does not ask us to make sense of God or the suffering."

The issue of suffering is taken up in a different spiritual context in Richard White's "Starting with Compassion." White draws on the Buddhist tradition, though, as his title suggests, he seeks to provide, with his account of compassion, a starting point for anyone interested in the spiritual life, since an authentic spiritual life must take us beyond our selves. Compassion can also be a path toward and expressive of a spiritual wisdom regarding the world and our place within it. Here there is a primacy of practice over theory. White first discusses the nature of compassion, which he contrasts with pity and empathy. He also contrasts a typical Western conception of compassion as a self-achievement (i.e., a personal virtue) with the Buddhist conception as a self-overcoming. Next, he considers and responds to some common objections to compassion by Western philosophers (viz., the Stoics, Kant, and Nietzsche), who consider it a vice insofar as it expresses weakness and abandons personal autonomy. White argues that compassion in fact often expresses inner strength and the abandonment of selfish concerns is a good thing. Finally, White explores some practical ways of enhancing compassion in our lives and thereby also achieving greater spiritual enlightenment.

In "Identifying with the Confucian Heaven: Immanent and Transcendent *Dao*," May Sim explores the question of whether Confucianism should be seen merely as a moral philosophy or as a moral philosophy *and* religion. Against those who deny its status as a religion, Sim seeks to show that Confucianism can be seen as affirming transcendent values and thus counting as a religion and offering a "spiritual way of life." In particular, though it differs from Western theistic religions in certain respects, Sim argues that Confucianism offers an account of the divine ("Heaven," or *tian*) that is the ultimate source of all things, and it also offers an ideal of ultimate personal transformation (i.e., "sagehood") that requires aligning oneself with a cosmic source of meaning and ethical purposiveness (i.e., "identifying with the Confucian Heaven"). She makes her case by exploring the goal of becoming Heaven-like in the writings of Confucius and Mencius, which requires that we align ourselves with the way (*dao*) of Heaven as expressed in the standards of ritual propriety (*li*) within a culture embodying the *dao*, or in our virtue-inclined human nature, or in the goodness inherent in the wider world.

In the final essay, "Agnostic Spirituality," John Houston writes on behalf of the agnostic who falls somewhere between the extremes of the confident, self-satisfied religious believer and the confident, self-satisfied unbeliever. He calls attention to a not uncommon phenomenon that is rarely considered by these extremes: viz., the person who deeply and perhaps desperately wants to believe in God (under some conception) because of the great goods of religious faith (understood here as *theistic* faith), but is simply *unable*. And when this involves the loss of a previously cherished faith, the resulting experience can be disorienting and sometimes crushing. Houston is thus concerned with a particular kind of agnosticism, viz., "open" or "Socratic" agnosticism, which claims ignorance of matters of religious faith and ultimate reality, but is still very much concerned with them. Houston then draws on scripture and the work of William James to make the case for an agnostic spirituality that seeks to maintain religious faith without belief, on the basis of hope, where one acts *as though* God exists.

It is my hope as the editor of this collection that these essays will prove both intellectually and spiritually beneficial for the reader.

CHAPTER I

Philosophy, Religion, and Spirituality

John Cottingham

The Role of Philosophy

Philosophy has long been a contested subject, and there have been, and still are, many different and often conflicting conceptions of its proper scope and aims. But if we go back to how its founding father, Socrates, conceived of the philosophical enterprise, we find one element that has continued to be central to much if not all subsequent philosophizing, that of *critical scrutiny* or *examination* (in Greek *exetasis*), encapsulated in Socrates' famous pronouncement at his trial, "the unexamined life is not worth living."[1] For Socrates, such "examination" meant, in the first place, a careful scrutiny of the meaning of our concepts: What do we really mean by justice, or piety, or courage? Can we define these notions? Do we really understand the criteria for their use? And so on. And of course this basic feature of philosophizing remains central today. Philosophers continue to be preoccupied with language, and with the correct analysis of concepts, both in general use and in the specialized disciplines; indeed, for a fair time during the latter part of the twentieth century, it was held that the analysis of language was the *only* proper object of philosophy.[2]

Yet alongside what may be called this technical or professional concern with meaning and language, philosophers have very often also had a commitment to "examination" in a deeper sense: they have felt a powerful drive to stand back from our day-to-day preoccupations and concerns and to inquire into the overall direction and purpose of our lives, and the significance of our human existence. This deeper project of examination also has its roots in Socrates, who was patently committed, like many of his

[1] ὁ ἀνεξέταστος βίος οὐ βιωτὸς ἀνθρώπῳ (*ho anexetastos bios ou biōtos anthrōpō*); Plato, *Apology* (ca. 390 BC), 38a. All translations are mine unless otherwise noted.

[2] Thus Michael Dummett went so far as to declare that with the rise of the modern logical and analytic style of philosophizing "the proper object of philosophy [has been] finally established, namely . . . the analysis of the structure of *thought*, [for which] the only proper method [is] the analysis of *language*" (M. Dummett, "Can Analytic Philosophy Be Systematic?" [1975], in *Truth and Other Enigmas* [London: Duckworth, 1978], 458).

successors in the Classical and Hellenistic philosophical worlds, to the search for a life of integrity and virtue. The wording of Socrates' famous pronouncement at his trial should remind us that philosophical "examination," for Socrates, involved not just a series of abstract conceptual puzzles, but a critical scrutiny of the entire character of one's life (*bios*). What is more, as is made clear in the *Apology*, Socrates' philosophical vocation was linked with an unwavering allegiance to the dictates of his conscience, the "god," as he put it, whose inner voice demanded his obedience.[3] Socrates reproaches his Athenian accusers for being very concerned with things like wealth and reputation, but not having the faintest concern for the improvement of the most precious part of themselves – their souls.[4] And he goes on to explain that the very activity for which he was famous – engaging his interlocutors in philosophical dialogue – was explicitly designed to "induce young and old to make their first and chief concern not for their bodies or their possessions, but for the highest welfare of their souls."[5]

This last aspiration evidently takes us beyond the narrow confines of philosophy construed as a specialized academic discipline and moves us out into the general territory of "spirituality and the good life," which is the subject of the present volume. In thinking about spirituality in this chapter, I shall aim to follow the Socratic model in both the ways just indicated. I shall begin at the linguistic or conceptual level, by looking critically at what is meant by the terms "spiritual" and "spirituality," particularly as they figure in our contemporary culture. I shall then move on to ask about the deeper significance for human life of that cluster of experiences and practices that are commonly grouped under the heading of the spiritual. By the end of the chapter, I shall hope to have thrown some light on the relationship between "spiritual" concerns of the kind that Socrates emphasizes, to do with the conduct of life and the "care of the self" (or "care of the soul"),[6] and the spiritual concerns that have typically been

[3] Plato, *Apology*, 40a2–c2. [4] Plato, *Apology*, 29d5–e3; cf. 30a6–b1; 31b; 36c.

[5] Plato, *Apology*, 30a. For more on this, see J. Cottingham, "Philosophy and Self-Improvement: Continuity and Change in Philosophy's Self-Conception from the Classical to the Early-Modern Era," in M. Chase, S. R. L. Clark, and M. McGhee (eds.), *Philosophy as a Way of Life: Ancients and Moderns* (Oxford: Blackwell, 2013), 148–66.

[6] For more on the notions of "care of the soul" (*epimeleia tēs psychēs*) and "care of the self" (*epimeleia heautou*) in ancient philosophy, see the magisterial study of P. Hadot, *Philosophy as a Way of Life: Spiritual Exercises from Socrates to Foucault* (Oxford: Blackwell, 1955), originally published as *Exercises spirituels et philosophie antique* (1987). See also M. Foucault, Seminar at the Collège de France on January 6, 1982, published as "Subjectivité et vérité" in *Cités*, ed. Y. C. Zarka (Vendôme: Presses Universitaires de France, 2000), vol. II, 143ff; trans. in M. Foucault, *The Hermeneutics of the Subject* (New York: Palgrave Macmillan, 2005), 1–19. Foucault shows how the notion of self-examination and care for the self resonates throughout subsequent Hellenistic thought, in the Epicurean

important to religious believers of the traditional theistic sort. Can one be spiritual without being religious? How far do the two domains overlap? And can there be a valid form of spirituality adapted to the secularist temper of our times? Can one preserve what is important about the Socratic ideal of care of the soul, while subtracting the traditional theistic framework for understanding the spiritual domain that became entrenched in Western thought with the rise of Christianity?

What Do We Mean by "Spiritual"?

Let us, then, start our "examination" at the linguistic level. A brief perusal of the relevant entry in the Oxford English Dictionary reveals that the term "spiritual" has a wide variety of meanings and uses. In one of the senses listed there, it has a distinctly dualistic flavor, meaning "of the nature of a spirit . . . incorporeal, immaterial"; and under this heading are cited Milton's lines, "millions of spiritual Creatures walk the Earth/Unseen . . . ."[7] These immaterialist connotations, present in the root noun "spirit," are particularly prominent in the use of the cognate term "spiritualism," which covers activities once popular in the early twentieth century, but now largely discredited, such as attending séances and attempting to communicate with the ghosts of the departed. But in contemporary usage, the terms "spiritual" and "spirituality" are, or can be, entirely free from such "spooky" connotations. The slogan "I'm spiritual, but I'm not religious" has become a cliché of our time, and those who employ it normally intend to dissociate themselves from any belief in supernatural entities (as well as from institutionalized religion, which they take to be committed to such entities, or to be objectionable for other reasons).

In this vein, Sam Harris, a prominent spokesman for the "new atheism," has insisted that acknowledging the existence and value of the spiritual is quite consistent with the uncompromisingly empiricist/naturalistic worldview he champions: "spiritual experiences often constitute the most important and transformative moments in a person's life. Not recognizing that

"therapeutic" conception of philosophy, and the Stoic notion of the care of the soul. For the Epicureans, see A. Long and D. N. Sedley (eds.), *The Hellenistic Philosophers* (Cambridge University Press, 1987), 25C; for the Stoics, see, for example, Seneca, *Epistulae Morales* (AD 64), x.

7 John Milton, *Paradise Lost* (1667), iv, 677. The context is a speech in which Adam, before the Fall, speaks to Eve of how he is aware of invisible angelic beings all around him, and can hear their "celestial voices . . . sole, or responsive to each other's note, singing the Great Creator."

such experiences are possible or important can make us appear less wise even than our craziest religious opponents."[8]

In the following two sections we shall look more closely at the nature and significance of the spiritual, including the "important" and "transformative" moments in life that Harris here admits and acknowledges. But keeping for the moment to the question of current linguistic usage, it seems clear that secularists such as Harris are not violating any rules of language in acknowledging the importance of spirituality while repudiating the theistic worldview and dissociating themselves from the beliefs and practices of institutionalized religion. Consider, for example, the two main components of spirituality, as the term is normally understood today, which I take to be spiritual *praxis*, and spiritual *experience*. As far as the first is concerned, praying to God, and other performances and activities that involve or presuppose the existence of a personal deity (or deities), evidently do not exhaust the class of spiritual practices. One thinks here of the spiritual techniques of fasting, meditation, and chanting in the Theravada Buddhist tradition, where there is no belief in a personal God. What is more, we can find a host of techniques and practices on offer in our contemporary culture, concerned, for example, with goals such as mindfulness, self-awareness, and inner tranquility,[9] which are widely regarded as having a "spiritual" aspect, without any suggestion that they are necessarily connected with a religion.

As far as concerns our second main component of spirituality, namely experience, it again appears that contemporary usage allows that an experience can count as spiritual without any suggestion that the content of the experience has to be interpreted in terms of some religious doctrine or doctrines. The kinds of experience Harris cites in his defense of atheist spirituality involve feelings of "selfless wellbeing," "self-transcendence," and "boundless love,"[10] and he maintains that "to seek to live a spiritual life without deluding ourselves, we must view these experiences in universal and secular terms."[11] This latter remark, however, raises the stakes, since it

[8] S. Harris, *Waking Up: A Guide to Spirituality Without Religion* (New York: Simon and Schuster, 2014). How far religious believers do actually subscribe to the radically dualistic ontology that Harris implicitly attributes to them is a question for another occasion.

[9] Compare, for example, a recent five-week clinical project that "used combined Tai Chi and mindfulness-based stress reduction" as an educational program. According to the study, "statements the boys and girls made in the process suggested that they experienced well-being, calmness, relaxation, improved sleep, less reactivity, increased self-care, self-awareness, and a sense of interconnection or interdependence with nature" (R. B. Wall, "Tai Chi and Mindfulness-Based Stress Reduction in a Boston Public Middle School," *Journal of Paediatric Healthcare*, 19 (2005), 230–7, opening abstract).

[10] Harris, *Waking Up*, 5, 14, 17, 18, 43.

[11] Harris, *Waking Up*, 203.

evidently goes far beyond the mere claim that one can have spiritual experience without being religious; it is phrased in such a way as to imply that religious accounts of spiritual experience are seriously mistaken, and that Harris's own preferred secular account is grounded in enlightened ("universal and secular") principles that should be acceptable to any rational inquirer. Yet from the fact that English usage allows certain experiences to be identified (by Harris and many others) under the description "spiritual and not religious," it does not automatically follow that they can be fully and adequately understood without any reference to religious categories of thought. To give an analogy: from the fact that certain phenomena are identified by many people as "mental and not physical," it does not follow that they can be fully and adequately understood without any reference to physical phenomena (if *that* followed, we would have an altogether too easy argument for mind-body dualism!).[12] Whether a fully adequate account of spiritual experience can indeed be supplied within a secularist framework is a question that remains to be decided.

A second but related caveat that needs to be entered here is that linguistic labels, even when sanctioned by ordinary usage, can often conceal questionable metaphysical presuppositions. Harris, like many militant atheists, wears the mantle of the impartial and empirically oriented scientist. Thus, in his book *Waking Up*, subtitled *A Guide to Spirituality Without Religion*, he tells his readers that "nothing in this book needs to be accepted on faith," since all the assertions "can be tested in the laboratory of your own life."[13] But the spurious image of the laboratory masks a vision of ultimate reality that is actually metaphysical, not scientific. Harris claims that his spiritual experiences disclose a reality where there are no true substances and there is ultimately nothing but an impersonal flux of conditions that arise and pass away, and "the conventional self is a transitory experience among transitory experiences."[14] Yet if the results of his reported spiritual experience are supposed to count as empirical confirmation of this impersonalist vision of reality, then Harris has left himself no justification for dismissing as "crazy" those countless theists whose own spiritual experience has, by contrast, seemed to them to disclose the nature of reality as deeply and ultimately personal. Talk of the "laboratory" of experience is not going to help very much here, since clearly everything is going to depend not on measurement of "data" or other such scientific

[12] Compare Antoine Arnauld's criticisms of Descartes's arguments in the Fourth Set of Objections to the *Meditations* (1641).

[13] Harris, *Waking Up*, 7. [14] Harris, *Waking Up*, 206.

procedures, but on the character of the experiences in question and how they are interpreted.

The upshot of all this is that whatever contemporary usage may or may not sanction regarding the current employment of the term "spiritual," all the interesting questions about the significance of the term, and whether it can be fully and coherently detached from the religious domain, are not going to be decidable on linguistic grounds alone; for they are inextricably bound up with the stance we take on more substantive issues about the *meaning* of the spiritual and the role it plays in our lives. To these more substantive questions we shall now turn.

Spirituality and the Cosmos

In many powerful accounts of spiritual experience in literature, two elements that are strikingly prominent are, first, that such experience has a profoundly *human* dimension, being connected with our deepest human responses and aspirations, and, second, that such experience has what might be called a *cosmic* dimension, being somehow concerned with the ultimate nature of reality as a whole, and our relationship to it. Few writers have produced more eloquent reflections on the character of spiritual experience than George Eliot, as in the following passage from her first novel, *Adam Bede*:

> Our caresses, our tender words, our still rapture under the influence of Autumn sunsets, or pillared vistas, or calm majestic statues, or Beethoven symphonies, all bring with them the consciousness that they are mere waves and ripples in an unfathomable ocean of love and beauty; our emotion in its keenest moment passes from expression into silence, our love at its highest flood rushes beyond its object and loses itself in the sense of divine mystery.[15]

The passage identifies some very typical and characteristic examples falling under the genre of spiritual experience as commonly understood: passionate reactions to the beauties of the natural world ("rapture" at "Autumn sunsets"); powerful responses to great works of art ("majestic statues," "Beethoven symphonies"); and the interactions, laden with deep significance, that arise between people who are in close personal relationships ("caresses," "tender words"). Although all three types of phenomenon are far from mundane – their heightened importance signals that they raise us above the humdrum world of daily routine and toil – they are all

[15] G. Eliot, *Adam Bede* (1859), bk. I, ch. 3.

nevertheless a precious part of our human birthright, indispensable elements of what it is to be a fully flourishing human being, and something without which our species would be immeasurably poorer.

Alongside (but by no means unrelated to) this very human dimension, there is also, as Eliot skillfully emphasized, something more. In having an experience that falls under one of the categories she describes, we are made dimly aware that what is happening to us somehow enables us to participate in something momentous – something that is more than a mere subjective psychological episode, and that connects us with an objective framework of meaning and value that is not of our own making. Language tends to falter here, since by its very nature this "cosmic" dimension (as I am calling it for want of a better term) transcends the domain to which our ordinary everyday language is fitted, adapted as it is to help us survive and cope with the immediate demands of the world around us. But as Eliot puts it, grappling with symbolic and metaphorical expressions in order to reach at what she wants to convey, there is a sense that these powerful and rapturous spiritual responses connect us with something greater – that they "are mere waves and ripples in an unfathomable ocean of love and beauty."

Note that Eliot herself is not being explicitly religious here – at least not in the sense that she is defending the truth of any specific religious dogma. Nor indeed was she herself religious in the conventional institutional sense, having a number of serious doubts about the metaphysical doctrines of Christianity. Influenced by David Strauss and Ludwig Feuerbach (both of whom she translated),[16] she inclined if anything toward an agnostic and humanistic stance, which valued Christianity more for its moral teachings than for its theological dogmas. Elsewhere in *Adam Bede*, the eponymous protagonist comes close to voicing what may well have been Eliot's own view of the matter when he says, "I've seen pretty clear ever since I was a young un, as religion's something else besides doctrines and notions."[17] The thought here is that the moral and practical components of Christianity – right conduct, and loving and generous emotions – are what count, rather than the theological ideas and theories embodied in this or that creed or catechism.

[16] The German liberal Protestant theologian David Strauss's *Life of Jesus* (*Das Leben Jesu*, 1836) created a stir at the time by treating the Gospel writings from a purely "historical" perspective, denying that the miracles, for example, were actual occurrences, and interpreting them purely on a mythical level. Eliot's English translation was published in 1846. More radically still, Ludwig Feuerbach's *Essence of Christianity* (*Das Wesen des Christentums*, 1841) interpreted the idea of God as a projection or externalization of man's moral nature; Eliot's English version appeared in 1854.

[17] Eliot, *Adam Bede*, ch. 17.

Yet although Eliot, in common with many nineteenth-century thinkers, was evidently attracted by what can broadly be called a humanistic interpretation of Christianity,[18] it is clear from the passage quoted at the start of this section that her vision of the content of spiritual experience cannot be understood *merely* in terms of human moral aspirations. The "unfathomable ocean of beauty and love" of which the passage speaks, let alone the talk of "divine mystery," implies that our human activities and emotions are not the entire story – they are but "waves and ripples," as Eliot puts it, in a greater whole. So it is not just that experiencing the beauties of nature or art or of close personal affection is very important and valuable in our lives (though that of course is true); more than that, such experience draws us forward and beyond ourselves, Eliot seems to be saying, and enables us somehow to be part of, or at one with, something mysterious that cannot be properly grasped or named, but that we sense as the unfathomable source from which flows all that is good and meaningful in human life.

If this is what spiritual experience at its deepest is (and I submit that most readers who honestly interrogate themselves will find that phenomenologically Eliot's description rings true, at least to some degree), then something like a "cosmic" dimension in our most profound spiritual experiences seems hard to deny. And then it begins to seem as if the whole project of secularizing, or "humanizing," or "demythologizing" spirituality, and hence the whole project of insisting that one can be "spiritual without being religious," may prove more problematic than it at first appeared. To be sure, the terms "religion" and "religious" are broad ones, which defy simple definition,[19] and as we have already seen, there are recognized spiritual practices that do not presuppose religious belief in the sense of allegiance to a theistic worldview. And certainly it would be absurd to suggest that spiritual experience is available only to those who are explicit "believers," as that term is normally understood in, for example, the Abrahamic religions. But even when all that is granted, the task of philosophical "examination" still requires us to reflect seriously about the character and content of the deep spiritual experiences under discussion. What exactly is the "cosmic" dimension that seems irresistibly to manifest itself to the experiencing subject? Is it just a vague sense the subject has that

[18] Perhaps the most famous example is Leo Tolstoy; see, for example, his *What I Believe* (*V chyom moya vera?*, 1885).

[19] There is a large literature on the vexed question of how to define the term "religion," which it would take far more space than is available to attempt to summarize here. A valuable starting point for discussion is Emile Durkheim's account in *The Elementary Forms of Religious Life* (*Les formes élémentaires de la vie religieuse*, 1912), trans. C. Cosman (Oxford University Press, 2001), ch. 1.

he or she is part of a wider process? Or is there (as is suggested by Eliot's talk of an unfathomable source of love and beauty) an inescapable *moral* dimension, something like an awareness of, or a confrontation with, an "enduring power, not ourselves, which makes for righteousness," in Matthew Arnold's solemn phrase.[20] For if the latter is the case (and we shall be exploring this in more detail in the following section), it may begin to look after all as if the experiences in question are comfortably locatable only within something very like a theistic worldview.

It is of course true that the account of spiritual feelings found in *Adam Bede* comes from an author who was brought up in and surrounded by a strongly entrenched theistic culture. So today's antireligious skeptic might argue that, in spite of her better rational self, Eliot's language inevitably bears the traces of the traditional religious outlook of her time; and further, that the modern advocate of "spirituality without religion" should be able, in our more fully enlightened and secularized milieu, to provide an account of the spiritual that dispenses with the theistic backdrop entirely. This is certainly the aim of Sam Harris, who tells us he wants to salvage the "important psychological truths" from the "rubble," or to "pluck the diamond from the dunghill of esoteric religion."[21]

It's remarkable, however, that despite these official aspirations to purge away all the religious elements, what we actually find in the descriptions that Harris and others who think like him give of their spiritual experience is language with a "cosmic" flavor very similar to that which we find in Eliot. As already noted, Harris talks of "boundless love," and a sense of "being at one with the cosmos." And in a similar vein, his fellow atheist Christopher Hitchens spoke toward the end of his life of deep experiences of the beauties of great music, or art, or the natural world, as giving him a sense of "what you could call the Numinous, the Transcendent."[22] But here we have a curious paradox. From the official standpoint of hard-nosed materialist-atheists, to describe such experiences as "transcendent," or "numinous," or as connecting them with an ocean of "boundless love" must necessarily be simply a *façon de parler* – a way of talking that lacks any ontological basis, or that does not point to any ultimate objective reality. For their officially held view maintains that the natural world studied by science is, ontologically speaking, all that there really is; and though there may be heightened or altered states of consciousness, like those Sam Harris

[20] M. Arnold, *Literature and Dogma* (1873), ch. 1. [21] Harris, *Waking Up*, 5, 10.

[22] Christopher Hitchens, in debate with Tony Blair (2010), quoted in Jules Evans, "The New Atheists Are Actually Transcendentalists," http://philosophyforlife.org/the-new-atheists-are-actually-transcendentalists/, posted January 24, 2014.

has expressed an interest in studying (produced, he says, by fasting, meditation, and "psychotropic plants"),[23] these are understood as purely subjective effects of various brain changes, arising as by-products of evolved physiological processes originally generated by the needs of survival in the ordinary natural world. The idea of anything more to the story than this, anything ontologically extra that transcends the material world, is, for Harris and those who think like him, simply an illusion, resulting from the fact that we humans are "deeply disposed to broadcast our own subjectivity onto the world"[24] (an idea derived from one of the founding fathers of modern atheism, David Hume, when he observed that "the mind has a great propensity to spread itself on external objects"[25]).[26]

But what in the scientific worldview that such atheists so prize could possibly license the idea that the jangling of particle interactions, unfolding impersonally without purpose or any intrinsic significance whatsoever, could constitute an ocean of love and beauty; or what could justify the notion of a deep harmony, between myself and these supposedly blank, impersonal, and purposeless phenomena, so that I can feel myself "at one with the cosmos"? To be fair to Harris's position, he does in his more cautious moments pull back from any implied commitment to what I have called the "cosmic" dimension of spiritual experience. Feeling at one with the cosmos, he observes at one point, "says a lot about the possibilities of human consciousness, but it says nothing about the universe at large ... nor does it suggest that the 'energy' of love somehow pervades the cosmos." All that such feelings do, he goes on to say, is "tell us a lot about the human mind": they tell us that such experiences do as a matter of fact occur if you adopt the right techniques (Buddhist-style *metta* meditation, for instance), or "tak[e] the right drug."[27]

Yet this kind of strategy, reducing spiritual experience to a mere subjective psychological state, has an enormous cost. It robs such experience of any significance beyond that of some kind of private "trip," which may make me "feel good," but does not disclose anything important about the way things are. Harris himself, as we have seen, speaks of spiritual experiences as among the most "important and transformative" experiences

[23] S. Harris, *The End of Faith* (New York: Norton, 2005), 210.

[24] S. Harris, "The Mortal Dangers of Religious Faith," interview at: www.amazon.com/gp/feature.html?docId=542154.

[25] D. Hume, *A Treatise of Human Nature* (1739–40), bk. I, pt. 3, sec. xiv.

[26] The foregoing paragraph draws partly on material from my *How to Believe* (London: Bloomsbury, 2015), ch. 2.

[27] Harris, *Waking Up*, 43–4.

humans can have. But if I simply take a pill that makes everything look green for twenty-four hours, even though such experience may, if replicated with many different subjects, be "scientifically well attested," there is no reason whatever to suppose that it is important or transformative in any interesting way – even if it makes me say "Wow!" and go round for a time with a euphoric smile on my face. Even if the experience is one of undifferentiated benevolence or love, or some other "oceanic" feeling,[28] it is not going to be transformative in any interesting way (as those who witnessed or participated in the short-lived vacuities of the "psychedelic" and "hippy" movements of the 1970s will be able to confirm), unless it is more than an interior episode. A psychological event or brain change might of course have great significance if it discloses something about what is going on outside me (if it is involved in my appreciating a great piece of music, or conversing with a loved one, for example), but then it is *ex hypothesi* more than just an interior change.

Authentic spiritual experience is not merely a psychological episode, but is inextricably bound up with a certain kind of spiritual *transformation*; and if we start to unpack the phenomenology of the change, we quickly see that it has a distinctively moral character, in the broad sense of that term. I have a sense of being confronted with something beyond myself that I perceive as good, or worthy of my admiration or love or respect, and as demanding a response from me whether I like it or not. To this vital moral dimension of spiritual experience we must now turn.

The Moral Dimension

Part of the problem in understanding what is meant by spirituality is that in our fragmented and compartmentalized modern culture, we tend to split the flow of our human existence into separate compartments. There is our "job" versus our "free time" – but where do philosophizing, or talking with a partner, or playing with one's children fit into that dichotomy? There are our "moral" sensibilities versus our "aesthetic" sensibilities, but to which set of capacities does a great literary work like Tolstoy's *War and Peace* or Jane Austin's *Persuasion* appeal? Or again, there is the "moral" domain versus the domain of "the natural world," but (as I have argued in other writings) it is impossible to read the "nature" poetry of William

[28] For this term, see A. Comte-Sponville, *The Little Book of Atheist Spirituality* [originally published as *L'esprit de l'athéisme*, 2006] (London: Bantam, 2008), 150ff. The term was discussed much earlier by Sigmund Freud in *Civilization and Its Discontents* [*Das Unbehagen in der Kultur*, 1929], §1; trans. in *The Penguin Freud Library* (London: Penguin Books, 1985), vol. XII.

Wordsworth properly without becoming aware that the poet's reflections are inextricable fusions of the moral and the aesthetic: his exaltation and joy at the beauty of the woods and fields is closely bound up with a deep sense of their goodness and of the "blessing" they bestow, a sense in turn linked to the upwelling in him of love and sympathy for humankind.[29]

If we turn to the "praxis" component of spiritualty – the performances, disciplines, and routines that have traditionally been part of a spiritual way of life – we can find this same comprehensiveness or inclusiveness as regards the faculties and capacities involved, and the same moral thread running through them all. Ignatius of Loyola was famous for his "spiritual exercises," designed to be undertaken systematically during the course of a retreat lasting many days.[30] Such exercises, or similar ones still widely practiced today in Ignatian and other forms of spirituality, include prayer, fasting, meditation, *lectio divina* (the attentive reading of Scripture), participating in communal worship, group activities such as singing Psalms, individual self-examination and confession, and prayer or reflective silence at key moments of the day (for example before eating, or before retiring).

Spiritual exercises are typically *multivalent* – they work on many different levels, including the emotional, the physical, the aesthetic, and the moral; and it is important to add that they operate in ways that are not always directly accessible to the conscious reflective mind. A paradigm case of a spiritual practice, familiar from the Benedictine and other monastic traditions, is the singing of Psalms. This originally involved learning the complete set by heart and reinforcing the memory through regular repetition, day by day and month by month. But the recitation is no mere intellectual exercise, but an embodied ritual, involving physical movements of standing and sitting and bowing, the taking up of each verse antiphonally, by alternating sides of the choir, and of course the music, the plainsong chant, which not only requires careful breathing and close attention to the rhythm of the words, but a constant listening by each singer, to match his intonation to that of his neighbors.[31]

[29] See J. Cottingham, "Human Nature and the Transcendent," in C. Sandis and M. J. Cain (eds.), *Human Nature*, Royal Institute of Philosophy Supplement, 70 (Cambridge University Press, 2012), 233–54, where I discuss key passages from Wordsworth's *The Prelude*.

[30] Ignatius of Loyola, *Spiritual Exercises* [*Ejercicios espirituales*, ca. 1525], trans. J. Munitz and P. Endean (Harmondsworth: Penguin, 1996). Ignatius's original Spanish text was first published posthumously in 1615, but a Latin translation (*Exercitia Spiritualia*) was published in Rome, with papal approval, in 1548.

[31] Further discussion of the multivalent aspects of Psalm singing and other spiritual practices may be found in John Cottingham, "Spirituality," in C. Taliaferro, V. Harrison, and S. Goetz (eds.), *The Routledge Companion to Theism* (New York: Routledge, 2013), 654–5.

One reason that music is so important here is that its effects on us, both as listeners and as participants, engage the whole person, physically, emotionally, intellectually, and also in deeper, more diffusive ways, operating below the threshold of consciousness, which we scarcely understand. Music at its best (and the same goes for the finest literature and visual art) has this ineffable quality – it speaks to something deep within us, yet at the same time somehow takes us outside ourselves to a more exalted plane. Such music is, as T. S. Eliot put it in one of his most religiously sensitive poems:

> music heard so deeply
> That it is not heard at all, but you are the music
> While the music lasts. These are only hints and guesses,
> Hints followed by guesses; and the rest
> Is prayer, observance, discipline, thought and action.[32]

The ability of great art to generate "self-transcendence" is something that many secularists are happy to acknowledge; indeed some have suggested that all we need of a "spiritual" kind can be supplied by music, art, or literature, thus making religion redundant. Salmon Rushdie has argued that literature can and ought to fill this role, and aim to capture what he calls "the soaring quality of transcendence":

> It is for art to capture that experience, to offer it to, in the case of literature, its readers; to be, for a secular, materialist culture, some sort of replacement for what the love of god offers in the world of faith.[33]

But one problem with this kind of position is that the implied exclusive dichotomy between the domain of religion on one hand and the domain of art on the other is in many respects misleading. For clearly some of the greatest visual art and literature and music in our culture is inherently religious. Those who juxtapose art and religion as opposites may well have in mind a very one-sided image of religion as what is purveyed by fundamentalists who subscribe to rigid dogmas and literalist interpretations of the Bible. Such fundamentalist approaches are, of course, to be found; but

[32] T. S. Eliot, "The Dry Salvages" [1941], subsequently incorporated into *Four Quartets* [1943]. I am grateful to Jay Parini for his comments on this passage in a talk on "Eliot's Four Quartets as a Pattern for Christian Living," given at Heythrop College, London in May 2016.

[33] S. Rushdie, "Is Nothing Sacred?," in *Imaginary Homelands: Essays and Criticism 1981–1991* (London: Granta, 1991), 425–6; cited in R. Stott, "The Wetfooted Understory: Darwinian Immersions," in G. Levine (ed.), *The Joy of Secularism* (Princeton University Press, 2011), 206. For a similar argument that art can and should be a replacement for religion, see A. de Botton and J. Armstrong, *Art as Therapy* (London: Phaidon, 2013).

elsewhere, for example in the great liturgical heritage of Catholic and Anglican and Orthodox Christianity, one can find forms of spirituality that are inextricably intertwined with some of the most resonant and "soaring" literature and art and music humanity has ever produced.

An even more important aspect of religious spirituality, which provides a further reason to suppose there is something suspect about the project of replacing it with art, is that it has an overwhelmingly *moral* purpose. Art of a secular kind is answerable to all sorts of standards, some detached from any moral concerns whatsoever; but the overriding aim of authentic spiritual praxis is to facilitate the emergence of a better self, purged of wasteful and destructive and self-absorbed inclinations and desires, and able to begin the task of growing, no doubt slowly and painfully, into the self one was meant to be – in short to embark on the traditional Benedictine task of self-transformation, or "conversion of life."[34] We are back with the Socratic idea of "care of the soul."

Moving our attention from spiritual praxis to the other component of spirituality we have been focusing on, namely spiritual experience, we find that the pervasive moral dimension is even more apparent. An experience that was merely diverting or titillating, or shocking or entertaining or enjoyable, or even just very emotionally moving, could not count as a spiritual experience; there has to be something deeper, more resonant, and more meaningful for the life of the subject and his or her moral development.

Such experience takes a specifically theistic form in many remarkable passages in the Hebrew Bible, as in one of the Psalms where the speaker is overwhelmed by a sense of divine power. God is described as the one who "breaks the cedars of Lebanon and makes Lebanon skip like a calf," who "shakes the wilderness and strips the forests bare, while all in the temple cry 'Glory.'"[35] The cry of "Glory" (in Hebrew *kavod* כָּבוֹד) signifies something weighty with significance, sacred, mysterious, a manifestation of the divine, as conveyed in the description of the pillar of fire and cloud that led the Israelites out of Egypt, or the cloud atop Mount Sinai where God's law was manifest to Moses.[36] We are not talking of "natural

[34] The Rule of St. Benedict, dating from the sixth century AD, speaks in chapter 58 of a *conversatio morum*, a difficult term to translate, but one that, as the context makes clear, implies a continuous reshaping and renewal of one's habits of behavior, character, and entire way of life.

[35] Psalm 29[28]:5–9. My discussion of this and the following examples (from Exodus and Isaiah) of spiritual experience as it figures in the Bible is based on a passage from chapter 5 of Cottingham, *How to Believe*.

[36] Exodus 13:21; 16:10; 24:16.

beauty" in the attenuated modern sense, but of something fearful that calls forth reverence and awe, like the burning bush, flaming but never consumed, where Moses was told to keep his distance.[37] These are not "impressive sights," of the kind familiar from television nature programs, but events pregnant with moral significance, as is clear from the lines from an earlier Psalm, where the forests are said to "sing for joy" because *the world is to be judged*.[38] In psychological or phenomenological terms, what is happening here is an experience where the subject is overwhelmed by the power and beauty of nature in a way that is somehow intertwined with awareness of one's own weakness and imperfection, and a sense of confrontation with the inexorable demands of justice and righteousness. In short, the spiritual experience in question involves the kind of awareness that enables one to see the world transfigured, so that it is irradiated with meaning and value, and the human subject, caught up in that mystery, is unmistakably called on to be no longer a spectator, a mere "tourist," but to *respond*, to be a morally responsive agent, part of a cosmos that is shot through with the divine.

The upshot of all this is that spiritual experience in what I have been calling its "cosmic" dimension is, in today's somewhat awkward philosophical jargon, "normative": we are dealing with intensely personal encounters, infused with awe and charged with moral significance, where the individual feels him or herself to be checked, to be scrutinized, and to be called on to respond and to change.

In the work of many creative artists, by contrast, particularly in the past two centuries, we see a resistance to any kind of alignment between art and morality. Yet one can certainly point to some nonreligious works of art that do seem to have a morally demanding aspect.[39] And it is also true that certain nontheistic meditative forms of spirituality, such as those found in Buddhism and other Eastern traditions, have ethical teachings attached to them. But the goals sought in those traditions, and enthusiastically taken up by the secularists we referred to earlier – involving notions like impersonal and boundless oceanic well-being – seem to have an essentially quietist character. The paramount objective is achieving bliss by detaching oneself from the stressful world of struggle, commitment, and dependency. To be sure, many of the Eastern sages are famous for enjoining right

[37] Exodus 3:5. [38] Psalm 96[95]:11–13.

[39] A possible example may be found in Rainer Maria Rilke's sonnet *Archaïscher Torso Apollos* [from *Der Neuen Gedichte anderer Teil*, 1908], which I translate and discuss in "The Self, the Good Life, and the Transcendent," in N. Athanassoulis and S. Vice (eds.), *The Moral Life: Essays in Honour of John Cottingham* (Oxford: Blackwell, 2007), 255–6.

conduct and the practice of virtue, so in this sense an ethical component is involved. But it is not a component that is intrinsically connected to the underlying vision of the cosmos; for the Eastern vision is one in which personal commitments and demands are based on an illusion, and ultimate reality is simply an impersonal continuum of conditions that arise and pass away. There is a fundamental contrast here with the kind of sacred vision found in some of the passages from the Bible quoted two paragraphs earlier, or with that of Isaiah, when he sees the temple shaking and billowing with smoke, and the earth and heaven filled with God's *glory* (here again we have the term that is so prominent in Jewish spirituality, *kavod*).[40] For when the prophet witnesses this vision, his first reaction is to cry "Woe is me!" The experience he has involves a vivid intermingling of the aesthetic with the moral, and even as he is overwhelmed by the "glory," he acutely feels his own failures and those of his people, so that he forthwith resolves to try to set things right. Such a vision, radically different from vague oceanic feelings of well-being and oneness, is a "normative" vision – one that carries with it inescapable demands. It is a vision that makes no sense without the two poles of the human condition that Blaise Pascal underlined – our wretchedness, or sinfulness, and our redeemability would we but turn toward the good.[41]

Coda: Philosophy and the Spiritual

It has been no part of my purpose in this chapter to disparage the recent interest in spirituality among contemporary atheist thinkers – on the contrary, I think it is thoroughly to be welcomed. But the favorable interpretation of theistic spirituality offered here, together with the reservations expressed about alternative nontheistic forms, may suggest to some readers that this chapter has, as it were, imperialistic ambitions, and aims to browbeat those who describe themselves as spiritual into admitting that they are really theists whether they know it or not. But polemical arguments seldom provide much enlightenment in philosophy, and would-be coercive philosophical strategies rarely succeed in getting anyone to shift their position. What I have been aiming to do, in a much lower key, is to suggest that when we unpack exactly what is involved in the activities and experiences we call spiritual, it is not easy to make fully adequate sense of

[40] Isaiah 6:1–4.

[41] *Misère de l'homme sans Dieu . . . Félicité de l'homme avec Dieu* (B. Pascal, *Pensées* [1670], ed. L. Lafuma [Paris: Seuil, 1962], no. 6).

spirituality, and of its importance for human life, without something very close to a theistic framework.

The theologian Karl Rahner once used the term "anonymous Christians" to describe those who do not adopt or have never heard of the Christian faith, but who may nevertheless achieve salvation through good works and through following their consciences, albeit, unbeknownst to them, none of this would have been possible but for the salvific sacrifice of Christ.[42] The phrase "anonymous Christian" is a controversial one that has irritated many critics, but for present purposes, we may perhaps extract from it a simple philosophical point, namely that one may respond to a divine reality without doing so *under that description* (just as someone may be aware of a flash of lightening, but not be aware of it under the description "electrical discharge"). Applying this to the case at hand, the gist of my argument has been that the profound importance for human life of those deep transformative experiences we call "spiritual," together with the moral response demanded from us through the working of such experiences, provides some support for thinking the reality glimpsed in such experiences is of the kind a theistic worldview envisages, even though it may not be experienced under that description. For either the moral demand is an illusion (something that those who take spiritual experience seriously are unlikely to want to say), or else there is something in the nature of the cosmos that grounds the demand. If there are indeed "irreducibly normative truths"[43] that we access through such experiences – moral truths, in other words, that are not reducible to factual truths about the natural world, which have objective authority over us and require us to act in certain ways – these will not fit easily within the prevailing naturalistic conception of the world where the only ultimate constituents of the world are the physical objects studied by science.[44]

[42] "Anonymous Christianity means that a person lives in the grace of God and attains salvation outside of explicitly constituted Christianity. Let us take a Buddhist monk, who, because he follows his conscience, attains salvation and lives in the grace of God: of him I must say that he is an anonymous Christian . . . If I hold that everyone depends upon Jesus Christ for salvation, and if at the same time I hold that many live in the world who have not expressly recognized Jesus Christ, then there remains in my opinion nothing else but to take up this postulate of an anonymous Christianity" (K. Rahner, *Karl Rahner in Dialogue: Conversations and Interviews, 1965–1982* [Spring Valley, NY: Crossroads Publishing, 1959], 135 [slightly adapted]).

[43] The phrase is Derek Parfit's, in *On What Matters* (Oxford University Press, 2011), pt. II, 464. It should be added that although Parfit recognizes the objectivity and "irreducible normativity" of these authoritative moral demands, he denies that there need be anything whatsoever in reality that grounds these truths.

[44] If naturalism fails, it is of course theoretically possible that the ultimate nature of the cosmos might be such as to accommodate other realities, of a nontheistic kind (such as Platonic forms perhaps), which might ground irreducibly normative truths of the kind accessed in spiritual experience. Another, more interesting possibility is that such normativity might be grounded in what Fiona Ellis

All this brings us back, in conclusion, to the role of philosophy in the deeper of the two Socratic senses referred to at the start of this chapter, namely what Pierre Hadot has called "philosophy as a way of life" – something of profound moral importance that impinges on the entire character and purpose of one's existence.[45] In this deeper sense, philosophy is part of a process of radical interior change – *metanoia* is the Greek term – a change of heart, a change of the kind that leads to a fundamental shift in the flow and direction of one's life.[46] As we have seen, spiritual practice in its traditional forms has aimed at just that – though one should perhaps add that philosophical inquiry tends to contribute to this process at an intellectual and reflective level, while the practices of spirituality characteristically engage more directly with a whole range of emotional, imaginative, and behavioral responses. But the truth of theism, if it is true, completes this picture in the most satisfying way possible, by ensuring that the process of change has an ultimate goal, being directed toward that which is objectively good and that wherein our ultimate fulfillment lies. Or, to close with a phrase from Michel Foucault, "there is, in the truth and in the access to it, something which fulfils the subject and completes, or transfigures, the very being of the subject."[47]

has called an "enriched" or "expansive" naturalism; see her *God, Value, and Nature* (Oxford University Press, 2014). These possibilities cannot be explored and evaluated with the space available in the present chapter.

45 See note 6 earlier in this chapter.

46 In its New Testament usage, the term *metanoia* may be translated as "repentance" or "conversion"; cf. Acts of the Apostles: "God hath granted repentance unto life [*metanoian eis zoēn*]" (11:18).

47 Foucault, *The Hermeneutics of the Subject*, 16. I am most grateful to the editor of this volume, David McPherson, for extremely helpful comments on an earlier draft of this chapter.

CHAPTER 2

The Problem of Impiety

Cora Diamond

In the first half of this chapter, I explain what I call the Problem of Impiety, and in the second half I explore some responses to the Problem.

I

The best way to explain the Problem is by looking at David Hume's essay "Of Suicide."[1] Hume was arguing that suicide would not in all cases be a violation of duty. Suicide was then generally taken to be a moral abomination and a violation of duty to God. It was usually prohibited legally as well. The general condemnation of suicide in Western thought, which forms the background to Hume's essay, went back to Augustine. Hume was probably an agnostic, but his essay on suicide was addressed to people who might be assumed to believe in God. What he was willing to describe as "true" religion played, he thought, a useful role in human life, but he took there to be also superstitious and fanatical forms of religion. He wanted to show that only if you accepted a superstitious conception of God could you defend an absolute prohibition on suicide, or hold that it was a violation of duty to God or an interference with divine providence.

More exactly, then, what was Hume arguing against? The prohibition on suicide was often defended by saying that killing oneself was an interference in a sphere that God had reserved for himself, that of deciding when a person's life should come to an end; and that God would be angered by anyone's committing suicide, precisely because it was an interference in the sphere he had thus reserved for himself – it was in a deep sense a rejection of God's sovereignty over life. But, Hume asked, how could we come to think that suicide was an interference in a sphere God

[1] D. Hume, "On Suicide" (also called "Of Suicide"), in *Essays: Moral, Political and Literary* (London: Grant Richards, 1903 [a printed version of the essay was suppressed by Hume prior to publication, 1755; first published edition of the essay in English, unauthorized, 1777]), 585–96.

had reserved for himself? Here we can see the significance of what Hume would take to be a conception of religion that is responsive to reason. For Hume takes it that, if you have a reasoned attitude to religion, you would think that God had given us our various powers, including our power to work out the consequences of our actions, and to do all sorts of things to change what would otherwise be the course of nature. If anything is a God-given power, that is. So he thinks that reasonable people should take the God they believe in to have given us the power to alter what the course of nature would otherwise be, with the intention that we use that power as best we can, working out what are good or bad consequences of possible interferences.

Hume asks us to think about the following sort of case: if I see that a boulder is going to fall on my head if I don't interfere in the course of nature, and that it will extinguish my life, I can interfere with the course of nature to ensure that I am not in the place where the boulder is going, or I can try to change the path of the boulder. No one, Hume thought, would take that to be an interference with God's will. And yet making sure the boulder does not hit me causes me not to die at the time I would have died if the course of nature hadn't been altered. So the unaltered course of nature cannot in general be taken as a guide to when God wants a person to die. There is an important general point here, namely, that no rational criterion is available to us for singling out some interferences in the course of nature and saying that they are absolutely ruled out for us, because they belong to a special sphere that God has set aside for himself. Only a superstitious conception of God, Hume thinks, can include the idea of some special sphere in which we are not allowed to interfere. The particular view of this sort that is his target takes the setting of the time of our deaths to lie within such a special reserved sphere, and treats as prohibited any interferences in the course of nature to make one's own death come earlier than it otherwise would. That, though, is just one specific kind of case, and the general point is wider.

To bring that general point home to his audience, Hume invites them to think about some people whom they will be quite willing to recognize as superstitious: the ancient Romans and the present-day French. The Romans held that diverting a river would "invade the prerogatives of nature."[2] This is, for Hume, a perfect example of a superstitious belief. And so is the contemporary French belief that inoculation against smallpox

[2] Hume is referring to the debate in the Senate, described by Tacitus, about diverting some of the waters flowing into the Tiber to prevent flooding.

is an interference with God's providence, because inoculation with a disease gives people a form of the disease, and the French idea was that it is strictly God's affair to give a person a disease; we can't do so for our purposes. Hume hopes that his readers will also recognize that French idea as superstitious. In Hume's day, nobody had argued, as people did later, that we should not have public health projects because they interfered with the divine will to give some people cholera; nobody had argued that we should not interfere with the pain of childbirth because God had linked childbirth and pain, and it wasn't for us to unlink them. But, if those cases had occurred in Hume's time and had been known to him, he would have treated them in the same way, as involving a superstitious notion of God. Any idea of God that takes there to be some realm that he has set aside, where we are not supposed to interfere, involves a superstitious conception of God; and the basic idea is that there is no rational criterion for recognizing such a sphere. It is superstitious to take some of the ways things happen in the course of nature, and to say: that's the way things are in the course of nature because God wants them so, and we therefore must not interfere, or we will arouse God's special anger. Whether a particular interference is a good idea must be looked at in terms of what is approved by the "sentiment of humanity"; it must be looked at without the idea of a set-aside realm of untouchable natural connections.

Now, impiety. The notions of piety and impiety are complex, and I focus here on only some of the elements in this complexity. One part of the notion of piety is the idea that we should treat the natural order of things with respect and awe. Another element is the idea of respect and gratitude as due to the sources of our life, which may be conceived to be God or the gods, our parents and ancestors, and our country. Another part of the notion of piety is the idea that actions that violate piety are properly regarded as outrageous or shocking. This outrage may manifest a sense that a wholly wrongful posture has been exhibited, a kind of will to dominate the natural order, a refusal to accept limitation, a challenge to God's sovereignty, or to honored and honorable traditions that should be taken as sacred.

Hume's basic argument in the essay on suicide constitutes a challenge to the whole way of thinking that accepts the notions of piety and impiety toward which I have just gestured. I'd emphasize again what he's doing when he notes that we properly recognize as superstitious the French idea that there is a kind of impiety in inoculating people against smallpox. He is trying to get his audience to alter their idea that suicide is outrageous in that it challenges God's sovereignty, that it is shocking in its impiety. He is, I think, attempting to get his audience to see that conventional ways of thinking about what is pious and what is impious are mere covers for our own superstitions. All ideas of a realm where we should not interfere, where it is impious to interfere, are challenged by his basic argument. The question whether some interference with the natural order is justified can be answered in all cases by considering how it will affect oneself and others; nothing is simply and automatically ruled out. Hume's argument goes further than just undermining ideas of piety tied to particular religious beliefs; it undermines as well, or is at any rate intended to, forms of natural piety, which need not be tied to specific religious systems, but which recognize comparable limitations in what we should take ourselves to be able to do.

To bring out some of the issues here, it will be useful to have a list of things that people have already done, or that have been talked about as possible things we might do in the future, with advances in technology:

1. The manufacture by Soviet scientists of two-headed dogs by transplantation of dog heads.
2. Artificially supported maintenance of the separated head of a fetus, for research on chemical activity in the brain.
3. The construction of embryos that are part human and part cow; part human and part goat, etc., as a source of tissues.
4. Mass production of animal life to exact genetic specification, treating animals as machines produced for research purposes.
5. Control over human reproduction, including in vitro techniques, surrogate motherhood, maintenance of the life of a pregnant but brain-dead woman (condemned by some Catholic authorities), pregnancies of post-menopausal women; and possibly for the future, cloning people, or possibly cloning embryos for use in research or as a source of tissues; transplantation of uteruses to men, making it possible for men to have babies.
6. Feeding of meat and bone meal to cows, which has given rise to bovine spongiform encephalopathy. This can be described as interference with the kind of creature the cow is, turning a graminivorous animal into a partly carnivorous one.
7. The combination of reproductive technology with the technology of slaughter, when the technique of artificial insemination is practiced on cows about to be slaughtered, using dye instead of semen, so that success or failure is visible when the animal is butchered.

8. Funding by the U.S. Department of Transportation of research in Germany and elsewhere using corpses of infants in crash-simulation studies. When the story came out in Germany, it had the headline, "Professor Horror: He Did Car Tests Using Dead Children," and gave the example of a corpse in a collision that resulted in injuries to liver and lungs, and twenty-seven breaks in the ribs.

I have wanted to bring out something of the variety of cases that might be thought to involve some or other form of impiety, some kind of interference with the right ordering of things, a failure to recognize what ought to be treated with respect and not interfered with. Hume's argument is meant to get us to give up the conceptual tools for such a criticism of any of these cases. So, in thinking about his sort of argument, we need to have before us such cases as these. The argument Hume provides to show that suicide cannot be taken as contrary to God's will and an interference in divine providence can be regarded as an argument that there is no rational criterion for setting apart any area as beyond our interference. The Problem of Impiety confronts us, then, when we have taken in that argument of Hume's.

I can now state the Problem of Impiety: a range of actions have, in the past, been taken to be morally ruled out, have been taken to be outrageous, where both the moral impossibility and the outrageousness were thought of as tied to divine ordinances or commands of some sort. If we do not make any appeals to divine ordinances of any sort, are we then left only the alternative of allowing all of these actions, in every case in which they would appear to be conducive to human welfare? If not, what alternative to divine prohibition is available as a basis for objection? In the next part of this chapter, I explain how the Problem is connected with questions about objectivity in ethics.

Hume's rhetorical strategy in the essay on suicide can help us to see the connection. I mentioned earlier Hume's reference to the Roman superstition that a river should not be diverted from its natural course. Hume's own picture is that we are frequently stopped from doing what we want by the way nature works, including the placement of rivers, but that we also alter nature, including the course of rivers, for our own ends. We may, perfectly appropriately, move a water course to irrigate a field or prevent flooding. And just as it is not in general a crime to move a water channel from its natural course, so it is not necessarily a crime for me to turn a few ounces of blood that have been coursing around inside my body from their channel, and to end my life that way. Hume is inviting us to view the person who cuts her wrists to end her life from a perspective in which what she does is divert a fluid from its natural channel. Hume's language is intended to put the event of suicide into a world viewed as this happening and that: water running here, and a millwheel turning; blood running there, followed by collapse of such-and-such body there. When we see this or that happening as having some moral character, we are as it were gilding it mentally, seeing it in light of our own moral sensibilities. We are providing the moral color. But the world to which we thus respond is simply the world of this happening and that; the moral colors are superadded by us. The world to which we morally respond is the same for all of us: events and psychological states without any moral color of their own.

What I want to emphasize here is not the obvious point that Hume takes the moral color to be superadded, to be something we contribute, but that it is part of Hume's picture that the world of happenings and states to which we add the moral color is supposed to be available to all of us. There is the change in the channel in which some blood is flowing. That's objective, that's there; then, supposedly, we can raise the question what is a morally appropriate or what is a superstitious response to the action of disturbing the channel of the blood. Familiar as the Humean conception may be, we should recognize it as a particular conception, not one that is the only possible understanding of our situation as moral agents.

Here I want to mention the ideas of Iris Murdoch and Akeel Bilgrami. Murdoch wrote that there are people, she meant including Hume, "whose fundamental moral belief is that we all live in the same empirical and comprehensible world";[3] we then may have different moral responses to what are the same facts. So that is one conception of the world. But other people, Murdoch says, see the world of the moral agent in very different terms. For example, they may have as their fundamental belief "that we live in a world whose mystery transcends us"; and that what is central in moral life is responsiveness to that mystery. There is a sense in which different people may be said, as moral beings, to see different worlds – that's another Murdoch point; and she notes also that the concepts with which one person makes sense of the world may be incomprehensible to someone else. You can't, on her view, simply pick out the given facts, and take people to differ merely in their judgments about how to act, given those facts. Moral concepts, she suggests, should be "regarded as deep moral configurations of the world, rather than as lines drawn round separable

[3] I. Murdoch, "Vision and Choice in Morality," *Proceedings of the Aristotelian Society*, 30 (1956), 32–58, at 47.

factual areas."[4] Bilgrami has argued, like Murdoch, that we need to recognize a view of the world different from Hume's. As Hume sees it, the world does not genuinely make normative demands; facts are simply brute and there. But it is alternatively possible to take the world as suffused with value, and ourselves as tasked with respecting it.[5] I'll return to these issues at the end of this chapter. Here I have wanted to suggest that the background of the Humean conception of superstition is a particular understanding of what is genuinely objective, genuinely there.

II

I come now to the second part of my chapter, in which I look at some possible ways of responding to the Problem of Impiety. Many of the views I consider are quite complex, and my survey won't be able to go into details. Further, in the case of each of the philosophers whom I consider (with the exception of the last), I focus on a single work, and not on the development of their views in other works, or their changes of mind. I want here simply to lay out something of what the ground looks like.

One way of responding to the Problem is suggested by Hume's essay: the Problem, from that point of view, isn't really a problem. Hume's argument suggests that only superstition would lead us to treat some type of interference in how the world works as off limits to us. This Humean sort of response can be seen in much public discussion of cases like that of cloning, or that of genetically engineered organisms. Cloning can be seen simply as a way of expanding the options for the creation of families, with nothing more uncanny or problematic about it than there is about expanding the options for making electricity by moving a river. And there are people who write about it in the same spirit in which Hume wrote about suicide. There are also people who write about creating transgenic animals in the same Humean spirit: there isn't in the species of animals anything that it even makes sense to ask that we should respect. Whether it's the case of transgenic animals or cloning people, this kind of approach looks to the foreseeable benefits and risks, and if the benefits outweigh the risks, that's all that counts. So this is a kind of utilitarian approach.[6]

[4] Murdoch, "Vision and Choice," 55.

[5] A. Bilgrami, "Occidentalism, the Very Idea: An Essay on Enlightenment and Enchantment," *Critical Inquiry*, 32 (2006), 381–411.

[6] A similar sort of approach could be justified from the point of view of Stoic ethics, which does not take any type of action as absolutely ruled out. There are, for example, Stoic arguments that challenge the prohibitions on incest, and that allow such things as the eating of amputated human limbs.

(Hume himself takes a somewhat different approach in other works. See especially his treatment of respect for dead bodies in "Of Moral Prejudices" and his discussion of designer babies in the same essay.[7] Hume's treatment of respect for dead bodies has some features in common with the second, third, and fourth approaches discussed here.)

The second approach I want to mention is that of Mary Warnock. In an essay on in vitro fertilization, she explicitly rejects the idea that what counts in considering such possibilities as cloning embryos as a source of organs for transplantation is simply the balance between the likely benefits and the risks.[8] Warnock would want to object to such things as allowing embryos to be farmed for transplantable organs. Her objection, though, isn't that such a system would be outrageous, but that feelings of outrage would be felt, and that law and morality need to take such outrage seriously. Such feelings are a deep and significant part of our nature as moral beings. She puts forward a basic principle, meant to be an alternative to strict utilitarianism: that feelings of outrage and similar feelings need to be respected, even when there is no likely harm of the sort that utilitarians take seriously. So respect for such feelings can provide a basis for regarding certain actions as impermissible. Cloning embryos for transplants might then be ruled out without appeal to any religious views. So Warnock has a solution to the Problem of Impiety – the problem whether there is any basis for objection, other than appeal to a religious system, to any of the kinds of actions that many people may take as simply ruled out. Warnock's response is: the feelings of outrage felt by people and the need for morality to respect such feelings provide a basis for objection to many such actions. It's important here that she doesn't take the feelings of outrage as indicating that there is anything wrong with what the feelings are directed against.

The trouble with Warnock's approach is that it takes equally seriously outrage that is merely part of conventional thinking, and outrage at what (it might be argued) genuinely deserves to be met with outrage. If the principle is that feelings of moral outrage should be treated with respect, this would include the feelings of outrage at sexual relations between people of different races. Warnock might indeed allow that feelings of outrage could be outweighed when they clashed with other human interests, but her approach (in "In Vitro Fertilization") doesn't necessitate questioning whether the outrage is justified. And there is another problem: someone supporting a utilitarian

[7] Hume, "Of Moral Prejudices," *Essays*, 573–8.

[8] M. Warnock, "In Vitro Fertilization: The Ethical Issues (II)," *The Philosophical Quarterly*, 33 (1983), 238–49.

approach might say: "Human feelings are malleable, and people should be educated out of some outrage. If creating cloned embryos for use in organ banks can be justified on utilitarian grounds when we ignore feelings of outrage, reeducation to change such feelings would be justified on utilitarian grounds, and we have no grounds for thinking this couldn't be done."

A third approach is that of Stuart Hampshire.[9] He held that any morality must contain some set of prohibitions touching on the basic areas of human life, defining our attitudes toward human life and death, the treatment of the dead, sexual relations and relations within families, and so on. We have to believe in some firm and insurmountable barriers to some sorts of action; we have to believe that certain sorts of actions are utterly ruled out. In a religious society, these prohibitions will be tied in with the religion; the prohibitions will be taken to rest on divine commands. But even in a secular society, morality needs to respect fundamental prohibitions in these central areas of human life. There is here expressed a picture of human nature as containing deeply dangerous elements that would be let loose once such restraints are no longer recognized. But we should note that this conception of morality does not involve any idea that there is some way of evaluating any such set of prohibitions. The moral theorist can recognize that we must have some ideas about what would be horrific and outrageous, but, on this sort of approach, the theorist provides no guidance concerning what should be regarded as outrageous. And so again there is nothing in this approach against, for example, a prohibition on interracial sexual relations as being horrific, and against the nature of things.

The third approach, as I have described it, does not make a case for a virtue of piety, but the fourth approach does. Here my example is Roger Scruton, who has argued for taking piety seriously as a virtue within a secular society like ours.[10] Piety, as he sees it, does not depend on a religious system or any kind of theological dogma. He has put his ideas about piety in various ways, and I focus on an essay in which he treats as the essence of piety respect for the dead, respect for our ancestors, for what we inherit from them and what we owe to them. We have inherited life itself from them, and owe to them the passing on of life. We need to respect the attitudes toward life and death, and toward sexuality, that are essential to the passing on of human life. These attitudes are defined by prohibitions,

[9] S. Hampshire, "Morality and Pessimism," in S. Hampshire (ed.), *Public and Private Morality* (Cambridge University Press, [1973] 1978), 1–22.

[10] R. Scruton, "Decencies for Skeptics," *City Journal* (Spring 1996), 43–9.

by the ruling out of certain sorts of action and even ideas as unthinkable, and these prohibitions are themselves part of our inheritance from the past. Piety, respect for the dead and for the prohibitions we inherit from them, is a social necessity. For we cannot simply invent for ourselves the attitudes and moral meanings we need. The prejudices of ordinary people, and their habitual respect for these inherited prohibitions, are in no way inferior to the prejudices of liberal enlightenment.

This approach has some similarities to what I've laid out as the third approach. For both Scruton and Hampshire, there is a social need for a set of prohibitions that shape our attitudes in fundamental areas of human life. And, for both of them, you can't judge the content of the prohibitions in question by thinking about what it would be good to have as the content of such prohibitions. Scruton claims explicitly that all we have to oppose the prejudices of tradition is the prejudices of liberalism. The only difference is that the prejudices of liberals never seem like prejudice to them. I don't know whether Scruton would take this to imply that even liberal criticism of the banning of miscegenation was a prejudice and that respect for the dead would properly have involved respect for the inherited view that had treated racial mixing as an abomination. I cannot see what resources he has with which to distinguish between that inherited prohibition and the inherited prohibitions he thinks we ought to respect because they are inherited, and we owe such respect to the dead. But this may be something of an oversimplification. I am not sure whether he is fully consistent on the issue of prejudice and reason. He wants to make the issue independent of rethinking on our part; but he does also want to take such things as a prohibition on pornography as justified because of what pornography expresses. Respect for the dead means, for Scruton, respecting the views we inherit from them, and respecting their interest in our passing on life; but these two things may be quite distinct.

The second, third, and fourth approaches all accept a fundamental part of the Humean argument. He argued that only if we have a superstitious conception of God will we believe in some special sphere of actions that are out of bounds for us. There is no rational criterion for picking out some things that we might be able to do, and then saying: "We are never to do those things, they lie in a sphere on which we must not encroach." If you accept that sort of argument, you can go on in two different ways. You can say there is no sphere in which we cannot interfere, so there is no absolute prohibition on suicide, or on cloning babies or whatever else it may be. Alternatively, you can accept the argument that there is no rational criterion for delimiting the area on which we must not encroach, and you can nevertheless say that we ought to recognize that there are things lying outside what we are entitled to do, although there is no rational way to establish what lies in that area. The second, third, and fourth approaches have that in common, and something else besides. According to each of these approaches, we should treat with respect the prohibitions that people do recognize; but the philosophers themselves, in each case, distance themselves to a greater or lesser degree from the prohibitions. Warnock, for example, thinks that we oughtn't to go in for cloning embryos and allowing them to develop for use as a bank of organs for transplantation, because people would find this outrageous, and we should respect that. But she doesn't say whether she finds anything outrageous in this. The respect she thinks we should have for people's attitude toward such a system is not based on her going along with the attitude. The moral theorist, Warnock herself, doesn't need to have any attitude in this area in order to respect the attitudes she finds there. Similarly with Hampshire: we need to have some prohibitions that set up impermeable barriers around doing certain sorts of things. But it is no part of his argument that anything in particular ought to be prohibited. So, whatever the actual prohibitions are, his position is not one of identifying with people who accept the prohibitions. And, in the case of Scruton, if you say that it's good to accept the prejudices that have come down to us, you may yourself indeed accept the prejudices, but you are to a degree standing apart from them if you say that there is no reasoning about this, and that you just accept these prejudices because they are the ones you have inherited. If you say, "I believe that incest is absolutely ruled out, but I don't believe the prohibition rests on some rational justification; it's simply what was passed down to me," you are, or so it would seem, undercutting your own claim genuinely to believe that incest is ruled out. Maybe there is some way of getting around this, but here I want simply to note the problem.

The other approaches I shall describe do not accept the idea that there is no rational way of establishing any of the boundaries that people may think it is impious to overstep.

I am not sure how to categorize the next kind of approach. Many thinkers would warn us of the dangers of overestimating our own capacities, and of underestimating the dangers when we interfere in some fundamental way in the natural world. They remind us of the story of Prometheus: we should take as a warning the idea of the anger of the gods at anyone stealing what belongs to them, and we should beware of overreaching ourselves. We can see Mary Shelley's novel *Frankenstein* as expressing this sort of concern. A good contemporary example of this sort of thought can be found in John McPhee's work. He writes about our attempt to control the course of the Mississippi, an attempt he takes as doomed to fail, and likely to create huge economic and human damage when it does fail. Again, many people would think that, if scientists attempt to create a virus from scratch, we have no idea what horrendous consequences this might have; it is sheer arrogance, they say, to go ahead with such activities in the face of the possible fearsome consequences. Bernard Williams has written about such Promethean fear – the fear that we may take far too lightly the character of our relation to nature. Promethean fear, he says, is "based on a sense of an opposition between ourselves and nature, [nature] as an old, unbounded and potentially dangerous enemy," an enemy we are liable to terribly underestimate.[11] Williams isn't arguing that the feelings ought to be respected simply because people have them. He thinks that such fears can remind us of what is genuinely fearful. And the fears are also connected with things in nature that are deeply valuable to us, to our sense of what is important in human life. Now Promethean fear warns us of interfering in certain areas, as does the sense that such interference would be impious. But I think that these are distinguishable modes of response. They may be combined, and they have in common that they see in human nature the tendency to interfere where we ought to hold back, a tendency tied to forms of arrogance. I am leaving unsettled here the question of what the relation is between Promethean fear and ideas about impiety.

I turn now to what we can see in the thought of Immanuel Kant. I begin with his discussion of a case mentioned by Hume, inoculation against smallpox. Although Hume speaks of the idea that inoculation is impious as a French superstition, controversy about inoculation was widespread in Western Europe and America. The argument against the practice was that, however fine the end of preventing people from getting a serious case of smallpox might be, the means – deliberately giving people a disease – was a usurpation of what was reserved to providence. Kant discusses this case alongside his discussion of suicide, which he takes to be prohibited as a violation of duty to self.[12] Suicide, the destruction of your own animal life, is as such also an attack on the subject of morality in your own person. Suicide is doing what it lies in your power to do to obliterate morality itself. Kant goes on to consider getting yourself inoculated against smallpox. He

[11] B. Williams, "Must a Concern for the Environment Be Centred on Human Beings?," in C. C. W. Taylor (ed.), *Ethics and the Environment* (Oxford: Corpus Christi College, 1992), 60–8, at 67.

[12] I. Kant, "The Metaphysical Principle of Virtue," Part II of *The Metaphysics of Morals*, trans. J. Ellington (Indianapolis, IN: Bobbs Merrill, 1964 [Metaphysik der Sitten, 1797]).

grants that you are entitled to run risks – for example, a sailor may set out to sea, even in a storm. But the sailor hasn't created the storm, while the person who chooses inoculation has the disease put into himself; and so being inoculated isn't merely running a risk for the sake of a benefit. Putting something into your body, something known to be capable of killing you, isn't the same as going to sea when a storm may threaten. If you die in the storm, you did not kill yourself; but if you die of smallpox, having chosen to be inoculated, is this a case in which you are the agent of your death? Does respect for yourself as a rational being require that you abstain from doing anything to your own body that would risk making you the agent of your own destruction? Kant thinks this is not an easy question.

My point, though, is that we see him, in his discussion of suicide and inoculation, as taking two questions that are familiar in European thought as questions about impiety, and interpreting both questions in a new way: as issues of respect for what is genuinely deserving of awe and respect, the moral capacities within us. Questions that everyone in his audience will recognize as questions about impiety are being reinterpreted and transformed by Kant: they become questions about duty to self. (The same transformation can be seen in Kant's treatment of sex.) I'm not suggesting that the questions cease to be questions about impiety, but rather that Kant is providing a new understanding of impiety itself, given his understanding of moral capacity as that which is genuinely deserving of respect informed by awe, that which is genuinely worthy of reverence. While Kant's application of these ideas reflects his upbringing, there is nevertheless a great distance from the sort of ideas we had in Warnock, Hampshire, and Scruton. If I am right in seeing Kant as giving us a transformed understanding of what is genuine impiety, he is providing a method for thinking about what is and what isn't impious. Suicide and what he takes as unnatural sexual practices are ways of treating our animal nature that implicitly derogate from our character as rational beings. They can be understood as primary examples of impiety, within the context of Kant's ethics; and the approach could be extended. So we can see Kant as providing a quite different kind of solution to the Problem of Impiety. He rejects the Humean argument that if we do not have a superstitious idea of God or the gods, we have no way to tell what sphere of actions is off limits to us, what interferences with nature go too far. We do not need any religious system in order to identify the limits. If there is a weakness in a Kantian solution to the Problem of Impiety, it is the difficulties in applying the ideas once we move away from the primary range of cases, for example to something like respect for the bodies of the dead. Not that you can't apply the sort of ideas I've sketched, but the application becomes less direct and less convincing.

I have not gone into details of how a Kantian moral philosophy provides a reinterpretation of impiety. Both divine law morality and Kantian morality can treat "impiety" as having both a narrow and a wider meaning. In a wide sense, any violation of a law that is worthy of reverence, that comes from a source worthy of reverence, is impious. But it is the narrow sense of "impiety" that is directly relevant to Hume's problem. What would be impious in this narrow sense within the context of Kantian ethics is a subcategory of perfect duties to oneself. The subcategory would include duties to oneself in regard to one's own animal nature, the animal nature of other human beings, and nonhuman nature; but again not all such perfect duties would correspond to impieties. This can be seen if we consider sexuality, and the contrast between what would from a Kantian point of view count as lack of moderation in marital sex and what would count as unnatural sex. Lack of moderation is a violation of duty to self, but it is the willful misuse of one's animal nature in unnatural sex that would constitute an abandonment of respect for oneself as a rational being. That is not a matter of degree. So what corresponds to impiety, within Kantian ethics, is violation of duties to self in regard to nature (one's own animal nature, that of other human beings, that of nonhuman animals, or inanimate nature), where the treatment of nature involves a denial or abandonment of respect for oneself as a rational being.

I turn now to Elizabeth Anscombe. She said very little explicitly about impiety, but some interesting ideas emerge in four of her works. First, she holds there are various practices of reason that are dependent on training in the particular practice. Recognizing that certain things aren't to be done because they are impious involves learning one such practice of reasoning.[13] This goes with a second idea: that conventional moral thought can be pernicious;[14] so she would reject the Warnock, Hampshire, and Scruton approaches because they do not take seriously enough that conventional pieties may be stupid or evil. Third, although she believes in a moral law given to us by God, she also believes that what is required by the moral law is something we can work out using our capacities to think through what sorts of actions are good and what are bad.[15] And fourth, she thinks that a

[13] G. E. M. Anscombe, "Rules, Rights and Promises" [1978], in *Ethics, Religion and Politics* (Oxford: Blackwell, 1981), 97–103.

[14] Anscombe, "Modern Moral Philosophy" [1958], *Ethics, Religion and Politics*, 26–42.

[15] Anscombe, "Modern Moral Philosophy," also "Contraception and Chastity" [1972, revised version 1975], in M. Geach and L. Gormally (eds.), *Faith in a Hard Ground: Essays on Religion, Philosophy and Ethics by G. E. M. Anscombe* (Exeter: Imprint Academic, 2008), 170–91.

kind of recognition of mystery, or a kind of mystical perception, is involved in some virtues. She doesn't mean by this something out of the ordinary. She thinks that the feeling for the respect due to a person's dead body is a perfectly ordinary feeling. Take "the knowledge that a dead body isn't something to be put out for the collectors of refuse to pick up": "This . . . is mystical," she says, "though it's as common as humanity."[16] So too the sense of respect for life that is reflected in the prohibition on murder: this is a kind of mystical perception. So too is a sense of something wrong in treating sex as mere casual satisfaction, like picking up an edible mushroom you happen to see, and eating it. The sense that sex isn't like that involves a mystical perception. There are, she thinks, some virtues that don't depend on any such mystical perception. You don't need any such perception to see the point of honesty about property, for example. Such honesty has obvious social utility. But, in the case of respect for life, what is involved is a sense of "respect before the mystery of human life"[17] – the kind of respect that might come out in refusing to treat some lives as more valuable than others. What she has in mind you can call a religious feeling, but it isn't connected with any particular religious system, and can be found in an incipient form in people who might not have much time for religion as any kind of organized system of beliefs and practices.

Anscombe's idea is that some virtues, like honesty about property, don't depend on a mystical perception and others, like respect for life and respect for the dead, cannot be given a utilitarian explanation and depend on a mystical perception. This distinction has in it the germ of a way of thinking about impiety. Interferences in the course of nature that go against the second sort of virtue could be thought of as impious. Take the case of the use of corpses in crash research. Many people have a sense of outrage and repugnance when they hear of this. A possible Anscombean approach here would not take those feelings as decisive (any more than they should be taken as decisive in the case of dissection in medical education): the question would be whether this treatment of corpses was a violation of the virtue of respect for the dead, and outrageous on that account. If it went against that virtue, it would thus count as impious, since that is a virtue of the nonutilitarian sort, the sort that depends on a mystical perception. So that is an example of how Anscombe's ideas could suggest a kind of response to Hume on impiety, a way of examining whether certain sorts

[16] Anscombe, "Contraception and Chastity," 187.

[17] Anscombe, "Murder and the Morality of Euthanasia" [1982], in M. Geach and L. Gormally (eds.) *Human Life, Action and Ethics: Essays by G. E. M. Anscombe* (Exeter: Imprint Academic, 2005), 269.

of action were ruled out as impious. Her ideas provide, not an account of impiety, but a possible line to be explored. There is an important contrast between her ideas and Kant's. In the Kantian reinterpretation of impiety, what plays a central role is the idea of reverence for our moral capacities, for ourselves as rational beings. In the Anscombean approach, what plays a central role is a kind of reverence or awe, and sense of mystery, before the life and death of human beings, and before the capacity to transmit life through sexual reproduction. So an Anscombean approach would be more directly applicable than Kant's to many of the cases listed earlier in this chapter. And it treats human beings essentially equally, whereas Kant's approach has a more limited kind of applicability to the treatment of people who have no rational capacity.

I have not tried to consider every thinker whose ideas suggest some approach to the Problem of Impiety. Here I will mention a few others. Simone Weil is one such thinker: she makes injustice into a kind of impiety, in that, in acting unjustly, we fail to be stopped by what is sacred about a human being.[18] I think also of Raimond Gaita, writing on respect for the dead, and how there is room for honoring a person, or indeed an animal, or dishonoring the person or animal, in how we treat the dead body of that person or that animal; also of Stephen Clark, writing on why we are right to be horrified by such things as the transformation of mammals into milk machines, of David Braine, writing on "respecting man's character as an animal in order to respect humanity itself." There is Michael Sandel's discussion of the taking up of a stance toward the world of "mastery and dominion," and Mathew Lu's wide-ranging investigation of the wrongness of cannibalism.[19] These approaches have in common a recognition of certain forms of respect as justified by what it is we are treating with respect, although many naturalistic approaches to ethics would not see in the things in question anything that could be taken to be worthy of such respect. One further sort of possibility is exemplified by some Stoic thinkers, who take piety seriously as involving respect for what

[18] S. Weil, "La personne et le sacré," *Ecrits de Londres et dernières lettres* (Paris: Gallimard, 1957), 11–44.

[19] R. Gaita, *The Philosopher's Dog* (Melbourne: Text Publishing, 2002); S. R. L. Clark, "Natural Integrity and Biotechnology," in D. S. Oderberg and J. Laing (eds.), *Human Lives: Critical Essays on Consequentialist Bioethics* (Basingstoke: Macmillan, 1997), 58–76; D. Braine, "The Human and the Inhuman in Medicine: Review of Issues Concerning Reproductive Technology," in L. Gormally (ed.), *Moral Truth and Moral Tradition* (Blackrock: Four Courts Press, 1994), 226–39; M. J. Sandel, *The Case Against Perfection: Ethics in the Age of Genetic Engineering* (Cambridge, MA: The Belknap Press of Harvard University Press, 2007); M. Lu, "Explaining the Wrongness of Cannibalism," *American Catholic Philosophical Quarterly*, 87 (2013), 433–58.

requires to be treated with respect, but who don't tie such piety to a realm of prohibited actions.[20]

III

Conclusions

First, the Humean sort of approach to the Problem of Impiety is not obviously correct, although it may appear to be the only reasonable approach if one assumes that only harms and benefits give us reasons for allowing or disallowing some interference in the course of nature.

A second conclusion is that there is a range of responses to the Problem that go halfway with Hume. That is, they assign importance to impiety-feelings, and argue that such feelings should be taken seriously. But they don't depart from Hume on the question whether such feelings have any basis that a moral thinker might investigate. They don't treat feelings of outrage at something as suggesting that the thing in question is outrageous, or might be outrageous, so that one could press the issue, and examine whether it was outrageous. There is a contrast between those views and the approaches of Kant and Anscombe. Kant and Anscombe differ deeply from each other, but they both take respect or reverence or honor for what should properly be honored to set limits to what we can legitimately do. If we look at their two approaches, we can see that piety goes with concepts of things that are worthy of our respect, and that how we treat nature (our own animal nature, or that of animals, or inanimate nature) can express disrespect for what is worthy of respect. It is therefore possible for us to recognize certain things as not to be done, as off limits, because they are expressive of such disrespect. Piety goes with an understanding of the world within which there are things requiring respect. For both Kant and Anscombe in different ways, the world is such that this makes sense. The world can also be understood differently, as bare of such proper objects of respect.[21] Wordsworth calls such a conception of the world

[20] See, for example, K. Vogt, *Law, Reason, and the Cosmic City: Political Philosophy in the Early Stoa* (Oxford University Press, 2008).

[21] My summary leaves out the interesting case of Wittgenstein's ethical views, as expressed in the "Lecture on Ethics." The world (on his view) is bare of what I am calling proper objects of respect; it is nonsense to speak as if some feature of things could make it essential for us to act in a certain way, or be worthy of reproach if we didn't. But exactly that nonsense is ethics. That sort of view could be said to leave room for piety (and indeed it is no accident that the primary example for Wittgenstein,

impious;[22] and the point is that, with a conception of the world as just a bunch of stuff or a bunch of nonmysterious facts, nothing requires treatment as having a dignity or integrity that needs to be respected, and so, in our reasoning about action, there's no room for asking what we need to honor or respect. There's no room to examine whether something expresses disrespect or contempt for what must not be treated so. Thus, for example, there is no room for the issue of respect for the dead in thinking about whether we can bash their bodies for research. I'm suggesting that there are conceptions of the world within which the idea of impiety makes sense, and conceptions of the world within which it doesn't. Here I have come again to the ideas of Iris Murdoch and Akeel Bilgrami, about the very different moral visions people have of what the world is. And that is where I stop.

in his earlier writings, of what is morally prohibited is suicide), but does not treat it as intelligible, in the way in which both Anscombe and Kant (on my account of their views) treat it as intelligible.

22 W. Wordsworth, "The Excursion" [1814], in *Poetical Works*, ed. T. Hutchinson, new edition revised by E. de Selincourt (Oxford University Press, 1969), 591–698, at 637.

CHAPTER 3

The Virtue of Piety

Robert C. Roberts

Euthyphro and Socrates

Socrates' conversation with Euthyphro[1] about piety is set in the ironical situation that Socrates, a wise old man whose piety before the god has dominated his life, on his way to an inquiry preliminary to his trial for impiety, tries to learn what piety is from Euthyphro, a young man who ignorantly claims to be an expert on piety, on his way to commit an impiety against his father. Thus the two contexts proper to the virtue of piety – relations between offspring and parents in a family, and relations of human beings to the divine – are represented together in the dialogue. But early in the dialogue, Socrates narrows the discussion to piety in the relation with the divine.

Plato's record of Socrates' last days marks the comprehensive moral importance of the virtue of piety by showing us that it was precisely Socrates' piety – his obedience to the god in practicing philosophy for the spiritual upbuilding of Athens and its people – that got him condemned to death for impiety; and that it was the impiety of people like Euthyphro – the willingness to do injustice that stems from an arrogant and ignorant unwillingness to examine oneself philosophically before the divine tribunal – that made possible Athens' judicial murder of the man who "was of all those we have known the best, and also the wisest and the most upright."[2] Let's begin by thinking about inter-human piety.

Filial Piety

Euthyphro takes a very modern line when he argues that ties of kinship should be irrelevant to ethics. The pursuit of justice should be utterly

[1] I am grateful to Douglas Henry for sharing with me his unpublished manuscript, "The Real Euthyphro Problem," which has inspired the reading of the *Euthyphro* presented here, and to David McPherson and Ryan West for very helpful comments on earlier drafts of this chapter.

[2] Plato, *Phaedo* [ca. 380 BC], trans. G. M. A. Grube, in J. M. Cooper (ed.), *Plato: Complete Works* (Indianapolis, IN: Hackett, 1997), 118a.

impartial, with the implication that, as painful as it may be, a son should be as ready to prosecute his father for a crime as any unrelated person would be. The pain of making yourself impartial when you revere your parent suggests that you haven't fully assimilated the modern moral outlook – that you're something of a throwback to a morality that endorses filial piety as a virtue. Euthyphro seems to suffer no such psychological hang-up.

Socrates expresses shock when he hears that Euthyphro is about to prosecute his own father for murder. We learn that the "murder" was at most a case of negligent homicide and was perhaps only an unfortunate accident. But the crime's mildness doesn't seem to be what dismays Socrates about Euthyphro's action. He is scandalized by the prospect of a *son's* prosecuting his *father*, perhaps even regardless of the charge and of its merit. In Plato's *Crito*, we learn the extent of Socrates' own piety toward the city that has nurtured him and provided a home for his life's work: though he regards the charge on which he is to be put to death as false and unjust, his veneration for Athens and his gratitude to her deter him from trying to escape from prison. Socrates is appalled by Euthyphro's apparent impiety, and notes with irony that he must be extremely wise, and confident of his wisdom to boot, to flout tradition in undertaking such an action.

What would piety be, in case Euthyphro had perfectly exemplified it toward his father? I propose that it would be an attitude, characterized by a special kind of caring, toward his progenitor *as his* progenitor. Piety is the perception of a relationship – thus of himself to his father and his father to himself – between himself as succeeding and resulting from his father and thus as being "subject" to his father, a recognition made possible by his caring about the relationships and the special kind of precedence and subsequence involved. What is this special kind of ascendancy that piety caringly ascribes to the parent? It is simply the progenitive relationship, both physical and social. The relevant kind of "superiority" is not that of morality, talent, power, wealth, or anything other than that his father is his *father* – that that man occupies that role and has that precedence. That is, our pious Euthyphro cares about his father *as* his father and thus about himself *as* the son of this father. Thus filial piety involves valuing fatherhood and sonship as such, as primal ordered goods, as fundamental to the structure of things human.

A primitive natural piety would explain why children without known fathers or mothers yearn to find them, or at least to find out something about them, to have some grasp of the parent's identity as pertinent to their own. As soon as children find out some basic things about the social structure of human existence, they are interested, on behalf of their own life, in their parentage. Like other healthy and natural passions, the reverential interest in one's parentage can be dulled or distorted, perhaps even obliterated, by a history of abuse, and more or less successfully transferred to other guardians. But in the best and least troubled kind of case, it develops into fully formed filial piety for one's own historical parents.

So if Euthyphro exemplified filial piety, he would care about his father as his father, himself as the son of his father, and the relationship so constituted. By contrast, Euthyphro's words would suggest that his ideological commitment to moral impartiality has stunted his piety almost to the point of extinction. But *how* would he have to care about his father and his relationship to him to exemplify filial piety? You can care about your parents and your relationship to them in a variety of ways. A way of caring about your parents is a function of what we might call your fundamental evaluative construal of them. Who do you think they are (so to speak)? Your fundamental construal will be what your parents mean to you. This construal will be dispositional and determinative, not usually explicit and occurrent. It will be a tendency to see – that is, *actually* construe – situations involving your parents in ways that are determined, in part, by the dispositional one.

Perhaps you see your parents as a ready source of cash. If you do, and then their financial fortunes diminish so that the cash dries up, you will be **disappointed**, and your disappointment can be analyzed as a construal of your parents as cashless, based on your love of them *as* your source of cash. Or if they voluntarily reduce the flow of cash from them to you, you might be **angry**, and your anger would be a construal of them as culpably restricting the cash, based on your love of them as your source of cash. And if they change their mind, you will be **glad**, and your gladness will be a construal of them as opening up the flow of cash, based on your concerned construal of them as your source of cash.[3]

You might construe them as competitors. Maybe your father was a successful businessman and vain about his success, and thought of himself as a self-made man, and drilled into his children that they would be worth exactly what they made of themselves, and that making something of

[3] So we have here two senses of "way of caring," the dispositional one and the occurrent one. The dispositional way of caring – what I call the basic concern in *Emotions: An Essay in Aid of Moral Psychology* (Cambridge University Press, 2003) and *Emotions in the Moral Life* (Cambridge University Press, 2013) – is the basis for the occurrent ways of caring (the emotions of disappointment, anger, gladness, and so forth).

yourself was a matter of equaling or besting the best in your field. So you came to see your father's success as a challenge, and your father as a rival of sorts, as the one you needed to equal or outdo to establish your credentials as a human being. This fundamental construal will have emotional consequences. You are **overjoyed** and **relieved** when you, like your father before you, are admitted to Yale. When others speak awestruck about your father's accomplishments, you feel a sinking **despair** of ever making anything of yourself. When he runs into difficulties later in life and his business falls on hard times and he's cut down to size a bit, **hope** rises in your heart that you may equal or even better his accomplishments. When you assess your own accomplishments, it is with **anxious apprehension** about how they will measure up. You find yourself comparing your accomplishments with your father's when he was your age, sometimes with **anxiety** and sometimes with **satisfaction**. Your fundamental construal of your father as your chief benchmark and competitor determines your emotional relationship to him, as well as to many others – your colleagues, your wife, your children.

But deeper in you is something else, a dimmer but more primordial construal of him – that seed of honoring from which the virtue of piety is supposed to grow. And you are conflicted in your competitiveness. You feel a loyalty to him, and in his later comparative humiliation the elation of your competitiveness is mixed with **compassion** and **empathic shame** and you find yourself using your own resources and ingenuity to rehabilitate, if possible, his tarnished reputation.

Our filially pious Euthyphro will care about his father in a way that Plato's Euthyphro doesn't seem to, but his caring must be formed by the fundamental construal that is characteristic for filial piety. The word that seems best to capture this construal is "reverence." Our better Euthyphro reveres his parents as his parents. His piety, then, will be reverence for his father as his father, and for their relationship as father and son. What kind of caring is reverence? A helpful place to start is Immanuel Kant's account of "respect" (*Achtung*) for the moral law. I will interpret it in terms of the account of fundamental construal and apply it to the case of one's parents as the objects of such construal.

> [*Achtung*] is properly the representation of a worth that infringes upon my self-love. Hence there is something that is regarded as an object neither of inclination nor of fear, though it has something analogous to both. The *object* of [*Achtung*] is simply the *law*, and indeed the law that we impose upon *ourselves*, and yet as necessary in itself. As a law we are subject to it without consulting self-love; as imposed upon us by ourselves it is

> nevertheless a result of our will; and in the first respect it has an analogy with fear, in the second with inclination.[4]

According to Kant, when someone appreciates the moral law for what it is, she construes it 1) as something of "worth" such that, in any contest with personal preferences, its worth trumps the preference; 2) as analogous to something both attractive (that inclines one toward it) and fearsome (that deters or inhibits). Thus *Achtung* sees its object as of overriding worth (the Jew or Christian might speak here of "glory"[5]) that both attracts and inhibits. I'm suggesting that the object of filial reverence is very much like this. Were Euthyphro to revere his father as his father, he would both cherish him as having a worth such as overrides the worth of many other things that Euthyphro values and respect him as setting limits to what Euthyphro is otherwise inclined to do. It is not, perhaps, *unthinkable* that a pious man would in some circumstances prosecute his father for a very great crime, but, as Socrates exclaims to Plato's Euthyphro when he reports what he is about to do, "most men would not know how they could do this and be right. It is not the part of [just] anyone to do this, but of one who is far advanced in wisdom."[6] Kant uses the word "holy" for a will whose appreciation of the moral law is so pure of morally adverse inclination that it has no need of inhibition. The holiness of the will will be subjective holiness. Subjective holiness is the ideal response (Aquinas would say the "connatural" one) to the objective holiness of the parent–child relationship – it's being "inviolate from ordinary use" in the words of the Oxford English Dictionary. The objective holiness of the parent–child bond would then be the inhibiting factor, to which the person who is reverent (but not necessarily holy himself) responds. The filially pious person who does prosecute his father would feel this inhibition as extreme spiritual distress and a sense of violating something holy. We've seen that Plato's Euthyphro seems to be without this distress.

Why does the commandment say, "Honor your father and your mother,"[7] and not "Love your father and your mother"? We might say that the word "honor" appears in the commandment because of what the commandment is specifically commanding: filial piety. Certainly you should love your parents, but here the emphasis is on their status as your parents and yours as their son

[4] I. Kant, *Groundwork of the Metaphysics of Morals*, trans. and ed. by M. J. Gregor, in *Practical Philosophy*, The Cambridge Edition of the Works of Immanuel Kant (Cambridge University Press, [1785] 1996), 56; italics original.

[5] See Exodus 34:29–35; II Corinthians 3:12–18.

[6] Plato, *Euthyphro* [ca. 390 BC], trans. G. M. A. Grube, in Cooper (ed.), *Plato: Complete Works*, 4a–b.

[7] Exodus 20:12.

or daughter, and your duties in consequence of this relationship. Since, as we've seen, honoring (revering) is a kind of caring, an emotional *attitude* is largely constitutive of the relationship, so that to speak of "your duties" here is not to speak primarily of discrete *actions* that a child might be thought under obligation to perform for her parents. In this way, filial piety is analogous to love.

Filial piety is often accompanied by gratitude to parents, as is natural since good parents – and even not-so-good ones – provide many good things for their children, and do so out of good will toward them. Still, the pious son's or daughter's reverence for the parents is not the same as dispositional gratitude, because such gratitude and such reverence are different construals: they are perceptions of different features of the parent–child relationship. Filial reverence sees the parent as progenitor, as antecedent and condition of one's existence in the nature of things, while gratitude sees the parent as the benevolent giver of good gifts. Yet piety, as a sensitivity to the parent–child relation and some appreciation of its excellence, readies its possessor for gratitude by making salient for him the actions and attitudes characteristic of a good parent.

In a book on the virtues of Abraham Lincoln and how he came to have them, William Lee Miller comments on an anomalous flaw in Lincoln's character. He notes that two of Lincoln's extraordinary natural traits that plausibly account for the self-confidence and sociability on which he built his amazing moral character – his physical strength and his talent for storytelling – he inherited from his father, Thomas Lincoln.[8] Miller reports that Abraham Lincoln is not known to have said anything complimentary of his father, and in autobiographical comments stressed his father's lack of education, commenting once that "He never did more in the way of writing than to bunglingly sign his own name."[9]

> The critic of Thomas Lincoln who is most convincing, partly by what he does not say and do, is Abraham, his son. He may have been unfair to his father, as ambitious and able sons sometimes are to not very talented and not very successful fathers, but his lack of filial piety is striking. If you are looking for some fault in Abraham Lincoln to offset his too consistent goodness, I suppose you might name his insufficient obedience to the commandment to honor his father.[10]

A nice example of filial piety is found in George Eliot's *Middlemarch*. Mary Garth has excellent parents in Caleb and Susan Garth. The Garths

[8] W. L. Miller, *Lincoln's Virtues* (New York: Alfred A. Knopf, 2002), 71ff.

[9] Miller, *Lincoln's Virtues*, 68. [10] Miller, *Lincoln's Virtues*, 60–1.

are a little straitened as to cash because Caleb cares more about meticulously improving land and buildings than he does about being paid for his work, but his wife has saved up enough money to apprentice their eldest son. Mary works as a kind of servant in the home of her relative, the wealthy but unsympathetic old Mr. Featherstone. When Fred Vincey (also a relative of Featherstone), a fun-loving and rather irresponsible young man who is in love with Mary, gets Mary's father involved in responsibility for Fred's debts, Mary and her mother both have to fork over their hard-earned savings.

> "I suppose your father wanted your earnings," said old Mr. Featherstone with his usual power of unpleasant surmise when Mary returned to him. "He makes but a tight fit, I reckon. You're of age now; you ought to be saving for yourself."
>
> "I consider my father and mother the best part of myself, sir," said Mary coldly.[11]

Mary's piety is no doubt mixed with love and gratitude, so it's impossible to apportion responsibility for such words to the one motive in distinction from the others.

It's a little clearer where the pious action derives less collateral support from the other attitudes. In a family discussion about where a grand-nephew and -niece might find the money for college tuition, my wife, Elizabeth, asked whether their father might contribute something. One of them replied, "I don't want to disrespect my father, but he's not good at holding onto money." Mary Garth's response might well have had gratitude at its root, inasmuch as her thought might have been, "Helping my folks in a strait is the least I can do, after all they've done for me" (though that isn't what she said, and what she did say sounds more like piety). In contrast, the very fact that my grandnibling felt the need to start with an apology for the father who has neglected his responsibility toward his child suggests that gratitude is not likely to explain the response. Responding in the style of Lincoln, he might have said simply, "We'll get no help from Dad." But feeling a respectful inhibition (see Kant), and wishing to avoid the bad light that saying so would have thrown on his father, he answered sensitively with a mild apology that seems to have been prompted by reverence for the man from whose loins he sprang – even though, due to carelessness or calculation, that father could spare no money to do his duty of seeing to his children's

[11] G. Eliot, *Middlemarch* (New York: Penguin Classics, [1871–2] 1994), ch. XXV, 258.

education. My grandnibling's devotion bears a distant similarity to Socrates' loyalty to the city of Athens despite its perverse and unjust decision to kill him.

Religious Piety

I have argued that the virtue of filial piety is reverence for one's parents, whereby one gives them their due as parents, regardless of whether they are good parents. The reason is that piety is directed at the *role* of parent, and thus at the particular parent as occupant of that venerable role. Extra admiration is warranted if the parent occupies the role well – approximates well to the ideal – but piety views the parent as inviting reverence in any case. The role is a kind of ideal, and so is an excellence and calls for treatment as such. But the notion of a role is odd when applied to God. If *being God* is a role, then the role and its occupant are identical (or at least inseparable). So the idea of piety toward God even in case God is not a good one makes no sense. God, being the only one, doesn't *conform* to any ideal; he *is* the ideal.

But who is God? Socrates and Euthyphro answer this question very differently, even though they seem to agree that it makes no sense to suppose that God is not entirely admirable. But their difference about who God is makes a big difference in their judgments about what to do. If filial piety is not properly conditional on parents' being personally flawless, and is even more clearly exemplified where parents are bad (as Kant's sense of duty is more clearly exemplified where the agent has no inclination to do her duty – or even has an inclination not to do her duty), piety toward the god requires denying that the god is in any way morally flawed. Socrates' objection to Euthyphro's theology and ethics is precisely that the gods so depicted have bad morals, and so can't be gods. Euthyphro's initial response is to assert the contrapositive of Socrates' conditional: "Zeus shackled his own father for swallowing his [other] sons unjustly, and … Cronus in turn had gelded his father for like reasons,"[12] so it is morally all right for me to prosecute my father. But Euthyphro's commitment to the morality of the Olympian gods is not firm against the onslaughts of Socrates' confident moral criticism. In his next definition of piety (piety is what *all* the gods agree to be right) he seems to allow the moral fallibility of individual gods. Socrates apparently advocates perfect being theology (in

[12] Plato, *Euthyphro*, 6a.

Republic, book 2), which presupposes that the theologian has an accurate concept of divine perfection. And divine perfection entails moral perfection. Thus the charge of impiety and theological innovation against Socrates seems justified from the point of view of the Greek tradition that Euthyphro represents. What from Socrates' point of view is scandalous impiety is piety for Euthyphro and the prosecuting Athenians, and what for him is piety is scandalous impiety for them.

So we have a version of what is known as "the Euthyphro problem": To what extent does the pious person derive her morals from her concept of God, and to what extent does she derive her concept of God from her morals? I deliberately put the question in the soft terms of "extent" to open a way between the dilemma's horns. Euthyphro seems to be deriving his moral judgments from his conception of the gods, while Socrates seems to be deriving his conception of the god from his conception of morals. – Or is this last correct? The god seems to guide him by the "sign," and so to be a source of guidance partially independent of Socrates' conscience. On the other hand, Socrates' moral development seems to make him more sensitive than others to the leading of the god. (Socrates doesn't seem to think that the god is just a fiction for his own conscience.)

I think the right approach to this question is dialectical. We can't help but use our moral intuitions (at whatever stage of development they occupy at the time) to understand God, but the sensitivity so constituted, along with sensitivity-engendering practices (for example, prayer, listening carefully to the tradition, dialectical criticism), enable us to hear from God things that transcend those intuitions. As we grow in piety, our understanding of God broadens and deepens, we understand better the gaps in our understanding, and we become better able to distinguish the voice of God from the voices of our environment and our rationalizing self-interest. The Christian, for example, wants to say *both* that God's law is written on our hearts *and* that God's ways are not our ways.

The ancient Greek conception of piety makes the virtue an attitude toward both God and parents. A similar connection can be traced in ancient Hebrew, and consequently also Christian, thought. Marilynne Robinson's character John Ames (in *Gilead*) is an elderly pastor who, nearing death, is writing a letter for his young son to read when he is older. In it he meditates, in a Christian vein, on matters of human life, and in one passage raises a question about the position of the fifth commandment, "You shall honor your father and mother," in the order of the Ten Commandments. His preferred interpretation is that this commandment is "the last in the sequence relating to right worship rather than the first in the series relating to right conduct."[13] If the idea that our attitude to our parents should be something like worship shocks a little, Ames didn't invent it. In Thomas Aquinas's discussion of the virtue of piety, which he classifies as a gift of the Spirit on account of the apostle Paul's remark that "When we cry 'Abba, Father!' it is the Spirit himself bearing witness that we are children of God . . .,"[14] he says, "since it belongs properly to piety to pay duty and worship [*officium et cultum*] to one's father, it follows that piety, whereby, at the Holy Ghost's instigation, we pay worship and duty [*cultum et officium*] to God as our Father, is a gift of the Holy Ghost."[15] The link Thomas sees between filial and religious piety is the construal of the worshiped object as Father. Both Paul and Thomas give a kind of psychological priority to the "worship" of parents, as though we'll understand something about the worship of God by consulting our experience of our parents. The relation between the reverence or honor that is due to God and that which is due to our parents is not equivalent, but analogical. Each "parent" has a kind of dignity that the proper reverence perceives and acknowledges, and the parent possesses her dignity as due to the order that God, who therefore has ontological priority, has ordained and established. So the virtue of piety is properly a disposition to an *integrated* construal of God and parents: God in similarity to parents and parents as provision of God.

Those who recognize the special dignity of parents due to the order established by God will also recognize a number of related dimensions that are characterized by that inhibiting glory that is perceived by the attitude of reverence. In "The Problem of Impiety" (Chapter 2 in this volume), Cora Diamond notes that a utilitarian way of thinking would commend doing some things that a pious person would feel strongly inhibited from doing, even to bring about great human good. Furthermore, this inhibition seems to be general in human nature, not limited to those who explicitly believe in God. Here are some of Diamond's examples:

1) manufacturing two-headed dogs by brain transplantation
2) using children's corpses in automobile crash tests to design cars that are safer for living children

[13] M. Robinson, *Gilead* (New York: Farrar, Strauss, and Giroux, 2004), 135. I am grateful to David McPherson for alerting me to this richly edifying passage, and reminding me of the whole novel.

[14] Romans 8:16.

[15] St. Thomas Aquinas, *Summa Theologica*, trans. Fathers of the English Dominican Province (Westminster, MD: Christian Classics, [ca. 1266–73] 1981), II–II, q. 121, a. 1.

3) maintaining the brains of decapitated fetuses in a hook-up devised for the study of chemical activity in the brain
4) the development by researchers in Massachusetts of embryos that are part human and part cow
5) mass production of cloned embryos for use solely in research, to make more easily available replacement tissues for patients
6) feeding ground-up sheep to cows

To my mind, the examples that involve tampering with humanity (2–5) are stronger than those that don't, but all can be construed as violations of the glory of creation. The stronger one's attunement to that forbidding glory, the more repugnance one will feel toward its violation. Professor Diamond thinks of the inhibiting factor in the pious theist as a response to a purported divine command or prohibition, but it seems to me that the most mature kind of piety is a response to what I've called "glory." (See the earlier discussion of Kant on reverence.) The order of creation expressed in the parent–child relation and the other dimensions of order are beautiful and precious, and piety is a response to this, rather than to a divine directive abstracted from it. (A theist might say that the perception of glory is the mode in which the believer receives God's command.) This would account for the feelings of piety among non-theists, who obviously won't believe in divine commandments.

Theists have a "problem of impiety," namely, that our piety is so vacillating, inconsistent, misguided, and weak: we are often dim-sighted of the inhibiting glory of creation, and so we are less good stewards than we might be and are called to be. And we may undertake various spiritual disciplines to toughen and sharpen the piety of our vision. But *our* problem of impiety is not the one Professor Diamond discusses. The problem she refers to is that people who feel inhibition about simply maximizing utility when doing so would involve altering the course of nature in ways like 1–6, yet are not theists, seem to have no way of distinguishing such cases from the feeling, which some people have historically had, that interracial marriage, for example, is a violation of nature and should be seen as an outrage. She mentions Stuart Hampshire and Roger Scruton as piety advocates who have this problem of impiety: they can provide no criterion for distinguishing proper from improper objects of piety's inhibition. Kant does somewhat better, offering a reinterpretation of impiety that detaches it from theology and attaches it to an anthropology of human dignity. For example, people ought not to commit suicide because to do so is to violate a duty to oneself as a being to whom reverence is due as having the dignity of practical rationality.

Diamond sees in some ideas of Elizabeth Anscombe the possibility of a better approach. Anscombe says that some virtues, such as chastity and respect for human life, require "mystical perception," such as that human corpses are to be treated with respect, and that casual sex is sordid.[16] (Examples of virtues not based on mystical perception are justice and respect for property.) To such perception, the human body can have a sacred or holy appearance, as can the act of sexual intercourse. Perhaps the insight that parenthood is venerable is another, this perception making it very difficult for a son to prosecute his father by use of the law. All these perceptual sensitivities can be overridden, not just in instances, but dispositionally so that the individual submerges the sensibility or erases it entirely. But in the well-reared, healthy, and unjaded, these natural sensitivities will be intact and, I should think, will be deepened, sharpened, and ramified as virtue matures. The Christian will have many centuries of careful reflection at her back to consult as to whether interracial marriage ought to be among the objects of her sense of abomination. The mature virtue of Christian chastity Anscombe describes obviously goes far, in reflection that reflects the reflections of Christian theologians and philosophers over two millennia, beyond the "mystical perception" that casual sex is base and unsavory. Its rationality depends on the dialectical character of the proper outcome of the Euthyphro dilemma, the thoughtful development of that basic sensitivity through wise and probing conversation about family life in light of the Christian revelation.

Part of the "problem of impiety," as Diamond thinks of it, is how to make sense of, and elaborate into a rational ethical stance, such intuitions as this mystical perception affords, *without resorting to theism*. While I don't doubt that Diamond's project of secularizing piety can succeed in a way, I think her chapter is testimony that the project is awkward and uncomfortable. She brings this out clearly in her discussions of the efforts of David Hume, Mary Warnock, Stuart Hampshire, Roger Scruton, and Immanuel Kant. The last four of these, at least, all feel the difficulty of the problem, and she nicely shows the weaknesses of their "solutions," and notes the conceptual discomfort we should feel with those solutions. Yet all of these thinkers, with the possible exception of Hume, feel that piety, at least in

[16] See G. E. M. Anscombe, "Contraception and Chastity," in M. Geach and L. Gormally (eds.), *Faith in a Hard Ground: Essays on Religion, Philosophy and Ethics by G. E. M. Anscombe* (Charlottesville, VA: Imprint Academic, 2008), 187.

relation to some objects, needs to be given a place in our moral thinking. It is perhaps significant that the thinker who has the most promising approach in Diamond's view (Anscombe) is a theist, though even Anscombe doesn't insist on a completely tight conceptual dependency of an endorsement of piety on theism.

I think the relation we should see between piety about such things as human corpses, sexual intercourse, and parenthood is the one that Steve Evans, adapting Thomas Reid, calls that of "natural signs," indeed, "theistic natural signs."[17] Our hesitancy to put the body of our recently deceased mom out with the garbage, or to fall into bed with just anybody, provided she's willing and we feel the urge, or to prosecute Dad in court, is a sense that there's something sacred about Mom's corpse, something holy about joining parts in intercourse with another person, something venerable about Dad, just because he's Dad. And it's natural to take these feelings, or their objects (or both) as signs (hints, if you will) that there's another Object of piety that makes sense of these lesser ones, that behind and before the natural order is *God.* It seems to me that the notion of a natural sign captures perfectly the nature, the psychological strength, and the logical status of the probative force of such experiences, their potential to connect creation with the Creator. The project of secularizing Anscombe's mystical perceptions can be seen as an effort to deny that they are theistic natural signs. But would it be irrational for the non-theist to entertain the possibility that mystical perceptions are theistic natural signs?

In a discussion of the rationality of moral improvement within "naturalism," Rosalind Hursthouse contrasts two cases. One is an atheist for whom the reasons characteristic of piety – God wants me to do it; to do so would be irreverent toward God; I am called to do it; before God I can do no other; to use my body that way would be to desecrate a holy temple – are not motivating, though this atheist can admit that piety is a kind of virtue in people in whom it supports other virtues like charity, justice, courage, and honesty. The other case is a person who has "lost [her] conviction that loyalty is a virtue."[18] Considerations that used to move her – that she's known so-and-so for a long time; that he would be hurt to hear her recount such-and-such about him, though he would never know she said it (let's say he's dead); that such-and-such institution has done a lot for her – no longer move her. She's lost her "feel" for such considerations, and now

[17] C. S. Evans, *Natural Signs and Knowledge of God: A New Look at Theistic Arguments* (Oxford University Press, 2010).

[18] R. Hursthouse, *On Virtue Ethics* (Oxford University Press, 1999), 233.

thinks they were a hobbling superstition and that it's best just to maximize the benefits of the present moment and present relationships, not to develop attachments to particular institutions or persons, but simply to exploit them for present use and enjoyment.

Hursthouse's cases are parallel in an obvious way: both subjects lack what some other people would regard as an important moral sensitivity or capacity for motivation. But Hursthouse thinks they are disanalogous in that a person who initially lacks the sensitivity that belongs to loyalty can be led to have that sensitivity by considerations that are rational by "naturalistic" standards, but the person who initially lacks the sensitivity that belongs to piety *cannot* be led by considerations that are rational by "naturalistic" standards to have *that* sensitivity. We can put her point in the terms of our discussion so far by saying that our reverence for past intimate ties to a person may possibly be retrieved by appeal to considerations that are rationally accessible even for someone who has lost, or seems to have lost, that sensitivity; while reverence for God as our Father cannot be so acquired or retrieved.

Some of the "naturalistic" considerations that, according to Hursthouse, might rationally lead a person who was insensitive to reasons for loyalty to be motivated by them are, "not many human beings are living the way I am," "their different ways of living are sustaining mine," their ways of living "are in part sustained by loyalty and gratitude," "these people's way of living works well because of their loyalty and gratitude," and "old people are rejoicing in relationships that go all the way back to their youth."[19] Hursthouse offers no comparable examples of considerations that a person advocating piety as a virtue might propose (maybe she thinks there aren't any), so I'll supply some possibilities: "Many people find that religious belief and practice give their life coherence and meaning that a merely secular outlook cannot give."[20] "Religious beliefs give groups cohesion and foster cooperation and the fruits thereof that merely secular beliefs do not."[21] "Religious beliefs can provide rational answers to questions like 'Why should a man not have sexual intercourse with his sister, or a chicken carcass?', questions that 'dumbfound' people with merely secular beliefs."[22]

[19] Hursthouse, *On Virtue Ethics*, 234.

[20] The quotation marks don't indicate actual quotation, but are there to make them parallel with the quasi-quotations in Hursthouse. Mine are mostly paraphrases of the source. Exceptions are the attributions to Putnam and Campbell and Woodberry.

[21] See J. Haidt, *The Righteous Mind: Why Good People Are Divided by Politics and Religion* (New York: Vintage Books, 2012).

[22] See Haidt, *The Righteous Mind*; for discussion see A. C. Pelser and R. C. Roberts, "Religious Value and Moral Psychology," in T. Brosch and D. Sander (eds.), *Handbook of Value: Perspectives from Economics, Neuroscience, Philosophy, Psychology and Sociology* (Oxford University Press, 2016).

"Religiously committed teenagers from blighted neighborhoods are more resistant to the use of illicit drugs than unbelieving teenagers with similar levels of social support."[23] "By many different measures religiously observant Americans are better neighbors and better citizens than secular Americans – they are more generous with their time and money, especially in helping the needy, and they are more active in community life."[24] "Religious belief seems to promote self-discipline and willpower with the many life-advantages that they bring."[25] "Conversionary Protestants were a crucial catalyst initiating the development and spread of religious liberty, mass education, mass printing, newspapers, voluntary organizations, and colonial reforms, thereby creating the conditions that made stable democracy more likely."[26] One of the marks of a virtue, in the Aristotelian tradition, is that it makes life better for its possessor and those with whom its possessor lives. All of these advantages that attach to a form of life that makes piety basic are broadly "naturalistic," unless "naturalism" is taken to rule out all belief in God. But to object that these considerations are not naturalistic because they favor a view of the world that isn't naturalistic would be to confuse the nature of the considerations with the nature of what the considerations favor. This may be the confusion that leads Hursthouse to deny that naturalistic considerations can be found for living a life of religious piety.

In connection with loyalty Hursthouse correctly insists on a point that applies also to piety, namely, that the "naturalistic" considerations adducible in favor of the virtue are not typically the reasons for which possessors of the virtue act when they exemplify the virtue. It would be silly for Socrates to explain why he has chosen to die at the hands of the Athenians rather than give up philosophizing with them by pointing to Jonathan Haidt's observations about the evolutionary advantages of religious beliefs.[27] The pious individual has a sense of God's presence and of being beholden to him. Similarly, the loyal person has a sense that it would be an

[23] See B. Johnson, "A Better Kind of High: Religious Commitment Reduces Drug Use among Poor Urban Teens," at: www.baylorisr.org/publications/recent-publications/j-l/recent-publications-byron-r-johnson/.

[24] R. D. Putnam and D. E. Campbell, *American Grace: How Religion Unites and Divides Us* (New York: Simon and Schuster, 2010); quoted in Haidt, *The Righteous Mind*, 267.

[25] See R. Baumeister and J. Tierney, *Willpower: Rediscovering Our Greatest Strength* (London: Penguin Books, 2011), ch. 8.

[26] See R. D. Woodberry, "The Missionary Roots of Liberal Democracy," *American Political Science Review*, 106 (2012), 244–74.

[27] See Plato, *Apology* [ca. 390 BC], trans. G. M. A. Grube, in J. M. Cooper (ed.), *Plato: Complete Works* (Indianapolis, IN: Hackett, 1997), 29c–30b.

offense against the object of her loyalty to gossip about his faults or to forget about him, or to stop feeling grateful to him for the favors he did her long ago. The reasons for which the pious or loyal person, *as* pious or loyal, acts, don't refer to the so-called naturalistic reasons, but to something that the virtue posits in its experience of performing acts of piety or loyalty. We might say that just as the pious theist "believes in God," the loyalist "believes in the reality of spiritual attachments." Thus, in refraining from speaking demeaningly about the absent or dead friend, the loyalist denies, in effect, that "what a person doesn't know can't hurt him." He feels that an act of disloyalty to his friend would be a betrayal, and so *would* hurt the friend, even if the friend never came to know of it. This may be one of those perceptions that Elizabeth Anscombe calls "mystical." Similarly, when Socrates goes about Athens trying to persuade the people "not to care for [their] bodies or [their] monies first, and to care more exceedingly for the soul, to make it as good as possible,"[28] he experiences his effort as he explains it to the court – as obedience to a summons from the god.

So religious piety is "externally" rational in that "naturalistic" reasons can be given for possessing the virtue. That is, piety can be defended on grounds that even religious unbelievers will see as good (though not sufficient) reasons. It is also "internally" rational, in that it has its own good reasons, the reasons yielded by the "grammar" of the virtue, the reasons that the possessor of the virtue has and can give for performing acts that exemplify the virtue, for example, Socrates' appeal to the absence of a prohibiting sign from his daimon about allowing Athenian law to take its course, or the Christian's appeal to the presence of the Holy Spirit as he rejoices in God as "Abba, Father."

Conclusion

Piety as a virtue is a developed and temporally stable disposition to appreciate the glory of God and his creation and thus to feel inhibited from actions that violate its order, including, importantly, the glory of parenthood and inhibition from actions and thoughts that violate it. The seeds of piety are found in everyone, though environments and individual choices work very different trajectories of the seeds' development, all the way from moribundity on one end of the spectrum to vital, well ramified, and satisfying sensitivity on the other.

[28] Plato, *Apology*, 30a.

CHAPTER 4

Homo Religiosus

Does Spirituality Have a Place in Neo-Aristotelian Virtue Ethics?

David McPherson

Introduction

Does spirituality have a place in neo-Aristotelian virtue ethics?[1] If we consult the major recent works on the subject, we might conclude that the answer is "no." The issue is often either ignored or explicitly excluded from consideration. I will discuss why this is and also why it is problematic. More positively, I will seek to show the importance of spirituality for a neo-Aristotelian account of "the good life."

In the first section, I will lay out my understanding of spirituality. In the second section, I will discuss why neo-Aristotelians have often ignored or explicitly excluded from consideration the issue of the place of spirituality in the good life. I will suggest that a lot turns on how one understands the "ethical naturalism" to which neo-Aristotelians are committed. In the third section, I will argue that through a deeper exploration of the evaluative standpoint from within our human form of life as "meaning-seeking animals" we can come to appreciate better the importance of spirituality for human beings throughout recorded history up to the present and why we can be described as *homo religiosus*. I will also discuss the draw to theistic spirituality in particular. In the fourth and final section, I will consider and respond to three important objections to giving spirituality, especially theistic spirituality, a central place within the good life: viz., (1) the wholeness objection; (2) the autonomy objection; and (3) the social peace objection.

[1] I take a neo-Aristotelian virtue ethic to be a perspective on "the good life" in which the virtues play a central role and where the account of the virtues bears a significant resemblance to Aristotle's account.

What Is "Spirituality"?

As a general working definition, by "spirituality" I mean *a practical life-orientation that is shaped by what is taken to be a self-transcending source of meaning, which involves strong normative demands, including demands of the sacred or the reverence-worthy.* This definition aims to capture a widespread and important phenomenon in human life, found among both theists and non-theists, and in what follows I will try to bring it into clearer focus by filling out each of its components.

First of all, spirituality is *practical*; it involves what we might call "spiritual practices": e.g., practices of prayer, meditation, self-examination, repentance, mindfulness, study, contemplation, worship, thanksgiving, communal living, charity, fasting, keeping the Sabbath, ritual observance, going on retreats or pilgrimages, imitating saints, habituation in virtue, and so on. Thus, spirituality in the fullest sense is more than just belief in God, or a spiritual force ("fate," "destiny," etc.), or the recognition of something sacred. Spirituality requires actions that will bring about and express a spiritual transformation, which involves growth toward spiritual fullness. We can also describe this as a process of sanctification (i.e., making holy), where one seeks to have a proper relationship in feeling and in action to what is seen as sacred or holy or reverence-worthy. In other words, one seeks to become more God-like or virtuous in accordance with a spiritually inflected understanding of the good life. The spiritual life in the fullest sense connects up then with the ethical life, and spiritual transformation always involves ethical transformation. Indeed, on a broad view of the ethical life, where it aims at the good life, we can say that the spiritual life is a species of the ethical life.

This practical aspect of spirituality, I contend, requires that we go beyond the popular slogan of being "spiritual but not religious." What often seems to be meant here by being "spiritual" is that one has a sense of a spiritual force or sacred value or something else of the sort that entails a rejection of reductive materialism. What often seems to be meant by being "not religious" is that one does not identify with "organized" or "institutional" religion.[2] As understandable as it might be that some people shy away from certain forms of organized religion, I think the slogan "spiritual but not religious" is misguided. Spirituality at its best, where one is intent on spiritual growth, leads to "organized" or "institutionalized" practices and often with others as one desires to be at home in the world in a

[2] My take here on the slogan is slightly different from John Cottingham's take in Chapter 1 of this volume.

communal life centered on a shared sense of the sacred or the reverence-worthy. In fact, it is no surprise that many people continue to be drawn to the great world religions (often in virtue of their time-tested practices and the spiritual wisdom built up within them over the ages), even if they end up with their own eclectic or syncretistic forms of spiritual practice.

"Spirituality" does sometimes have the connotation of being personal (or even individualistic) and focused on the quality of inward life, whereas "religion" can have the connotation of being communal, institutional, and focused on outward expression in rituals or practices. However, people also speak of "personal religion" and there are many communal and institutionalized forms of spirituality (e.g., Catholic, Jesuit, Benedictine, Orthodox Jewish, Islamic, Mahayana Buddhist, etc.). Moreover, as should be clear, I think inward life and outward practice go together in the best kinds of spirituality. Thus, in this essay, I make no strong distinction between spirituality and religion.[3] Indeed, I will be arguing for the view that we are *homo religiosus* by discussing the draw toward spirituality in human life.

Spirituality is not just practical; it is a practical *life-orientation*. In other words, spirituality involves a way of seeing and directing one's life as a whole. This relates to what has already been said about spirituality aiming at spiritual transformation. We can understand this in terms of living in a certain spiritual/ethical space: we see ourselves as *moving* toward or away from what we understand to be the good, which connects up with a vision of spiritual/ethical fullness.[4] We achieve fullness (or fulfillment) to the extent that we realize the good in our lives, viz., by acquiring and exercising the virtues. Otherwise put, the degree of fullness in our lives corresponds to our "placement" relative to the good. Moreover, we define our identity or selfhood in terms of the direction of our lives with respect to the good and the degree to which we have realized it in our lives. Because this orientation and degree of achievement can change over the course of our lives, our identity will be understood in terms of an unfolding story. Spirituality is thus a way of seeking to orient one's self better toward the good and thereby to achieve a greater placement relative to it so that one's whole life story is a movement – albeit with ups and downs – toward greater spiritual fullness.

[3] The language of spirituality and religion are in fact commonly used interchangeably: e.g., when people speak of both "spiritual practice" and "religious practice" without making a distinction between the two.

[4] In this paragraph I draw on ideas found in C. Taylor, *Sources of the Self: The Making of Modern Identity* (Cambridge, MA: Harvard University Press, 1989), ch. 2; Taylor, *A Secular Age* (Cambridge, MA: The Belknap Press of Harvard University), Introduction. This understanding of a life-orientation gives sense to talk about "the spiritual life" and "the ethical life."

Given that spirituality is concerned with the orientation of one's life as a whole, it is also fundamentally concerned with the issue of living *a meaningful life* (which is connected with a vision of fullness). The "meaning" that makes for a meaningful life here is "strong evaluative meaning," i.e., meaning or value (used equivalently) with which we *ought* to be concerned and toward which we ought to orient our lives. In contrast to weak evaluation, where something is judged to be good – a "weak good" – simply in virtue of being desired, in strong evaluation, something is judged to be good – a "strong good" – according to qualitative distinctions of value in terms of higher and lower, noble and base, sacred and profane, and so on that are seen as normative for our desires.[5] Hence spirituality is a practical life-orientation that is *shaped by what is taken to be a self-transcending source of meaning, which involves strong normative demands.*[6] The concern here for strong evaluative meaning and for living a meaningful life is part of what makes us distinctively "the meaning-seeking animal."[7] In other words, we have not only "material needs," but also "spiritual needs," viz., needs for strong evaluative meaning, which implies a non-reductionistic view of our human form of life.[8] We are also meaning-seeking animals in that our concern for a meaningful life is often seen as connected with a concern for "*the* meaning of life." In other words, we are concerned with how our lives fit into the grand scheme of things and whether there is a cosmic or "ultimate" source of meaning to which we must align our lives. Through spirituality, then, we seek to find our "place" in the cosmos.

Finally, spirituality is a practical life-orientation that is integrally shaped by *demands of the sacred or the reverence-worthy.* The first thing to note is that the terms "sacred," "holy," and "reverence-worthy" – which I use interchangeably – are strong evaluative terms. What is sacred makes normative demands on us for certain ways of feeling and acting in relationship to it; i.e., it is *worthy* of being valued in particular ways. For example, if

5 On "strong evaluation," see C. Taylor, *Human Agency and Language: Philosophical Papers I* (Cambridge University Press, 1985), Introduction and chs. 1–2; Taylor, *Sources of the Self*, pt. 1.

6 Subjectivist views of value thus cannot offer a genuine form of spirituality on this definition. Also, the phrase "what is taken to be" is meant to indicate that one could be mistaken about the self-transcending source of meaning. I should note further that one could also speak of "*sources* of meaning," but for simplicity's sake I speak of "a source of meaning," which, as expressive of a *worldview*, can be taken to be inclusive of different specific sources of meaning.

7 I borrow this term from J. Sacks, *The Great Partnership: God, Science and the Search for Meaning* (London: Hodder & Stoughton, 2011), ch. 1, though I fill it out in my own way.

8 On material vs. spiritual needs, see J. Cottingham, *The Spiritual Dimension* (Cambridge University Press, 2005), 3; J. Cottingham, "Spirituality," in C. Taliaferro, V. Harrison, and S. Goetz (eds.), *The Routledge Companion to Theism* (New York: Routledge, 2013), 654–5; and R. White, *The Heart of Wisdom: A Philosophy of Spiritual Life* (Lanham, MD: Rowman & Littlefield, 2013), 1–8.

we regard human life as sacred – as when we affirm the "sanctity of human life" – then this demands feelings of reverence and concern as well as actions that protect the inviolability of human life and promote human well-being.[9] We can also say something similar if we regard the natural world as sacred, as many deep ecologists do. And of course if we regard God as sacred or holy – as theists do – then this calls forth feelings of reverence, awe, worship, and loving devotion and requires actions expressive of these feelings.[10] This idea that the sacred makes normative demands on us fills out what was previously said about the spiritual life being a species of the ethical life. In the spiritual life, the good life is seen as in part constituted by a sense of the sacred.

We can better understand the notion of the sacred if we consider its contrast term, the profane. Sometimes this is understood as that which violates or destroys what is sacred; i.e., the profane is what desecrates. However, we should consider here another meaning of the profane: viz., the ordinary or mundane. A sense of the sacred, by contrast, involves the recognition of something *extraordinary*, which provokes feelings of reverence, awe, wonder, and the like. Thus, it has a sense of *transcendence*, as something set apart from ordinary modes of human experience.[11] Moreover, sacred goods – e.g., the sanctity of human life, God's holiness, one's own sanctification, etc. – *transcend in value* the goods that make up ordinary modes of human flourishing, such as individual survival, growth toward biological maturity, physical health, procreation, and ordinary enjoyments.[12] In other words, sacred goods are constitutive of a spiritual fullness the value of which transcends that of ordinary modes of human flourishing, which, we will see, are what neo-Aristotelian ethical naturalists

[9] In my view, the sacred always involves a normative requirement of "inviolability," but the understanding of this can differ between things that are regarded as sacred.

[10] As should be clear from my examples, one does not need to be a theist in order to have a sense of the sacred, since God – even for theists – is not the only entity that can be considered sacred (or reverence-worthy). Indeed, this should not be surprising if human beings are *homo religiosus*. A number of recent books defend non-theistic views of spirituality; e.g., see: A. Comte-Sponville, *The Little Book of Atheist Spirituality*, trans. N. Huston (New York: Viking, 2006); A. de Botton, *Religion for Atheists: A Non-believer's Guide to the Uses of Religion* (New York: Vintage, 2012); L. Ferry, *Man Made God: The Meaning of Life*, trans. D. Pellauer (University of Chicago Press, 2002); M. McGhee, *Transformations of Mind: Philosophy as Spiritual Practice* (Cambridge University Press, 2000); R. Solomon, *Spirituality for the Skeptic: The Thoughtful Love of Life* (Oxford University Press, 2002); T. Nagel, *Secular Philosophy and the Religious Temperament: Essays 2002–2008* (Oxford University Press, 2010); and R. Dworkin, *Religion without God* (Cambridge, MA: Harvard University Press, 2013).

[11] See R. N. Bellah, *Religion in Human Evolution: From the Paleolithic to the Axial Age* (Cambridge, MA: The Belknap Press of Harvard University, 2011), ch. 1; C. Taylor, "Recovering the Sacred," *Inquiry*, 54 (2011), 113–25.

[12] See Taylor, *A Secular Age*, Introduction and ch. 3.

tend to focus on.[13] Sacred goods also transcend other goods such as money, power, fame, and honor. We can observe this transcendence in value of sacred goods over all of these various goods in that sacred goods can require the sacrifice of these other goods when they come into conflict.

What is sacred thus imposes especially strong demands; indeed, it also exceeds the demands placed on us by other strong evaluative judgments, such as those pertaining to "dignity" and "nobility."[14] Thus, when we speak of the "sanctity of human life" rather than "human dignity," we capture an even stronger normative demand. We could say something similar with respect to the "life of sanctity" and the "life of nobility." The spiritual life – or the life of sanctity – makes a particularly strong demand on us to change our lives, to bring about a thoroughgoing conversion or transformation of self in alignment with what is seen as sacred or holy. As John Cottingham puts it, it requires a "radical re-orientation of the self," or "rebirth," to use the language of the Christian gospels.[15] This demand for a thoroughgoing conversion is needed in part because the spiritual life is a high-aspiring kind of life; it aims at sanctification – culminating in the state of saintliness – through cultivating a proper relationship in feeling and in action to what is seen as sacred.[16] Another reason why a radical transformation of self is needed – at least according to many great spiritual traditions – is because human nature, in its untransformed state, is seen as "out of joint." This might be captured in terms of the problem of sin – as in the major monotheistic faiths – or the problem of selfish craving (*tanha*) and suffering (*dukkha*) – as in Buddhism – or in some other terms. In short, human life is seen as in need of redemption or salvation and this requires a radical transformation of self.[17]

[13] Although the terms "fullness" and "flourishing" can be used interchangeably, "flourishing" has a biological connotation, whereas ethical/spiritual "fullness" involves strong evaluation: it is a normatively higher mode of life.

[14] In Taylor's terms, sacred demands are "hypergoods": "goods which not only are incomparably more important than others but provide the standpoint from which these must be weighed, judged, decided about" (Taylor, *Sources of the Self*, 63).

[15] Cottingham, "Spirituality," 659; see also Taylor, *A Secular Age*, 430–1, 435–6, 604–5, 623, 729–30.

[16] William James writes (in his lecture on "Saintliness"): "The highest flights of charity, devotion, trust, patience, bravery to which the wings of human nature have spread themselves have been flown for religious ideals" (W. James, *The Varieties of Religious Experience: A Study in Human Nature* [New York: Barnes & Noble Classics, (1902) 2004], 230).

[17] In Buddhism, the ideal in fact is one of "emptiness" (*sunyata*), i.e., the proper recognition that we are "not-self" (*anatta*). We might say that this ideal of emptiness is really a matter of transcending a lower, narrower mode of selfhood for a higher, wider, more fulfilling mode of selfhood. On this interpretation, the lower mode is seen as a mode of being a self that is dominated by selfish craving, while the higher, wider mode of selfhood is that which is achieved in communion (affective

With this account of spirituality in place, I want to turn to discuss why the issue of the place of spirituality in the good life has often either been ignored or explicitly excluded from consideration by neo-Aristotelian virtue ethicists and why this is problematic.

Neo-Aristotelian Virtue Ethics: What Kind of Ethical Naturalism?

On the face of it, this stance of neglect or exclusion seems problematic given the prevalence and importance of spirituality in human life throughout recorded history up to the present. Moreover, it is worth noting that this stance departs from Aristotle's own stance, as seen in his account of the contemplative life. For Aristotle, understanding (*nous*) is something we share with God, and thus it is a "divine element" – or we might say "sacred element" – within us that we should seek to actualize as far as possible. He writes:

> We ought not to follow the makers of proverbs and 'Think human, since you are human,' or 'Think mortal, since you are mortal.' Rather, as far as we can, we ought to be pro-immortal, and go to all lengths to live a life in accord with our supreme element; for however much this element may lack in bulk, by much more it surpasses everything in power and value.[18]

In fact, Aristotle also thinks that the political life can be undertaken as a divine or sacred task, as he writes: "while it is satisfactory to acquire and preserve the good even for an individual, it is finer and more divine to acquire and preserve it for a people and for cities."[19]

As mentioned at the outset, I think the issue of whether there is a place for spirituality in neo-Aristotelian virtue ethics turns on how one understands the "ethical naturalism" to which neo-Aristotelians are committed. All neo-Aristotelians accept some version of ethical naturalism that maintains that *ethics is to be founded on claims about human nature.* More specifically, all neo-Aristotelians seek to articulate an account of what it is to live well as the kind of beings we are, where this involves living in accordance with a certain understanding of the virtues. In doing so, they follow Aristotle's procedure in the *Nicomachean Ethics*, where he begins with an argument for a particular conception of the "human function" –

identification) with other sentient beings, as expressed in the Buddhist ideals of compassion (*karuna*) and loving-kindness (*metta*). I cannot pursue this issue in detail here.

[18] Aristotle, *Nicomachean Ethics*, trans. T. Irwin, 2nd ed. (Indianapolis, IN: Hackett, [ca. 325 BC] 1999), 10.7, 1177b27–8a2.

[19] Aristotle, *Nicomachean Ethics*, 1.2, 1094b10–12.

viz., to live well as rational social animals – and then moves on to specify an account of the virtues that achieve this.

Most neo-Aristotelians no longer accept anything like Aristotle's metaphysical biology that underpinned his function argument; however, many still seek to found ethics on biological considerations. In particular, neo-Aristotelians such as Philippa Foot, Rosalind Hursthouse, and Alasdair MacIntyre seek to found a virtue ethic on an account of what it is to flourish *qua* human being, where this is understood as being on par with what it is for plants and nonhuman animals to flourish *qua* member of their particular species. In other words, they attempt to found a virtue ethic on considerations of human beings within the "natural, biological order of living things."[20] Hursthouse writes: "[If] there is any truth in ethical naturalism, our ethical evaluations of ourselves ought to exhibit at least a recognizably similar structure to what we find in the botanists' and ethologists' evaluations of other living things."[21] Here we can see a further specified understanding of ethical naturalism where it involves a *quasi-scientific approach to ethics* that appeals to a quasi-scientific account of human nature and human flourishing. For Hursthouse, e.g., whether we are good, flourishing specimens of our kind depends on whether our actions, emotions, and desires are conducive to attaining what she regards as the four naturalistic ends of social animals: viz., (1) individual survival; (2) the continuance of the species; (3) characteristic freedom from pain and characteristic enjoyment; and (4) the good functioning of one's social group.[22] Moreover, as *rational* social animals, it is important that these ends be pursued in a "rational way" through the use of practical reason and the acquisition and exercise of the virtues.[23]

Finally, there is an even further specified understanding of ethical naturalism where it involves an *opposition to supernaturalism*. For some neo-Aristotelians, the three understandings of "ethical naturalism" described here go together. Consider again Hursthouse:

> There is, of course, room for disagreement over what we are. It might be said, for example, that what human beings *are* are possessors of an immortal soul through which they can come to know and love God for eternity. But 'ethical naturalism' is usually thought of as not only basing ethics in some

[20] R. Hursthouse, *On Virtue Ethics* (Oxford University Press, 1999), 206. See also P. Foot, *Natural Goodness* (Oxford University Press, 2001), 15–16, 24–5; A. MacIntyre, *Dependent Rational Animals: Why Human Beings Need the Virtues* (Chicago, IL: Open Court, 1999), 64–5, 77–9.

[21] Hursthouse, *On Virtue Ethics*, 206. [22] Hursthouse, *On Virtue Ethics*, 202, 207.

[23] Hursthouse, *On Virtue Ethics*, 208–10, 222. The last two paragraphs draw some from D. McPherson, "Cosmic Outlooks and Neo-Aristotelian Virtue Ethics," *International Philosophical Quarterly*, 55 (2015), 199–200.

> way on considerations of human nature, but also as taking human beings to be part of the natural, biological order of living things. Its standard first premise is that what human beings *are* is a species of rational, social animals, and thereby a species of living things – which . . . have a particular biological make-up and a natural life-cycle. . . . We might say that the fifth end [of human beings] was the preparation of our souls for the life hereafter, or that it was contemplation – the good functioning of the theoretical intellect. But to adopt the first is to go beyond naturalism towards supernaturalism, and even philosophers have baulked at following Aristotle and endorsing the second.[24]

One might quibble with the use of the term "supernaturalism" here. The main target is evidently theism; however, "supernaturalism" seems to capture only God's transcendence and fails to capture the theistic belief that God is also in some sense immanent within the natural world.[25] In any case, it is clear that Hursthouse means to exclude appeals to theistic views in her version of ethical naturalism. Other neo-Aristotelians likewise exclude theistic and other "supernatural" views, while many simply ignore the issue and thus implicitly exclude theistic and other supernatural perspectives from consideration in their accounts of the good life.[26]

My concern here is primarily with the general neglect and exclusion of the topic of spirituality and its place in the good life among neo-Aristotelians, and I want to suggest that it is especially the second understanding of ethical naturalism (the quasi-scientific approach) that is problematic, though this may also give us reason to question the third understanding (anti-supernaturalism). But I think we should affirm the first understanding of ethical naturalism (the attempt to found ethics on claims about human nature); indeed, I want to argue that it is part of human nature to be drawn to spirituality.

[24] Hursthouse, *On Virtue Ethics*, 206, 218.

[25] See Fiona Ellis's *God, Value, and Nature* (Oxford University Press, 2014), where she argues (compellingly, I think) that there is a version of "expansive naturalism" that is compatible with theism, which requires going beyond "scientific naturalism" and other forms of expansive naturalism (such as John McDowell's) currently on offer.

[26] John McDowell and Martha Nussbaum take issue with the second understanding of ethical naturalism (the quasi-scientific approach), but nevertheless accept a version of the third (anti-supernaturalism); see J. McDowell, *Mind and World* (Cambridge, MA: Harvard University Press, 1994), Lecture IV; J. McDowell, *Mind, Value, and Reality* (Cambridge, MA: Harvard University Press, 1998), ch. 9; M. Nussbaum, "Transcending Humanity," in *Love's Knowledge: Essays on Philosophy and Literature* (Oxford University Press, 1990), 365–91. Like Hursthouse, Philippa Foot seems to accept all three understandings of ethical naturalism in *Natural Goodness*. An interesting case is Alasdair MacIntyre, who is a theist but does not address the place of spirituality in the good life in his most extended defense of a neo-Aristotelian ethical naturalist perspective in *Dependent Rational Animals*, which endorses the first two understandings of ethical naturalism.

Homo Religiosus

The main complaint that I want to lodge against the version of neo-Aristotelian ethical naturalism that involves a quasi-scientific approach is that it does not adequately account for the first-personal evaluative standpoint from within our human form of life as meaning-seeking animals. Indeed, I think this is true as well of some, like John McDowell, who also question the third-personal, quasi-scientific approach and go some ways toward accounting for our first-personal evaluative standpoint. McDowell rightly notes that neo-Aristotelians who endorse the quasi-scientific approach neglect the strong evaluative category of "the noble," which is central to Aristotle's ethics.[27] For Aristotle, virtuous actions are performed "for the sake of the noble" where this is seen as constitutive of a normatively higher, nobler, more fulfilling mode of life (*eudaimonia*).[28] Thus, there is a major disanalogy between human happiness or flourishing (*eudaimonia*) and the flourishing of nonhuman animals. Aristotle strikingly states: "we regard neither ox, nor horse, nor any other kind of animal as happy; for none of them share in this sort of [noble] activity."[29] In fact, Aristotle uses the term *makariotēs* ("blessedness") interchangeably with *eudaimonia* ("happiness") to describe the ultimate aim of human life. For instance, he writes: "happiness appears to be one of the most divine things, since the prize and goal of virtue appears to be the best good, something divine and blessed."[30] Similar to the case of "the noble," I contend that the third-personal, quasi-scientific approach – and McDowell too – neglects the place of the strong evaluative category of "the sacred" within human life.

The experience of the sacred, like other strong evaluative experiences, is made possible for us because of our human distinctiveness as language animals. Through language – which is part of our acquired "second nature," as McDowell puts it – we can possess concepts like "the sacred" and "the noble" that light up the world for us in a strong evaluative manner such that we experience it in a fundamentally different way from non-linguistic animals: from our first-personal evaluative standpoint we

[27] See J. McDowell, "Eudaimonism and Realism in Aristotle's Ethics," in R. A. Heinaman (ed.), *Aristotle and Moral Realism* (Boulder, CO: Westview Press, 1995); McDowell, *Mind, Value, and Reality*, 9–10, 26, 91–3, 169.

[28] Aristotle, *Nicomachean Ethics*, 3.7, 1115b11–12; see also 2.3, 1104b29–35; 2.4, 1105a29–34; 4.1, 1120a22–3. I have substituted "the noble" for "the fine" in the quotation in order to follow McDowell's translation of *to kalon*.

[29] Aristotle, *Nicomachean Ethics*, 1.9, 1099b30–2; see also 10.8, 1178b24–32.

[30] Aristotle, *Nicomachean Ethics*, 1.9, 1099b16–18; see also 1.8, 1099b1–5; 1.10, 1100b7–01a22; 10.8, 1178b24–32; cf. M. Nussbaum, *The Fragility of Goodness: Luck and Ethics in Greek Tragedy and Philosophy*, updated ed. (Cambridge University Press, 2001 [1986]), 327–36.

experience the world in light of a conceptual framework whereby certain things are seen as worthy of our concern and fit to be valued in strong evaluative terms; i.e., the world makes normative demands on us. We might say that this enables a "transfiguration" of the world. On this point, consider the following passage from John Cottingham where he describes a sense of the sacred that is found in common human experiences of natural beauty, great works of art, and the moral demand:

> [These experiences] involve not so much a revelation of supernatural entities as a heightening, an intensification, that transforms the way in which we experience the world. Terms like 'transfiguration' or 'epiphany' come to mind here, but not in the sense that there is necessarily an explicit invocation of metaphysical objects that transcend ordinary experience, but rather because the categories of our mundane life undergo a radical shift: there is a sudden irradiation that discloses a beauty and goodness, a meaning, that was before occluded.[31]

While theists might interpret such experiences as "intimations of the divine reality that is the source of all truth, beauty, and goodness," non-theists can also have these experiences; they are part of "our ordinary human birthright."[32]

It is part of "our ordinary human birthright" to be drawn toward the sacred, I contend, because of our nature as meaning-seeking animals. As mentioned previously, it is a distinctive feature of human life, as contrasted with the life of nonhuman animals, that we are concerned with living a meaningful or worthwhile life, where this is understood in strong evaluative terms: we are concerned to orient ourselves within ethical/spiritual space by acknowledging and seeking to align our lives properly with certain strong goods (i.e., normative demands). The most important among such goods will be sacred goods because they are experienced as deeply meaningful and as making particularly strong demands on our lives such that they play a central guiding role in our practical life-orientations. Such a life-orientation, as discussed, will also often involve seeking to find our place in the cosmos. As meaning-seeking animals, we understand specific strong goods as meaningful (and as the goods they are) against the background of our overall cosmic outlook: i.e., our sense of how our lives fit into the grand scheme of things and whether there is a cosmic or "ultimate" meaning and purpose for human life. Indeed, it seems that such strong

[31] J. Cottingham, *Philosophy of Religion: Towards a More Humane Approach* (Cambridge University Press, 2014), 61–2.

[32] Cottingham, *Philosophy of Religion*, 63.

goods require an affirmation that human life does in fact have an ultimate meaning and purpose (since their existence in a world that is at bottom devoid of purpose would be very odd).[33] It is in this context that questions about God's existence and the like become especially significant and can acquire a sense of urgency. It is also in this context that we can especially appreciate the importance of spirituality for human beings throughout recorded history up to the present and why we can be described as *homo religiosus.*

If it is indeed the case, as I have argued, that human beings are *homo religiosus* – i.e., naturally drawn to spirituality understood as a practical life-orientation that is shaped by what is taken to be a self-transcending source of meaning, which involves strong normative demands, including demands of the sacred or the reverence-worthy – then a certain virtue is crucial to human well-being that has tended to be neglected or seen as no virtue at all: viz., the virtue of piety, which, as I understand it, is the virtue concerned with a proper relationship in feeling and in action to the sacred or the reverence-worthy. It is worth noting that Rosalind Hursthouse does briefly discuss the possibility of piety as a virtue in her version of neo-Aristotelian ethical naturalism.[34] She allows that piety helps religious believers to foster other virtues that promote the four naturalistic ends described earlier, but she says:

> [In] so far as their piety prompts them to pray, to refrain from blasphemy, to go to church, to spend time thinking about God and trying to get closer to an understanding of Him, the atheist, by her own lights, must think that they are not acting rationally, because the right reasons they think they have . . . for doing these things, are no reasons at all. Though the character trait indeed fosters the four ends, it does not do so in the way characteristic of our species, namely in a rational way. Moreover, although . . . piety undoubtedly brings great joy and serenity to its possessors, no atheist can regard such joy as 'characteristic of human beings', that is, as something that reason can endorse. . . . Hence, employing the normative idea of 'our characteristic way of going on', our atheist will conclude that piety is not, after all, a virtue.[35]

It is not clear why the atheist must see the theist as "not acting rationally," since one might think that reasonable people could come to different conclusions about ultimate questions, such as whether God exists. But the bigger problem – which is illustrative of the problems I have identified in this essay with Hursthouse's version of neo-Aristotelian ethical naturalism – is that she

[33] I take this up further in McPherson, "Cosmic Outlooks and Neo-Aristotelian Virtue Ethics."
[34] Hursthouse, *On Virtue Ethics*, 232–4. [35] Hursthouse, *On Virtue Ethics*, 233.

narrowly construes piety as theistic piety and misses the more fundamental concern of piety with a proper relationship to the sacred or the reverence-worthy.[36]

However, I think it is also worth considering here the draw to theistic spirituality in particular.[37] At the heart of the theistic worldview is the belief that the universe is a personal order, as opposed to an impersonal order. As William James puts it: "The more perfect and more eternal aspect of the universe is represented in our religions as having personal form. The universe is no longer a mere *It* to us, but a *Thou*, if we are religious [i.e., theists]; and any relation that may be possible from person to person might be possible here."[38] In other words, the theist holds that the ultimate nature of reality is personal rather than impersonal due to having been created by a person (God) and – at least on the theistic view I want to put forward – for the central purpose of love, which is most fully realized in communion between persons (both human and divine).[39] So why then might someone be drawn to theistic spirituality?

First of all, theism provides a teleological worldview (centered on the telos of interpersonal love) according to which the universe in general and human life in particular are seen as permeated with meaning; or as Gerard Manley Hopkins puts it: "The world is charged with the grandeur of God."[40] This meets our human need as meaning-seeking animals to address the issue of the meaning of life, i.e., to see how our lives fits into the grand scheme of things in a meaningful and worthwhile way, which

[36] For more on piety and impiety, see the essays by Diamond (Chapter 2) and Roberts (Chapter 3) in this collection. Paul Woodruff also defends reverence – or piety – as a virtue for theists and non-theists alike. But he tends to understand it in a way that makes it more like the virtue of humility. He writes: "Reverence begins in a deep understanding of human limitations; from this grows the capacity to be in awe of whatever we believe lies outside our control – God, truth, justice, nature, even death. . . . Simply put, reverence is the virtue that keeps human beings from trying to act like gods" (P. Woodruff, *Reverence: Renewing a Forgotten Virtue*, 2nd ed. [Oxford University Press, 2014], 1). On my view, the virtue of piety involves awe or reverence for what is sacred and not simply for what is outside our control; indeed, it sets limits on our will with the knowledge that we can (and some people do) transgress these limits.

[37] The following draws some from D. McPherson, "Seeking Re-enchantment," in P. J. Rossi (ed.), *Seekers and Dwellers: Plurality and Wholeness in a Time of Secularity* (Washington, DC: The Council for Research in Values and Philosophy, 2016), 37–45.

[38] W. James, *The Will to Believe and Other Essays in Popular Philosophy* and *Human Immortality* (New York: Dover, [1897] 1956), 27–8.

[39] None of this denies the value of nonpersons. Indeed, theism, as I understand it, entails the view that the created world is intrinsically good. Moreover, a kind of communion is possible between persons and nonpersons, but it is not the fullness of interpersonal communion.

[40] G. M. Hopkins, "God's Grandeur" [1877], in *The Major Works* (Oxford: Oxford World's Classics, 2002).

shapes our practical life-orientations toward strong goods, including the sacred or the reverence-worthy. A theistic teleological worldview shapes our practical life-orientations in this way because the universe is seen as an enduring moral order that expresses "ultimate moral purposes" to which we must align our lives.[41]

This also connects up with a second way in which human beings can be drawn to theistic spirituality, which concerns the deep human need, especially in the face of great suffering and evil, to believe or at least to hope that ultimate reality is concerned with our fate and is on the side of the good and that tragedy does not have the final word. A theistic moral and personal order that expresses ultimate moral purposes addresses this need. William James sees this as crucial to the "pragmatic [or practical] significance" of theistic spirituality, and he remarks that a belief or at least a hope in a theistic moral order "not only incites our more strenuous moments [of working to bring about good in the world], but it also takes our joyous, careless, trustful moments, and it justifies them."[42] We can add that it also provides support for the common spiritual practice of petitionary prayer (consider, e.g., the central Christian prayer, the "Our Father," in this light).[43]

A third way that one can be drawn to theistic spirituality arises from the profound feeling of gratitude for existence (which we can call "existential gratitude"[44]). This feeling typically involves seeing life as a gift or a blessing. However, the notion of life as a gift or a blessing seems to make most sense when there is *someone* (viz., God) who is the giver of the gift or the bestower of the blessing. Such a feeling of existential gratitude seems natural for human beings – unless things have gone terribly wrong – and since theism provides a natural home for this

[41] The phrase "ultimate moral purposes" is from F. Nietzsche, *The Gay Science*, trans. W. Kaufmann (New York: Vintage Books, [1882/1887] 1974), §357. Nietzsche thinks that such a view is no longer believable in the modern world (at least among the more "refined"), but I think this is still very much an open debate; see J. Cottingham, *On the Meaning of Life* (New York: Routledge, 2003), ch. 2.

[42] W. James, *Pragmatism* (Indianapolis, IN: Hackett, [1907] 1981), p. 51; cf. 49–51. John Cottingham also writes about the "buoyancy of the good": "despite the cruelty and misery in the world, the struggle for goodness will always enjoy a certain kind of buoyancy" in a theistic worldview (Cottingham, *On the Meaning of Life*, 72–3).

[43] The topic of prayer is explored in an interesting way in Cormac McCarthy's *The Road*. In an interview about the novel, McCarthy remarked: "sometimes it's good to pray. I don't think you have to have a clear idea of who or what God is in order to pray. You could even be quite doubtful about the whole business" (www.oprah.com/oprahsbookclub/Cormac-McCarthy-on-Writing).

[44] See M. Lacewing, "Can Non-theists Appropriately Feel Existential Gratitude?," *Religious Studies: An International Journal for the Philosophy of Religion*, 52 (2016): 145–65.

feeling, we can see why someone might be drawn toward theistic spirituality. Consider, e.g., the following statements by the character Dmitri Karamazov in Dostoevsky's *The Brothers Karamazov*: "I'm tormented by God. Tormented only by that. What if he doesn't exist? . . . So then, if he doesn't exist, man is chief of the earth, of the universe. Splendid! Only how is he going to be virtuous without God? A good question! I keep thinking about it. Because whom will he love then – man, I mean? *To whom will he be thankful, to whom will he sing the hymn?*"[45]

This passage also points to a human need to be orientated toward an ultimate object of love, devotion, reverence, and even worship, which is explored throughout Dostoevsky's writings.[46] Such a need seems to be expressed not only in the life of the devout theist, but also in the lives of non-theists who seek a "God-substitute," whether in the form of a "religion of humanity" (*à la* Comte, Mill, Feuerbach, Marx, etc.), or Nietzsche's *Übermensch*, or a deep ecological perspective. But the question is whether such "God-substitutes" are as adequate objects of love, devotion, reverence, and worship as a personalistic God. The theist argues that God – if God exists – is worthy of our fullest love, devotion, reverence, and worship in virtue of God's perfect goodness, love, wisdom, and so on.[47] According to Alasdair MacIntyre: "finite beings who possess the power of understanding, if they know God exists, know that he is the most adequate object of their love, and that the deepest desire of every such being, whether they acknowledge it or not, is to be at one with

45 F. Dostoevsky, *The Brothers Karamazov*, trans. R. Pevear and L. Volokhonsky (New York: Everyman's Library, [1880] 1990), 592; my emphasis.

46 In *The Adolescent*, the "holy peasant" Makar remarks: "[To] live without God is nothing but torment. And it turns out that what gives light is the very thing we curse, and we don't know it ourselves. . . . It's impossible for a man to exist without bowing down; such a man couldn't bear himself, and no man could. If he rejects God, he'll bow down to an idol – a wooden one, or a golden one, or a mental one. They're all idolaters, not godless, that's how they ought to be called" (F. Dostoevsky, *The Adolescent*, trans. R. Pevear and L. Volokhonsky [New York: Everyman's Library, (1875) 2003], 373). Likewise, at the end of *Demons*, Stepan proclaims: "The whole law of human existence consists in nothing other than a man's always being able to bow before the immeasurably great. If people are deprived of the immeasurably great, they will not live and will die in despair. . . . For every man, whoever he is, it is necessary to bow before that which is the Great Thought" (F. Dostoevsky, *Demons*, trans. R. Pevear and L. Volokhonsky [New York: Everyman's Library, (1872) 1994], 664).

47 This sort of argument is implicit in views that see the idea of God as a projection of our longings or highest ideals. However, as John Cottingham notes: "talk of God as a projection does not in the end advance the debate between theists and atheists very much, since it cannot settle the question of whether the impulse to project our longings outward to an external source does or does not have an objective counterpart" (Cottingham, *On the Meaning of Life*, 10–11). It does seem to suggest something very important about us as human beings that we project our longings in this way: viz., we are in some sense *homo religiosus*.

God."[48] If this claim is accepted, then it constitutes a further way that one might be drawn to theistic spirituality.

Responding to Objections

Even if we acknowledge that human beings are in some sense *homo religiosus*, there might still be concerns about allowing spirituality to have a central place in our lives. In this last section, I want to consider and respond to three important objections to giving spirituality, especially theistic spirituality, a central place within an account of the good life for human beings.

The first objection is *the wholeness objection*. It is based on the worry that the high aspiration of the spiritual life to a thoroughgoing spiritual transformation can threaten our wholeness as human beings insofar as it can at times require the sacrifice of our ordinary human flourishing and perhaps lead to its denigration. In other words, the concern here is that spirituality can lead to a kind of self-mutilation.

This objection has been put forward forcefully by Martha Nussbaum. Her criticisms are focused particularly on aspirations to "transcend humanity," viz., by aspiring to a God-like existence that takes us beyond our ordinary human flourishing.[49] We can think here of the ideals of the contemplative life in Plato and Aristotle, or the theistic hope for eternal life, or even certain highly demanding ideals of saintliness that require a thoroughgoing ethical-spiritual transformation (as exemplified, e.g., by St. Francis). Nussbaum regards the aspiration to such transcendence as in fact arising from the unease we experience with respect to the vulnerability, neediness, and finitude inherent in human life.[50] She believes that such an aspiration is ultimately self-defeating:

> [What] my argument urges us to reject as incoherent is the aspiration to leave behind altogether the constitutive conditions of our humanity

[48] A. MacIntyre, *God, Philosophy, Universities: A Selective History of the Catholic Philosophical Tradition* (Lanham, MD: Rowman & Littlefield, 2009), 5–6. These remarks, it should be noted, seem to take us beyond the sort of quasi-scientific ethical naturalism that MacIntyre defends in *Dependent Rational Animals*.

[49] See M. Nussbaum, *The Fragility of Goodness*; Nussbaum, "Transcending Humanity," in *Love's Knowledge*; Nussbaum, "Transcendence and Human Values," *Philosophy and Phenomenological Research*, 64 (2002), 445–52; Nussbaum, *Upheavals of Thought: The Intelligence of the Emotions* (Cambridge University Press, 2003), pt. III; Nussbaum, "Judaism and the Love of Reason," in R. E. Groenhout and M. Bower (eds.), *Philosophy, Feminism, and Faith* (Bloomington: Indiana University Press, 2003).

[50] Nussbaum, *The Fragility of Goodness*, pt. II; Nussbaum, "Transcending Humanity," 368, 377; see also Taylor, *A Secular Age*, 625.

> and to seek for a life that is really the life of another sort of being – as if it were a higher and better life for *us*. It asks us to bound our aspirations by recalling that there are some very general conditions of human existence that are also necessary conditions for the values that we know, love, and appropriately pursue.[51]

However, what is precisely at issue is whether spirituality (as including the aspiration to spiritual transformation and spiritual fullness) is in fact *integral* to our humanity. If this is so – and I have argued that it is because of our being meaning-seeking animals – then we should also be concerned that denying a place for spirituality in human life would be its own form of self-mutilation, or threat to human wholeness.[52] Nussbaum is right to raise the concern that certain forms of spirituality can be self-mutilating, but I do not think that the solution here is to abandon altogether a spiritual life with high aspirations to spiritual transformation and spiritual fullness. The solution, I contend, is to live the spiritual life in such a way that we best realize what is integral to our humanity and thereby achieve true spiritual fullness.

It is worth noting that Nussbaum herself acknowledges that "there is a great deal of room, within the context of a human life . . . for a certain sort of aspiration to transcend our ordinary humanity. For . . . it is all too plain that most people are much of the time lazy, inattentive, unreflective, shallow in feeling; in short, that most human action falls well short of the fully human target of complete virtue."[53] The issue, then, is not about whether we have an ideal of transformation for human life – as very few people, if any, would want to affirm completely our "ordinary humanity" at it is – but rather it is about the nature of the ideal and whether it in fact helps us to realize best what is most admirable in our humanity.

The second objection I want to consider is *the autonomy objection*, and it pertains particularly to theistic forms of spirituality. According to this objection, if we make God the ultimate object of our love and concern, then this threatens our autonomy as human beings. The exact nature of this objection depends on how one understands the term "autonomy." The word itself suggests the idea of "self-legislating," which could be seen as synonymous with a subjectivist view in which we "legislate" for ourselves what is good and bad on the basis of our *de facto* desires. We would thus be

[51] Nussbaum, "Transcending Humanity," 379.

[52] See Taylor, *Sources of the Self*, 519–21; Taylor, *A Secular Age*, 604–5, 625–34, 639–40; Taylor, "Critical Notice of Martha C. Nussbaum, *The Fragility of Goodness: Luck and Ethics in Greek Tragedy and Philosophy*," *Canadian Journal of Philosophy*, 18 (1988), 805–14.

[53] Nussbaum, "Transcending Humanity," 378.

autonomous when we pursue such desires without external constraints. Such a view of autonomy would be opposed to any strong normative demand on us, whether it relates to God, or our own potential, or other human beings, or the natural world.

However, another way of understanding autonomy is in terms of our making decisions "independently of the arbitrary will of another, acting in the full light of reason, free from internal or external interference with [our] rational processes."[54] This view, it seems, is fully compatible with a theistic perspective where love and devotion to God is based on our free judgment that God is worthy of such love and devotion and where following the will of God means aligning ourselves with a purposeful moral framework in which the good is understood as independent of God's act of willing it. In short, a theist can reject theological voluntarism.

But even if we acknowledge the compatibility between this second notion of autonomy and a theistic perspective, there are still some who see theism as threatening another kind of autonomy: viz., a freedom from divine judgment or "ultimate" moral responsibility. Something like this seems to be behind comments that Thomas Nagel makes about the "fear of [theistic] religion," which he thinks has motivated much of the problematic scientism and reductionism in modern intellectual life. Nagel wants to encourage his fellow nonreligious colleagues to resist the influence of this fear on their intellectual life. However, he acknowledges that he is also subject to this fear of religion, which he says is distinct from the fear of the baleful effects of religious institutions. It is a "fear of religion itself." He writes: "I want atheism to be true and am made uneasy by the fact that some of the most intelligent and well-informed people I know are religious believers. It isn't just that I don't believe in God and, naturally, hope that I'm right in my belief. It's that I hope there is no God! I don't want there to be a God; I don't want the universe to be like that."[55] Nagel refers to this as the "cosmic authority problem." It is not entirely clear what all is behind this fear of religion, but an important part of it seems to be related to the thought that there is an all-powerful, all-knowing Being who can hold us accountable for everything we think and do, even the most shameful things that we might keep hidden from others.[56] While I think such a reaction is quite understandable, it does not necessitate that one should reject theism

[54] Cottingham, *The Spiritual Dimension*, 43.

[55] T. Nagel, *The Last Word* (Oxford University Press, 1997), 130.

[56] Roger Scruton argues (somewhat provocatively) that an underlying motive for contemporary atheist culture (especially in its militant forms) is "the desire to escape from the eye of judgment [whether human or divine]" (*The Face of God: The Gifford Lectures 2010* [New York: Continuum, 2012], 2).

altogether, especially if a better view of the matter is possible. For instance, the thought that God knows what we do and think and can hold us accountable might form an important part of our sense of moral "conscience," at least according to the etymological meaning of the term as "knowledge-with." But in order for this not to be oppressive, I believe it needs to be accompanied by a view of God as a kind of loving and merciful parent rather than a vindictive and wrathful judge. To be seen and loved for who we really are in this way can in fact be morally and spiritually liberating.[57]

The third and final objection I want to consider is *the social peace objection*. It claims that religion poses a serious threat to the modern social order, which is based on relationships of mutual benefit and is especially concerned to promote peace and prosperity.

Hume offers an important example of someone who gives voice to this objection in his critique of religious perspectives that take us beyond a primary concern with maintaining a social order based on relationships of mutual benefit. We can think here of his rather uncharitable interpretation of a religious transformation ideal in terms of the "monkish virtues." Hume gives the following odd list of monkish "virtues": celibacy, fasting, penance, mortification, self-denial, humility, silence, and solitude. Many of these are practices or vows rather than virtues, but certainly he should have at least mentioned the primary "theological virtues" of faith, hope, and love. In any case, he writes of his list: "for what reason are they everywhere rejected by men of sense, but because they serve to no manner of purpose; neither advance a man's fortune in the world, nor render him a more valuable member of society; neither qualify him for the entertainment of company; nor increase his power of self-enjoyment?"[58]

One can of course contest Hume's account of a religious transformation ideal here and the claim that a representative of such an ideal would be

One should also recall here the remarks from Dmitri Karamazov: "if [God] doesn't exist, man is chief of the earth, of the universe. Splendid! Only how is he going to be virtuous without God? A good question! I keep thinking about it. Because whom will he love then – man, I mean? To whom will he be thankful, to whom will he sing the hymn?" I don't think the point is that one can't be virtuous without God, but that belief in God can be helpful for becoming virtuous.

57 See Cottingham, *Philosophy of Religion*, 166–8 for a helpful analogy between the believer's relationship to God and the psychoanalytic relationship, where allowing oneself to be truly seen by a compassionate Other (i.e., God or the analyst) can in fact be liberating rather than oppressive and it can be "a powerful vehicle for continued moral growth and integration" and allow one "to move away from preoccupation with the self and its flaws and conflicts, and to turn outwards in love and compassion towards one's fellow creatures."

58 D. Hume, *Enquiries Concerning Human Understanding and Concerning the Principles of Morals*, ed. L. A. Selby-Bigge, rev. P. H. Nidditch, 3rd ed. (Oxford University Press, [1748/1751] 1975), 270.

"useless" to society or this-worldly life. Certainly a St. Francis or a Mother Teresa or a Jean Vanier does much to benefit others, though it will likely not be only in the terms of the modern social order with its relationships of mutual benefit (especially economic benefit). However, Hume's critique of such religious transformation ideals in fact goes beyond saying that they are useless to the modern social order to claiming that they are dangerous to it. In his *Dialogues Concerning Natural Religion*, Hume has the character Philo respond to the claim that religion is beneficial to society by saying:

> How happens it then . . . if vulgar superstition be so salutary to society, that all history abounds so much with accounts of its pernicious consequences on public affairs? Factions, civil wars, persecutions, subversions of government, oppression, slavery; these are the dismal consequences which always attend its prevalency over the minds of men. If the religious spirit be ever mentioned in any historical narration, we are sure to meet afterwards with a detail of the miseries which attend it.[59]

While one might think (as I do) that Hume (via Philo) is too extreme, polemical, and one-sided in these remarks – for they neglect how religions, through their ethical teachings, have often fostered love of neighbor, compassion, peace, etc., even if they have also sometimes been used for ill – nevertheless, it is important to note that fears about the dangers of religion are of course still present today. For instance, we often find reminders about the history of religious violence, especially the so-called wars of religion in early modern Europe, by liberal political philosophers in their attempts to justify a liberal political order that would privatize religion and thereby neutralize it.[60] There is also the view among the most militant atheists that it would in fact be best to eradicate religion completely if possible, since, for one thing, even if religion is privatized, there is always the danger that it can "go public." Such views usually maintain a very strong connection between religion and violence, as we see in the following remark by Steven Weinberg: "With or without religion, good

[59] D. Hume, *Dialogues Concerning Natural Religion* [1779], in *Principal Writings of Religion*, ed. J. C. A. Gaskin (Oxford University Press, 1993), 122. In various places Hume distinguishes between "true" (i.e., deistic or "philosophical") religion, to which he is more positively disposed (though I don't think he actually embraces it, despite calling it "true" religion), and "false" (i.e., revealed, historical) religion, which he often describes condemningly as "superstitious" or "fanatical." The aspect of Hume's critique of religion outlined here, he would hold, applies to the majority of cases of religious belief and practice in his day and our own.

[60] See J. Rawls, "Justice as Fairness: Political not Metaphysical," in S. Avineri and A. de-Shalit (eds.), *Communitarianism and Individualism* (Oxford University Press, 1992), 188; J. Rawls, *Political Liberalism*, 2nd ed. (New York: Columbia University Press, 2005), xxiii–xxiv.

people can behave well and bad people can do evil; but for good people to do evil – that takes religion."[61]

However, the danger of violence is present with any high ideal for human life, whether religious or nonreligious, as we can see in the destruction wrought by a number of atheistic or nonreligious regimes in the twentieth century. The solution here is not to do without any high ideal for human beings, since this would again be a form of self-mutilation and it would prevent the ethical and spiritual transformation needed in human life (given that our human nature, in its untransformed state, is "out of joint"). Rather, the solution is to articulate and defend high ideals for human life that can avoid and prevent violence and destruction.[62]

With respect to each of the preceding three objections – viz., the wholeness objection, the autonomy objection, and the social peace objection – I have argued that they do not undermine the place of spirituality in the good life for human beings. Instead, what we need is the right kind of spirituality. It is here again that we need the important yet too often forgotten virtue of piety. As aforementioned, the virtue of piety is a matter of achieving a proper relationship in feeling and in action to the sacred or the reverence-worthy. This is cultivated through certain spiritual practices, which we might also call practices of piety: e.g., practices of gratitude for the gift of life; practices of humility that help to avoid human hubris (the practice of the Sabbath is an example here[63]); practices of charity, forgiveness, and reconciliation; practices of prayer, contemplation, and self-examination; and so on. These practices of piety help to avoid certain problematic directions the religious impulse can take, as identified in the foregoing objections. More positively, these practices are important for achieving ethical and spiritual fullness.[64]

61 S. Weinberg, "A Designer Universe," *The New York Review of Books*, October 21, 1999.

62 See Taylor, *Sources of the Self*, 515–21; Taylor, "Reply and Re-articulation," in J. Tully (ed.), *Philosophy in an Age of Pluralism: The Philosophy of Charles Taylor in Question* (Cambridge University Press, 1994), 225; and: www.templetonprize.org/ct_statement.html.

63 See M. Sandel, "Mastery and Hubris in Judaism: What's Wrong with Playing God?," in *Public Philosophy* (Cambridge, MA: Harvard University Press, 2005); see also Samuel Fleischacker's essay (Chapter 7) in this collection.

64 An earlier, much shorter version of this essay was published in the fiftieth anniversary special issue of *Religious Studies*; see *Religious Studies: An International Journal for the Philosophy of Religion*, 51 (2015), 335–46.

CHAPTER 5

Desire and the Spiritual Life

Fiona Ellis

Introduction

How important is desire to the spiritual life? And how important is the spiritual life in any case? Different answers have been given to these questions, for there are conflicting interpretations of the nature and value of these notions, although some of the disagreements are terminological. According to a position which it is Nietzsche's purpose to expose, and which he associates with a religious outlook, desire is undesirable, and it must be transcended if life is to be properly spiritual. A template here for the atheist's antireligious stance, the familiar line being that a spirituality infected by religion involves an antipathy and even hatred for all things pertaining to *this* world, *this* life, and *our* humanity. It gains stark expression in the following words of Nietzsche, the target in this context being the Christian idea of God:

> God having degenerated into a *contradiction of life* instead of its transfiguration and eternal *yes*! God as declared aversion to life, to nature, to the will to life! God as the formula for every slander against 'the here and now', for every lie about the 'beyond'! God as the deification of nothingness, the canonization of the will to nothingness![1]

On this way of thinking, then, religion involves an aversion to life and nature, this aversion is expressed in the postulation of an anti-natural and lifeless "beyond," and we are to suppose that it is built into the religious person's creed that the spiritual life is oriented toward this "beyond." Janet Soskice captures the general idea when, in the context of describing a widespread (mis)conception of the spiritual life, she talks of something "still and luminous, turned to the future and far from our daily lives."[2] We can note that she registers this objection as a Christian theologian. Where does desire – or the lack of it – come into the disputed picture? We are to

[1] F. Nietzsche, *The Anti-Christ* [1888], §18, in *The Anti-Christ, Ecce Homo, Twilight of the Idols*, eds. A. Ridley and J. Norman, trans. J. Norman (Cambridge University Press, 2005), 15–16.

[2] J. Soskice, *The Kindness of God* (Oxford University Press, 2008), 12.

suppose that the anti-natural and lifeless "beyond" corresponds to the religious person's heaven, that it involves the transcending of all desire, and hence, that the properly spiritual life must involve aspiring to such a condition. As Ivan Soll puts it in the context of criticizing the "dream" of Schopenhauer (and, more generally, that of Buddhism, Stoicism, and Christianity), the aspired-to condition here is one in which "one no longer experiences desires, longings, and wants . . . an existence in which we want for nothing."[3] A putatively "angelic ideal" that, he claims, is more properly described as "a diabolical piece of work" once we see that it involves wanting nothing. The deification of nothingness, we are to suppose, the final two sentences of his paper exhorting us to remember "the crucial but commonly ignored truth, that desire is itself desirable. Long live desire!"[4]

We have a conception of the spiritual life that takes us beyond desire, and hence, beyond life itself, assuming that desire and life are equivalent and that spiritual life, thus conceived, is a form of death. It is criticized by Nietzsche, Nietzscheans, and some theists too, Soskice's objections pre-empting an alternative conception of spiritual life that is firmly rooted in *this* world. What of Nietzsche's relation to the spiritual life? Robert Solomon tells us that "Nietzsche may have rejected religion in its many forms . . . but he never rejected spirituality. On the contrary . . . he attempted to 'revalue' and revise our concept of spirituality . . . to *naturalize* spirituality, to get away from 'other-worldly' religions and philosophies, and to reappreciate or 'reenchant' everyday life."[5] We are to suppose that the envisaged re-enchantment brings the return of desire. The theme is familiar, and it should come as no surprise that a similar "revaluation" of spirituality has preoccupied many contemporary atheists, like, for example, Solomon himself.[6] As he puts it, "[w]hatever else it may be, spirituality is passion. The spiritual life is a passionate life."[7]

We have two ways of thinking about the spiritual life that, on the face of it, are diametrically opposed, although it is assumed on both sides that we should be aspiring to live in this way. According to the first position, it is a requirement of such a life that desire is transcended. The nature and limits of the relevant concepts is unclear, but the position is associated with a

[3] I. Soll, "On Desire and Its Discontents," *Ratio*, 2 (1989), 182–3.

[4] Soll, "On Desire and Its Discontents," 184.

[5] R. Solomon, *Spirituality for the Skeptic: The Thoughtful Love of Life* (Oxford University Press, 2007), 5.

[6] Other notable examples are André Comte-Sponville's *The Little Book of Atheist Spirituality* (London: Bantam Press, 2009), and Sam Harris's *Waking Up: Searching for Spirituality Without Religion* (New York: Simon and Schuster, 2014).

[7] Solomon, *Spirituality for the Skeptic*, 28.

religious outlook, although there is no requirement that it be comprehended in God-involving terms, Schopenhauer being an important case in point. The second position involves a rejection of this rejection of desire, claiming to the contrary that desire is central to the spiritual life. It is likewise unclear how broadly or narrowly these concepts are to be understood, but we can note that a blank acceptance of desire per se is surely as problematic as its wholesale rejection. After all, not all desires are desirable, like, for example, the desire to destroy someone's life for the hell of it or to stuff one's face to oblivion. The starting point of the pro-desire position is that the first, "religious," option is a recipe for death – it is in this sense that the heaven it promises is more properly viewed as a hell – worse than a living hell, we are to suppose. So desire provides the essential life-giving ingredient, although to repeat the worry, we must surely discriminate between desires in this context if the life in question is to be remotely worth living, and it is central to both the positions at hand that not just any life will do. Finally, we must allow that a proponent of the religious option has a response to the supposed objection from desire, for I have noted already that she is not invariably opposed to life on earth, and it has not been shown that her opponent has the monopoly on desire.

The disagreements are less stark than first appears, and in what follows I want to defend the claim that the spiritual life involves desire in a manner that narrows the gap between our disputants. My initial task will be to get a preliminary fix on the concept of a spiritual life by isolating some points of agreement. This will give a starting point from which to tackle the question of the role played by desire, the next problem being to determine the limits of *this* concept. The category of appetitive desire is a common starting point in such discussions, and there is a motive – consonant with the drive toward naturalism – for making it the paradigm for thinking properly and more generally about desire per se. It will become clear that it cannot cover all of the conceptual ground, and that our disputants are committed by their own lights to rejecting a conception of the spiritual life that is reducible to such terms.

Desire involves some hidden complexity, and this means that we must be clear about what is at issue if we are to respond appropriately to claims about its relevance for the spiritual life. Schopenhauer tends to be brought in as an example of how not to proceed, but we shall see that there are insights in his position that are consonant with some recent themes in the philosophy of desire and spirituality. I shall argue that the position toward which he is gesturing – not always consistently or successfully – is to be applauded, and that it grants us the right to allow that desire is central to the spiritual life. As for Nietzsche himself, it will remain unclear what *his* conception of the spiritual life really amounts to. However, we shall question the validity of some of his antireligious protestations, and take seriously the possibility that his position has more in common with his target than he would have us believe, even while allowing that it itself degenerates into the contradiction of life.

The Spiritual Life: Some Preliminaries

Our disputants agree that the spiritual life, properly understood, is fundamental to human flourishing. Solomon tells us that it embraces love, trust, reverence, and wisdom, as well as tragedy and death; that it involves "a sense of ourselves as identified with others and the world"; and that it is that by virtue of which the self is transformed.[8] He makes clear that such transformation concerns the self's "expansion" rather than its "abandonment" – a clear admonition to those for whom the spiritual life involves trading in our humanity for an empty dream.

Soskice agrees that the spiritual life is part and parcel of what it is to be properly human, that love and morality are central in this regard, and that it has nothing to do with rejecting *this* life in favor of some "beyond," or *this* human self for a disembodied spirit. Thus, we are told that what we need to attend to with love is "a changing world full of creatures of change – not Cartesian minds ontologically distinct from extended matter, but extended wholes";[9] that our physical natures are an essential part of the picture of the spiritual life as a good;[10] and that we must reject the dualism of reason and desire that leads us to suppose that desire and appetite are "delusions and snares" on the spiritual path.[11] We might compare John Cottingham's insistence that we give precedence to "the individual's embarking on a path of practical self-transformation, rather than (say) simply engaging in intellectual debate or philosophical analysis," his further claim being that the "spiritual" dimension of human existence "cover[s] forms of life that put a premium on certain kinds of intensely focused moral and aesthetic response, or on the search for deeper reflective awareness of the meaning of our lives and of our relationship to others and to the natural world." Cottingham writes as a theist but concedes that even the most convinced atheist would grant the significance of a spiritual life in *this* sense.[12]

[8] Solomon, *Spirituality for the Skeptic*, 6–7. [9] Soskice, *The Kindness of God*, 26.
[10] Soskice, *The Kindness of God*, 29. [11] Soskice, *The Kindness of God*, 27–9.
[12] J. Cottingham, *The Spiritual Dimension: Religion, Philosophy and Human Value* (Cambridge University Press, 2005), 3–5.

We have what seems to be a conception of the spiritual life that is amenable to a naturalist outlook, there being no hint of any aversion to life in the here and now. But where does this leave the "angelic" dream or "lie" of figures like Schopenhauer? For although Schopenhauer's interest in the spiritual life embraces most of the things we have mentioned so far – love, wisdom, self-transformation, a sense of ourselves as identified with others and the world, morality, aesthetics, and meaning – it does express a rather strong aversion to life in the here and now. Is this simply a throwback to unenlightened times or is there more to the position than meets the typical atheist's eye? I have hinted already that this latter diagnosis may well be appropriate, and I want now to develop this thought, beginning with a more general discussion of the nature and limits of desire, desire being the thing that, for Schopenhauer, provides the surest obstacle to a properly spiritual life.

Desire: Some Clarifications

Philosophers and others have tended to treat the question of the nature of desire far too simply. So says Mark Platts in a discussion of the role desire plays in morality, his further claim being that this simplifying tendency is encouraged by an undue attention to appetitive desires.[13] An attention along these lines will be important to one for whom a concern with our physical natures is paramount, for appetitive desires are central to our animal nature. Furthermore, it seems plausible to suppose that they can be comprehended without any need to introduce the "otherworldly" ingredients to which the religiously minded are prone – to put it in terms that are familiar from those who protest along these lines, they are amenable to naturalistic treatment. We can note at this preliminary stage that it has not been shown that a more complex conception of desire must involve a rejection of our animal nature, although it may well involve rejecting the assumption that all of our desires are appetitive. As for the idea that non-appetitive desires bring a commitment to "otherworldly" ingredients, everything hangs on the question of the limits of *this* world, and it is not ruled out that there are conceptions of these limits that invite if not demand such ingredients.[14]

[13] M. Platts, "Moral Reality and the End of Desire," in M. Platts (ed.), *Reference, Truth and Reality: Essays on the Philosophy of Language* (London: Routledge & Kegan Paul, 1980), 79.

[14] See my *God, Value, and Nature* (Oxford University Press, 2014) for a lengthy vindication of this thought.

Appetitive desires have a biological function, and they involve distinctive bodily sensations. They make their presence *felt* in this respect, and when this happens, the desiring subject is motivated to satisfy the relevant desire, such satisfaction leading to the elimination of the relevant sensations and being a source of enjoyment in its own right. So, for example, the felt desire for food leads me to seek out something to eat, the feeling of hunger disappears as I fill myself up, and the whole process is a source of contentment.

This much applies to my hungry cat, but the picture is more complex in the case of human beings, for things have significance for us in the way that they do not for other animals, and even appetitive desires involve some sense of the value that comes from their satisfaction.[15] So, for example, I want to eat the biscuits because they'll abate my hunger or because they taste so good. I can also want to eat them because they were made by somebody I love, although this latter desire takes us beyond the realm of the appetitive in the sense that I can have it without feeling hungry, and the value of satisfying it involves reference to somebody other than myself.[16]

Appetitive desires do not exhaust the range of desires that we have, for there is more to human life than wanting to fill oneself up and feel the pleasure this affords. Platts goes so far as to say that most of our desires are non-appetitive, the category of most interest to him being those in which the attention is deflected away from the subject and her satisfactions to the object and its independent value.[17] His focus is the case of moral value, and the desires in question are said to be motivated by the subject's conception of the independent desirability of their objects.[18] Contrast the felt desire for food where the object's desirability is purely a function of its being desired:

[15] The transformation of lust into erotic love is a key case in point, highlighted in Roger Scruton's *Sexual Desire* (London: Weidenfeld and Nicholson, 1986). For the case of hunger, see Leon R. Kass's *The Hungry Soul: Eating and the Perfecting of Our Nature* (University of Chicago Press, 1994). Kass argues that through cultural formation (second nature) we transform animal feeding into human eating, which can also take the form of fine dining and feasting, where the categories of the noble and the sacred have relevance. I thank David McPherson for helpful discussion on this issue.

[16] The distinction at issue here can be related to Thomas Nagel's distinction between motivated and unmotivated desires in his *The Possibility of Altruism* (Princeton University Press, 1970), 29–32. Stephen Schiffer makes a similar distinction between reason-following and reason-producing desires in his "The Paradox of Desire," *American Philosophical Quarterly*, 13 (1976), 195–203. Maria Alvarez offers a helpful discussion of these distinctions in her *Kinds of Reasons: An Essay in the Philosophy of Action* (Oxford University Press, 2010), 74. See also Mark Platts's *Moral Realities: An Essay in Philosophical Psychology* (London: Routledge, 1991), 43–5.

[17] Platts, "Moral Reality and the End of Desire," 80.

[18] Platts, "Moral Reality and the End of Desire," 77.

the biscuits seem good to me because I'm hungry, and they would not be remotely appealing if I were not.[19]

The general idea here is that we have desires that have nothing to do with wanting to satisfy our bodily appetites, and that are oriented, rather, toward something whose value is not a function of its capacity to deliver such satisfaction, and that serves to elicit the desire in the first place. The position can be traced back to Plato and Aristotle,[20] and it involves conceiving of desire as a representation of the desired object as good in some sense, and with the power thereby to draw the subject outside of herself. The further crucial thought is that it is by virtue of so responding that she is somehow redeemed. Thus Platts, in the context of envisaging what it would be like to lack such desires, talks of an existence that is "empty, brutish, and long."[21]

The relevant desires are object-directed, and Platts claims that "it is at least arguable that any description of a desire using the form *desiring object x* can be rewritten using the *desire that* construction."[22] Talbot Brewer agrees that there are desires that involve being responsive to value, and that they are central to a properly human existence. As he puts it, they allow us to make sense of "our depth, of the intelligibility of our life quests, or of the yearnings that draw us to our ideals and to each other."[23] However, he denies that their objects can be captured in propositional form,[24] understandably so, given that "propositionalism," on his way of thinking, "banishes all evaluative content from desires."[25] Brewer's target is the "narrowly naturalistic, value-denuded" version of the position according to which desire is an attitude toward a proposition whose content can be characterized in purely non-evaluative terms.[26] The relevant attitude is that of wanting the proposition to be true, and one has it when disposed to act on the world in ways calculated to make the proposition true. It is in the context of so acting that the desire is satisfied.[27]

The case of Platts suggests that the position is not bound to take this "value-denuded" form, although he himself is open to the possibility of there being desires that resist propositional treatment. Brewer's further

[19] This is akin to Charles Taylor's distinction between weak and strong evaluation in his "Responsibility for Self," in A. Rorty (ed.), *The Identities of Persons* (Berkeley: University of California Press, 1976), 281–300.

[20] See Plato's *Symposium* 210d–211b, and Aristotle's *Nicomachean Ethics*, 1.1, 1094a3.

[21] Platts, "Moral Reality and the End of Desire," 80.

[22] Platts, "Moral Reality and the End of Desire," 76.

[23] T. Brewer, *The Retrieval of Ethics* (Oxford University Press, 2009), 14.

[24] Brewer, *The Retrieval of Ethics*, 19. [25] Brewer, *The Retrieval of Ethics*, 24.

[26] Brewer, *The Retrieval of Ethics*, 15. [27] Brewer, *The Retrieval of Ethics*, 17.

objection to such treatment is that it fails to accommodate the desires that are of most significance to his purposes, namely, those that draw us to our ideals and to each other, and by virtue of which we can be said to possess a depth. The desires themselves are said to involve a depth in the sense that their objects exceed the desirer's explicit articulation thereof, and cannot, in any case, be reduced to a state of affairs that the subject, by virtue of desiring, is disposed to produce – hence their resistance to propositional treatment. The further claim is that we are capable of penetrating and extending this depth as we come to a more adequate conception of the goods the relevant desires draw us toward.[28]

Brewer takes himself to be articulating and defending a version of the Platonist/Neo-Platonist claim that we have desires that attract us to the highest good.[29] These desires are related to one another as motivating intimations of a goodness that is variously and progressively revealed and realized in the activities we pursue on their basis, when, for example, we are motivated by artistic, moral, or philosophical excellence. Desire is the state we are in when we "feel the tug" of the relevant values, and it is this tug that moves us to act accordingly, when, say, we act with compassion or set about writing something of philosophical worth.[30] Brewer makes clear that this supposedly "world-making" concession offers no hostage to the disputed position, and that to suppose otherwise is to fail to distinguish between the desire's object and its expression. As he puts it, "[t]he object of such a desire is that towards which it draws our evaluative focus, not the state of the world that we are inclined to bring about when our evaluative attention is focused in this way."[31]

Desire thus understood has a teleological structure, and we ourselves *qua* desiring beings are engaged in an ongoing quest to articulate and to embody an adequate conception of the good. Brewer contrasts this with the picture according to which living is simply a matter of throwing one's causal weight around the world in response to some state of affairs one seeks to bring about, and he objects to this picture not simply because it fails to accommodate the ongoing narrative of a properly human existence, but because it leaves no room for the desires that motivate such a narrative in the first place. We know already that such desires are oriented toward the good, and Brewer claims that it is an effect of so desiring that one is taken outside of oneself. It is in this context that he talks of desire's "'unselfing'

[28] Brewer, *The Retrieval of Ethics*, 51. [29] Brewer, *The Retrieval of Ethics*, 56.
[30] Brewer, *The Retrieval of Ethics*, 46. [31] Brewer, *The Retrieval of Ethics*, 46.

influence,"[32] claiming that it frees us "from that most banal and obsessive of human distractions, the self."[33] The idea is familiar from Platts.

The Spiritual Life, Again

We have a picture of desire that promises to make sense of at least some of the features that, by the lights of our disputants, are fundamental to a properly spiritual life. The idea that it draws us to our ideals and to each other accommodates the values – love, trust, reverence, and wisdom – that are so important to Solomon, and it is surely a consequence of being so drawn that we are given a sense of ourselves as identified with others and the world. It is a further feature of the position that desire is deepened and refined over time as the subject struggles to understand and to articulate the values it brings into view. It is in this sense that she is said to be caught up in a "life-quest." Crucially, however, this is no mere intellectual exercise, and Brewer makes clear that the journey at issue here is irreducibly practical, and expressed at various levels of evaluative response. He would be happy to grant with Cottingham, then, that we are concerned with "forms of life that put a premium on certain kinds of intensely focused moral and aesthetic response, or on the search for deeper reflective awareness of the meaning of our lives and of our relationship to others and to the natural world." We can note finally that it is fundamental to the overall picture that the transformation that comes from engaging in this desire-fueled quest has nothing to do with relinquishing the self in favor of something beyond this world and our humanity – as if one becomes something other than a human self or nothing at all. So we can grant with Solomon that the self is *expanded* rather than *abandoned*, this metaphor being entirely appropriate to Brewer's talk in this context of the self's growing depth.[34]

This is all very well, but the conception of desire to which we have been introduced has its origins in a Platonist/Neo-Platonist way of thinking, and we are familiar with the complaint that Platonism involves reference to "otherworldly" ingredients, undermines the significance of the here and now, and points us in the direction of just the kind of "angelic ideal" that stands opposed to life and desire. As Roger Scruton has described Plato's image of spiritual ascent, it involves the discarding of desire and its

[32] Brewer, *The Retrieval of Ethics*, 63. [33] Brewer, *The Retrieval of Ethics*, 63–4.

[34] We might for this reason worry about the "unselfing" language Brewer and Platts use, implying as it does that the self itself is to be transcended. I think they would agree, however, that the real point is not that we should be escaping the self per se, but that our egoistic tendencies should not be given exclusive dominion. This point will be important when we come to consider Schopenhauer.

replacement with an "act of serene contemplation of the Form of the Beautiful."[35] We are reminded of Soskice's talk of something "still and luminous, turned to the future and far from our daily lives," and Scruton's later and more pejorative reference to a "bloodless philosophical passion" that offers a natural prelude to the Nietzschean protestations with which we began.

I have hinted already that these supposedly "otherworldly" ingredients may be rather more significant than our disputants suggest, and that everything hangs on the question of how we are to comprehend the limits of the world against which they are supposedly defined. The Nietzschean encourages us to suppose that it incorporates all that pertains to life, nature, and humanity, the implication being that the move the Platonist envisages involves a declared aversion to these things, and, ultimately, the "deification of nothingness." We know also that Schopenhauer is a familiar target in this context, his metaphysical framework being one that is said to express the offending nihilism to the cost of our proper humanity and spirituality, and to also involve an explicit rejection of desire. It will be helpful then to look more closely at his position with a view to determining whether, and in what sense, he falls foul of the relevant objections, and where this leaves the question of the relation between the spiritual life and desire. It is to this task I now turn.

Schopenhauer on Desire

The textual evidence suggests that Schopenhauer does, indeed, preach a transcending of desire, taking it to be a "delusion and snare" on the spiritual path, to repeat Soskice's terminology. Desire, as he sees it, is fundamental to our nature as willing beings, will being the craving, malevolent force that constitutes the innermost essence of things, and that is expressed at every level of life as it strives to maintain itself in existence.[36] It is expressed in human life at the level of desire, and desire thus understood involves a lack or deficiency that brings suffering to its subject.[37] This lack can be filled and the suffering abated because desires can be satisfied. However, they can be satisfied only temporarily, and are

[35] R. Scruton, *Death-Devoted Heart: Sex and the Sacred in Wagner's* Tristan and Isolde (Oxford University Press, 2004), 136.

[36] A. Schopenhauer, *The World as Will and Representation*, trans. E. F. J. Payne (New York: Dover, [1818] 1969), vol. I, 110.

[37] Schopenhauer, *The World as Will and Representation*, 196.

compelled to rear up again, giving rise to more suffering, demanding similar satisfaction, and so on ad infinitum. Hence:

> Absolutely every human life continues to flow on between willing and attainment. Of its nature the wish is pain; attainment quickly begets satiety. The goal was only apparent; possession takes away its charm. The wish, the need, appears again on the scene under a new form; if it does not, then dreariness, emptiness, and boredom follow, the struggle against which is just as painful as is that against want.[38]

The result is that:

> The subject of willing is constantly lying on the revolving wheel of Ixion, is always drawing water in the sieve of the Danaids, and is the eternally thirsting Tantalus.[39]

Schopenhauer's verdict is that:

> [s]o long as our consciousness is filled by our will, so long as we are given up to the throng of desires with its constant hopes and fears, so long as we are the subject of willing, we never obtain lasting happiness or peace . . . without peace and calm, true well-being is absolutely impossible.[40]

The idea that desire involves a lack in the subject that demands to be filled fits the case of bodily appetites, and it is familiar that such desires can involve suffering, witness the discomfort that comes from being excessively hungry or thirsty. Pain occurs when the deprivation is severe, but it does not follow that desire is an intrinsically painful state, and even appetitive desires can be "suffered" with pleasure, the force of the term in this latter context serving to capture the sense in which they can be said to "assail" us.[41] As I put it previously, they make their presence *felt.* Schopenhauer is concerned with the desires of human beings. So he grants the value we attach to the things we desire – hence the reference to our "constant hopes and fears" – and is not, in any case, concerned exclusively with the bodily appetites. Rather, his focus is any desire whatsoever, and I have noted already that he takes them to be expressions of a hungry and malevolent will. The further crucial claim is that they are exclusively self-concerned. As one commentator has put it, it's a matter of "each individualisation of [the will] wanting its own way, I wanting mine, you yours, others theirs, each

38 Schopenhauer, *The World as Will and Representation*, 231–4.

39 Schopenhauer, *The World as Will and Representation*, 196.

40 Schopenhauer, *The World as Will and Representation*, 196.

41 Thomas Nagel uses this term in the context of discussing appetitive desires in his *The Possibility of Altruism*, 29.

asserting itself, subjecting others or subjected to them, each implicitly saying, 'I', 'I', and tolerating others only as they serve it (making the I more I)."[42]

The Platonist would object that Schopenhauer has failed to acknowledge those desires that involve being responsive to something independently valuable, and that display an "unselfing" influence in this regard. Schopenhauer promotes an analogous deflection away from the self, the difference being that the state of mind he envisages in this context is one in which the self is no longer given up to the "throng of desire." So there is a deflection away from the *desiring* self. As noted, however, he is operating with a conception according to which desire is exclusively egoistic. It follows therefore that he is recommending a deflection away from egoism, i.e., from the very distractions that, for the Platonist, are silenced by the desires that attract us to an independent source of value.

Schopenhauer makes abundantly clear that there is more to the self than egoism, the main point of his work being to discourage the reader from such distractions and toward the very things that, it has been agreed, are central to a properly spiritual life. This is spelled out in his discussion of aesthetic and moral experience – contexts in which, for a time at least, consciousness is no longer "filled by our will."[43] As Schopenhauer puts it, we "*lose* ourselves entirely in [the] object"[44] when we attend to it aesthetically, and the man of virtue "no longer makes the egoistical distinction between himself and the person of others, but takes as much in interest in the sufferings of other individuals as in his own."[45]

All of this requires that there is something beyond will, and although Schopenhauer sometimes gives the impression that there is not, he makes clear eventually that the nothingness envisaged and feared by his critics ("as children fear darkness") is equivalent to blank non-existence only on the misguided assumption that will is everything.[46] This assumption is challenged

[42] W. M. Salter, "Schopenhauer's Contact with Theology," *Harvard Theological Review*, 4 (1911), 298.

[43] For aesthetic experience, see book III of *The World as Will and Representation*; for compassion and asceticism, see book IV.

[44] Schopenhauer, *The World as Will and Representation*, 178.

[45] Schopenhauer, *The World as Will and Representation*, 378.

[46] Hence: "[w]e freely acknowledge that what remains after the complete abolition of the will is, for all who are still full of the will, assuredly nothing. But also conversely, to those in whom the will has turned and denied itself, this very real world of ours with all its suns and galaxies, is – nothing." A footnote adds that what is at issue here is the "beyond of all knowledge" to which the Buddhists refer (Schopenhauer, *The World as Will and Representation*, 412). For an interpretation along these lines, see W. M. Salter's "Schopenhauer's Contact with Theology"; G. Mannion, *Schopenhauer, Religion, and Morality* (Aldershot: Ashgate Publishing), 2003; and J. Young, *Schopenhauer* (London: Routledge, 2005).

in his account of aesthetic and moral consciousness, and if we accept with Brewer that the relevant responses are desire-involving in some sense, then, terminology notwithstanding, he is conceding to a Platonist conception of desire and granting hereby that there are desirable desires.

Thus far there is nothing remotely anti-life in any of this except insofar as "life" is taken to be equivalent to an unrelenting egoism. It is familiar, however, that Schopenhauer's position culminates in a description of mystical experience, that this is his soteriological ideal, and that it involves a wholesale rejection of anything pertaining to this world and our humanity (proper or otherwise). After all, the will has been abolished in its entirety,[47] and this is said to bring an analogous "abolition and disappearance of the world" (subject and object included).[48] As he puts it himself, "there is certainly left only nothing."[49] He quickly adds, however – and these are the final words of the book – that "what remains after the complete abolition of the will is *for all who are still full of the will*, assuredly nothing. But also conversely, to those in whom the will has turned and denied itself, this very real world of ours with all its suns and galaxies, is – nothing."[50] He refers in this context to an "ocean-like calmness of the spirit," and offers the terms "ecstasy," "rapture," "union with God," and "Nirvana" as ways of referring to the state of mind at issue here, even while granting that all such conceptualizations are inadequate. The further crucial claim is that we have a foretaste of what it involves in moral and aesthetic experience.[51]

We seem to be returned to Soskice's "still and luminous" something that is "far from our daily lives" in the sense that it transcends human existence. The idea that it transcends human existence is problematic on the assumption that being human exhausts our reality, although blank nothingness might be thought to be preferable if such existence involves unrelenting pain. Schopenhauer takes pain to be intrinsic to egoistic desire, and I have already questioned this assumption as far as appetitive desire is concerned. What of egoistic desire more generally? It does not make its presence felt in the manner of hunger or thirst, and is not therefore suffered in this (innocuous) respect. Rather, it is more a matter of the subject making *her* presence felt as she does what is required to get what she wants, i.e., throws her causal weight around the world in Brewer's pejorative sense.

47 Schopenhauer, *The World as Will and Representation*, 408.
48 Schopenhauer, *The World as Will and Representation*, 410.
49 Schopenhauer, *The World as Will and Representation*, 411.
50 Schopenhauer, *The World as Will and Representation*, 411–12; emphasis mine.
51 Schopenhauer, *The World as Will and Representation*, 410–12.

Could desire in *this* sense be a source of pain? Schopenhauer draws this conclusion on the ground that it is like trying to drink water from a sieve, the implication being that we are *failing* to get what we want. Given that egoistic desires can be satisfied in one clear enough sense, he must mean that the satisfaction is not genuine, and that, to continue the image, egoistic desires are like sieves that filter out what we really want. They are a source of pain in *this* sense.

The Nietzschean interprets this as an objection to desire per se, claiming that what Schopenhauer really wants – and what he thinks we all really want – is the permanent stilling of desire. The evidence for this – alongside the fact that Schopenhauer objects to desire's endless recurrence – is that the ideal he proposes involves a state of mind in which desire has been discarded once and for all. Add to this that we are essentially desiring beings, and that desire is desirable in any case, and the picture does indeed become a piece of diabolical work.

I have denied that desire is invariably desirable, and interpreted Schopenhauer's objection to desire as an objection to egoism. There is no need to go so far as to say that egoism should be eradicated, the important point being that it must not be given free reign. The Platonist avoids this implication by introducing a level of desire in which the focus is deflected away from the hungry self toward an independent source of value, and I have argued that Schopenhauer operates with a terminological variant upon this idea. What of the ocean-like calmness of the spirit to which he refers? Does this not mean that desire has been discarded, and hence, that the satisfaction he has in mind demands its (and our) elimination? Yes, on the assumption that calmness of spirit is equivalent to blank nothingness, but Schopenhauer has denied that this is so, even while granting that there are limits to what can be said and known in this context. But how could such a state be of relevance to our daily lives? Is it not simply an angelic ideal in which we want for nothing and our aspiration to which involves wanting nonexistence? I have already challenged this latter claim on Schopenhauer's behalf. As for the idea that it is too far removed from our daily lives to make any real difference, the response to this objection is found in Schopenhauer's claim that the relevant state of mind is foretasted in moral and aesthetic experience. For this suggests that it precisely *is* relevant to our daily lives, assuming that such lives accommodate the relevant responses. (If they do not, then we are back with an unrelenting egoism.) We can note finally that this state of mind must also be desire-involving in some sense – at least, this is so if we accept that the relevant human experiences can be analogously described. This is borne out by

Schopenhauer's use of the terms "ecstasy" and "rapture" to refer to it, their etymology testifying to just the kind of "unselfing" influence that, for the Platonist, is intrinsic to desire.

Conclusions

The position at which we have arrived grants us the right to say that desire is intrinsic to the spiritual life in the sense that there is a kind of desire that draws us toward the values that are fundamental to such a life, although this is not to deny that some desires have the opposite effect,[52] and that others can be comprehended in purely biological terms. What of the worry that the ingredients to which we are committed hereby are too otherworldly to be taken seriously? They certainly count as such if "world" is comprehended in purely egoistic terms, but there are no good grounds for accepting such a limited conception, and neither theist nor atheist could plausibly deny that the life of the spirit is otherworldly in *this* sense. What of the sense that leads the typical naturalist to reject Platonism on the ground that it involves the postulation of a second, supernatural realm? Again, everything depends on what "natural" means in this context, and if the point of moving in a supernatural direction is simply to avoid scientism, then we are obliged to take this option very seriously indeed.[53] It is worth noting also that supernaturalism is not best viewed in the overly literalist terms assumed by those for whom it is a framework for the intellectually challenged – terms that suggest that Plato really did commit to the existence of a two-decker universe.[54] We might add that it is equally misguided to interpret the heaven of the theist or the nirvana of the Buddhist in these literalist terms – as if it is the *contradiction of life* instead of its transfiguration and eternal *yes*![55]

[52] Schopenhauer would say that desires of the first category are motivated by malice and aimed toward another's misfortune. Nonhuman animals have no such desires, and the idea that they stem from our (improper) humanity is illustrated in Seiriol Morgan's brilliant paper "Dark Desires," *Ethical Theory and Moral Practice*, 6 (2003), 377–410. This paper offers a salutary lesson to those who believe that we are degraded by virtue of being animals. As Morgan illustrates, our darkest desires come from our humanity. I thank David McPherson for alerting me to Morgan's paper and for clarifying this point.

[53] See my *God, Value, and Nature* for some detailed thoughts along these lines.

[54] Compare John McDowell: "Plato is a naturalist of the Aristotelian sort, with a penchant for vividly realized pictorial presentations of his thought" ("Two Sorts of Naturalism," in *Mind, Value, and Reality* [Cambridge, MA: Harvard University Press, 1998], 177, n. 19).

[55] Hence John McDade: "Perhaps I have been in heaven, because whenever God has acted in my soul, that has been heaven; when in the Mass I have felt supported by saints around me, that has been heaven; when I have seen grace work in others, that too has been heaven; when charity has flowed through me, that has been heaven; when I have desired God, when I have been drawn into Christ's offering of himself that has been heaven and will be heaven because that is the life of God enfolding

What I have just said – or rather, what Nietzsche has just said – suggests that the position of his target is not so far removed from his own preferred alternative. It has been left unclear how Nietzsche himself conceives of life's transfiguration, but the idea that he is defending a form of spirituality puts paid to the idea that his preferred life of desire involves an unrelenting egoism, although it remains open that he is doing no such thing.[56] The Platonist sees desire as the state we are in when we feel the tug of the values they reveal, the implication being that, without this tug, we should cease to desire. Does this mean that Nietzsche cannot accommodate such desires? Presumably not if he rejects the relevant values, although it remains open that he is operating with a modified conception of value – one moreover that could be seen as a product of the desire-involving journey we have described. The alternative is to suppose on his behalf that there is no objective source of value, and that the life of desire can be reconstructed in its absence. This is one way of interpreting Robert Pippin's conception of Nietzsche's anti-nihilistic task, the aim, as he puts it, being to divorce our longings from transcendent aspirations,[57] and to arrive at "a picture of striving without the illusion of a determinate, natural lack that we can fill."[58]

The idea that we have aspirations that are transcendent is one way of giving expression to desire's "unselfing" influence, and I have noted already that there are conceptions of this influence that we would do well to avoid – those, in particular, that make it look as if we are being moved in the direction of a realm that could have no bearing on our proper human existence and that serves to contradict everything it involves. So the notion of a transcendent longing is not invariably problematic, and it may be exactly what is needed if we are to accommodate the ingredients of a properly spiritual life. As for the idea that we should be courting a picture of striving without the illusion of a determinate, natural lack to be filled, the Platonist

me. The difficulty is not that we can't see what it will be like after death; it's that we now only haltingly know what is going on now. We are perhaps already in 'deep God'" ("Heaven, Then and Now," *New Blackfriars*, 83 [2002], 48). See also Bret W. Davis, who challenges the assumption that, for the Buddhist, being in nirvana involves being somewhere else: "nirvana is not some place outside this world ... [r]ather nirvana implies a different way of being-in-*this* world" ("Zen after Zarathustra: The Problem of the Will in the Confrontation between Nietzsche and Buddhism," *Journal of Nietzsche Studies*, 28 [2004], 98). It is made clear in this wonderful paper that Buddhism has nothing to do with nihilism, and that Nietzsche was quite wrong to accuse it on this score. Davis does not discuss Schopenhauer, and it would be interesting to see whether he would vindicate his position on analogous grounds.

56 This is how Stephen G. Post describes his position in his "The Inadequacy of Selflessness: God's Suffering and the Theory of Love," *Journal of the American Academy of Religion*, 56 (1988), 224.

57 R. Pippin, "The Erotic Nietzsche: Philosophers without Philosophy," in S. Bartsch and T. Bartscherer (eds.), *Erotikon: Essays on Eros, Ancient and Modern* (University of Chicago Press, 2005), 181.

58 Pippin, "The Erotic Nietzsche," 187.

agrees that this picture must be avoided, and would no doubt accept with Schopenhauer that it is appropriate, at best, to the case of egoistic desire.[59] So it is denied that desire is simply a matter of wanting to fill oneself up. Rather, it can involve an attraction *beyond* the self toward the values that motivate it in the first place. Self and desire are deepened in the process, and we might even say of such a desirer that she is in a condition of eternal thirst. However, she is not the eternally thirsting Tantalus, for she is receiving something in the process, namely, the goodness to which she is (eternally) drawn by virtue of desiring in this way.[60]

Where does this leave Nietzsche? One option is to treat his position as a version of Platonism, and I have suggested already that the gloss Pippin provides is compatible with such an interpretation.[61] The alternative is to say on his behalf that the life of desire can be purely self-generated where this involves denying that it involves *any* kind of "unselfing" influence. The picture makes sense as far as appetitive desire is concerned, for these desires are hard-wired into our animal nature, springing up in response to our biological needs. However, the life of desire in *this* sense could not sustain a properly spiritual existence, and it is unclear what it would mean for there to be a conception of desire that is equal to this task if divorced from anything other than itself. Indeed, there is a question of whether such desire could even sustain itself, insofar as we are remotely clear about what we are seeking to sustain in this context.[62] My own view is that a satisfactory resolution of these issues will demand a considerable concession to Platonism, that the real diabolical work comes with its denial, and that Nietzsche comes close to conceding this point. Long live desire indeed![63]

[59] Plato himself moves beyond the "lack" conception of desire, most notably in Diotoma's speech in *The Symposium* where the emphasis is on giving of oneself rather than taking for oneself. Compare R. L. Markus: "this 'desire' is now of a being already complete or 'perfect' . . . indeed, complete to overflowing, no longer is it thought of as a lack. This desire is not for something to be obtained – the beloved – but for giving something of itself" ("The Dialectic of Eros in Plato's *Symposium*," *Downside Review*, 233 [1955], 226).

[60] Compare Levinas, who talks of a "hunger that nourishes itself not with bread but with hunger itself" (*Totality and Infinity: An Essay on Exteriority*, trans. Alphonso Lingis [Dordrecht: Kluwer, 1991], 179).

[61] For a challenge to the assumption that Nietzsche's will is to be comprehended in egoistic terms, see J. Golomb, "Will to Power: Does It Lead to the 'Coldest of all Cold Monsters'?," in J. Richardson and K. Gemes (eds.), *The Oxford Handbook of Nietzsche* (Oxford University Press, 2013), 526–48. See also Davis, "Zen after Zarathustra," and my "Two Erotic Ideals," *Religious Studies*, 51 (2014), 41–59.

[62] Platts envisages the *failure* of desire in such a context, concluding that "the price of abandoning moral realism can be the end of desire" ("Moral Reality and the End of Desire," 79).

[63] I thank my wonderful friends and colleagues for discussion of these issues, especially Anna Abram, Michael Barnes, John Cottingham, David McPherson, Sarah Coakley, Clare Carlisle, and Mike Inwood.

CHAPTER 6

Between Heaven and Earth
Sensory Experience and the Goods of the Spiritual Life

Mark R. Wynn

Introduction

There are, of course, many ways of conceiving of the goods of the spiritual life. In this chapter, I am going to concentrate on one such conception, drawing on Thomas Aquinas's account of the infused moral virtues. Aquinas's discussion allows us to distinguish a kind of spiritual good that is concerned not simply with our relation to created things, nor simply with our relation to God, but with our relation to created things so far as that relation is properly ordered to our relation to God. Such goods lie, as it were, between heaven and earth, and to mark this fact, I'll refer to them as hybrid goods. Thomas makes a helpful interlocutor for these purposes both because his work is authoritative for one central strand of Christian reflection and also because, at least on these matters, it is representative of a much wider tendency of thought, which spans non-Christian as well as Christian traditions.

Having introduced Aquinas's category of infused moral virtue, and drawn out some of its implications for our understanding of the nature of spiritual goods, I'll then examine the claim that the senses can contribute to the realization of such goods. While the first part of the chapter builds on themes from Aquinas, the second will use William James's influential discussion of conversion experience to chart some of the ways in which a person's sensory experience may be more or less closely aligned with his or her theological context. It is of course a commonplace of accounts of the spiritual life that our thoughts and feelings, attitudes and behavior are all important constituents of spiritual well-being. In this discussion, I aim to show how the goods of the spiritual life can be realized not only when our lives are properly ordered in these respects, but also in virtue of the quality of our experience of the everyday sensory world.

Following this general approach, let's begin by considering the relevance of Thomas Aquinas's category of infused moral virtue for our understanding of the nature of spiritual goods.

Aquinas on the Goods of the Spiritual Life

Thomas Aquinas had, of course, inherited from Aristotle the idea that there are "acquired" moral virtues – that is, virtues that derive from some process of habituation, whereby the repeated performance of, for example, courageous acts leads to the formation in the person of the habit of acting courageously, so that thereafter they not only do the courageous thing, but do it as a person of courage.[1] He had also inherited from his theological forebears the idea that there are theological virtues – of faith, hope and charity – that are the product not of any process of habituation but of divine activity or "infusion."[2] It is against this conceptual background that Thomas develops his account of infused moral virtue.

The idea that there are such virtues is not original to Aquinas: his Dominican predecessor Peraldus seems to have been committed to much the same idea.[3] But what is novel to Aquinas is the attempt to hold together an Aristotelian account of the "acquired" moral virtues, a traditional view of the theological virtues as infused, and the idea that there are infused moral virtues.[4] We can see how Thomas understands the distinction between acquired and infused moral virtues by turning to his discussion of temperance, so far as it concerns the consumption of food in particular.

Acquired and infused temperance are both concerned with our relations to food (and with the regulation of other bodily appetites); so both are "moral" rather than theological virtues, in the sense that both are concerned, in the first instance, with the ordering of our habits of thought, desire, and action in our relationship to created things – and to keep to this example, in our relationship to food in particular. But while acquired temperance is concerned simply with a person's flourishing as a member

[1] Aristotle, *The Ethics of Aristotle: The Nicomachean Ethics* [ca. 325 BC], trans. J. A. K. Thomson, rev. H. Tredennick (Harmondsworth: Penguin, 1976), bk. II.

[2] See St. Thomas Aquinas, *Summa Theologiae*, I–II, q. 62.

[3] For a helpful discussion of the relationship between Aquinas and Peraldus on this point, see J. Inglis, "Aquinas's Replication of the Acquired Moral Virtues," *The Journal of Religious Ethics*, 27 (1999), 3–27.

[4] Inglis notes that in his account of the moral virtues, Peraldus had allowed that human beings "can prepare for, but not cooperate in, the reception of moral virtue" ("Aquinas's Replication," 11). By admitting the acquired moral virtues, Aquinas gives a role to cooperation, and not only to preparation. Following Augustine, the bulk of the tradition had no place even for preparation.

of the kind *human being* (and independently, therefore, of any reference to one's "supernatural" calling), infused temperance has as its ultimate end a person's relationship to God. And for Aquinas, this difference in teleology makes for a difference in etiology and in epistemology: acquired but not infused temperance can be produced by our own efforts, and the requirements of acquired but not those of infused temperance can be understood simply by the exercise of reason, and independently of "revelation."

We can see Aquinas elaborating on this general picture in the following passage. Here, he distinguishes between the "rules" that are appropriate to the acquired and infused forms of temperance:

> It is evident the measure of desires appointed by a rule of human reason is different from that appointed by a divine rule. For instance, in eating, the measure fixed by human reason is that food should not harm the health of the body, nor hinder the use of reason; whereas [the] divine rule requires that a man should chastise his body and bring it into subjection [1 Cor. 9:27], by abstinence in food, drink and the like.[5]

So we can judge the appropriateness of a given pattern of consuming and desiring food from two perspectives. First of all, we can adopt the vantage point of "reason." Here, we are concerned with those habits of consumption that will, to put the point minimally, do no harm to the body. Such harm will ensue both when we consume too much and when we consume too little, and what counts as excess and deficiency here is, of course, relative to our human nature: the patterns of consumption that make for excess and deficiency will vary, depending on whether we have in view porpoises, or tortoises, or human beings.[6] We can speak of a rule of "reason" in this context because harm-inducing patterns of consumption can be identified through the relevant empirical investigation, and without reference to scripture or "revelation." So, in sum, there is a standard of right eating that is relative to human nature, accessible to reason, and that can be enacted simply by human effort, that is, via the inculcation of the right habits of thought, action, and desire.

According to Thomas's text, there is evidently a further perspective from which we can judge the appropriateness of a given pattern of consuming and desiring food. In this case, we are to appeal not to a reason-grounded, human-nature-relative understanding, but to what is revealed in the

[5] Aquinas, *Summa Theologiae*, ed. T. Gilby (London: Eyre & Spottiswoode, [ca. 1266–73] 1964–74), vol. 23, I–II, q. 63, a. 4.

[6] There is also, of course, a person-relative measure of right consumption, as Aristotle observes with reference to Milo the wrestler (*Nicomachean Ethics*, bk. II).

scriptures about the connection between various habits of consumption and our relation to God. When Aquinas talks here of "chastising the body," rather than simply avoiding harm of the body, he is citing the following text from Paul's first letter to the Christian community in Corinth:

> Everyone who competes in the games exercises self-control in all things. They then do it to receive a perishable wreath, but we an imperishable. Therefore I run in such a way, as not without aim; I box in such a way, as not beating the air; but I discipline [chastise] my body and make it my slave, so that, after I have preached to others, I myself will not be disqualified.[7]

From this reference to an "imperishable wreath," it is clear that Paul's concern in this passage is with the person's relationship to God in eternity; and when he imports this text into his discussion of infused temperance, Aquinas is indicating that he takes the goal of abstinence, and of "chastising the body," to involve the person's relationship to God not simply here and now, but in the afterlife. So the divine rule that is the measure of right consumption of food turns out to be grounded in a conception of the person's future life with God.

Generalizing from this case, we can say that the infused moral virtues are like the theological virtues, and unlike the acquired moral virtues, in having as their goal relationship to God – but whereas the theological virtues aim directly at our well-being in relationship to God, the infused moral virtues aim at that well-being only indirectly, that is, via our relation to created things. As Aquinas puts the point: "The theological virtues are enough to shape us to our supernatural end as a start, that is, to God himself immediately and to none other. Yet the soul needs also to be equipped by infused virtues in regard to created things, though as subordinate to God."[8] So the role of infused moral virtues is, in brief, to draw our relationship to "created things" into our relationship to God. We could see the infused moral virtues as, therefore, a kind of hinge: they bring together the "acquired" moral virtues and the theological virtues, since they share their subject matter with the acquired moral virtues, and their teleology with the theological virtues. In this way, the infused moral virtues are directed at a good that lies between heaven and earth, namely, a good that is realized insofar as our relations to created things are properly ordered by reference to our relationship to God. And knowing

[7] 1 Corinthians 9:25–7; the translation is taken from the New American Standard Bible.
[8] Aquinas, *Summa Theologiae*, I–II, q. 63, a. 3, ad. 2.

the nature of these hybrid goods, and what it takes to attain them, depends on familiarity with the relevant divine rule, which in turn requires acquaintance with revelation.

We can clarify the nature of these hybrid goods by thinking a little more closely about the respective "rules" that serve as the measure for the acquired and infused moral virtues. The divine rule that provides the standard for a given infused moral virtue does not cancel the rule that is the measure of the acquired counterpart of that virtue. Hence, to return to the case of acquired and infused temperance, abstinence involves "chastising of the body," but not harm of the body. (It is for this reason, of course, that in Christian tradition, the young and infirm are standardly exempt from the full rigor of penitential fasting.)[9] So the rule that is appropriate to infused temperance does not involve any breach in the corresponding rule of reason. And that is because the first rule is relatively demanding: in eating in accordance with the divine rule, I do not harm the body, but at the same time, I restrict my consumption further than would be required simply for the sake of preserving bodily health. To put the point in general terms, in adhering to the relevant divine rule, I thereby adhere to the corresponding rule of reason, so that my conduct is fitting both relative to my human nature and relative to a further, God-directed teleology. So the infused moral virtues orient us to the created order and at the same time to God, and in so doing, they realize not only spiritual goods but also the goods that are the object of the acquired moral virtues, whose measure is not a divine rule but a rule of reason.

We have been thinking about the nature of the goods that are the object of the infused moral virtues, noting their hybrid character, and their relationship to the goods that are the object of the acquired moral virtues. And we have seen that these goods arise insofar as a person's thoughts,

[9] Aquinas himself notes this exemption with approval: "In children there is a most evident reason for not fasting, both on account of their natural weakness, owing to which they need to take food frequently, and not much at a time, and because they need much nourishment owing to the demands of growth, which results from the residuum of nourishment. Wherefore as long as the stage of growth lasts, which as a rule lasts until they have completed the third period of seven years, they are not bound to keep the Church fasts: and yet it is fitting that even during that time they should exercise themselves in fasting, more or less, in accordance with their age." Aquinas adds that under special circumstances, even children are required to fast: "Nevertheless when some great calamity threatens, even children are commanded to fast, in sign of more severe penance, according to Jonas 3:7, 'Let neither men nor beasts . . . taste anything . . . nor drink water'" (Aquinas, *Summa Theologiae*, II–II, q. 147, a. 4, ad. 2, trans. Fathers of the Dominican Province, Benziger Brothers edition, 1947, available here: http://dhspriory.org/thomas/summa/SS/SS025.html#SSQ25OUTP1). So the prospect of a great calamity establishes that it is not just "fitting" for children to fast but required, though this is still not to say that under these conditions their fasting may involve harm of the body.

feelings, and behavior are properly aligned with some theological truth, such as a truth concerning our future life with God. In concluding this discussion of infused moral virtue, I want to think a little further about what it is for our thoughts and behavior to be properly aligned in this sense.

For this purpose, let's shift our attention from Aquinas's discussion of infused temperance and turn to his treatment of the cardinal Christian virtue of neighbor love. Although Thomas does not put the point in these terms, we can think of charity, or *caritas*, so far as it is directed to human beings, as a further example of an infused moral virtue. Like infused temperance, charity so understood concerns our relations to the created order (here the virtue's focus is of course our fellow human beings rather than food) and folds those relations into our relationship to God. And as with infused temperance, so here, Aquinas grounds the appropriateness of neighbor love in an appeal to our future life with God.

Of course, charity is the object of a dominical command, and for Christians, that is sufficient to establish its obligatoriness.[10] But for Aquinas, there is another, more theoretical rationale for Christian charity, which is evident in the following passage, where he is considering whether the angels are properly the objects of neighbor love. To a modern readership, this might seem a rather arcane concern, but in structural terms, what Aquinas says here is no different from what he says when discussing the scope of neighbor love in other respects, as when he considers whether it properly extends to one's enemies, or one's body, or to non-rational creatures. So what he says in this passage is representative of this larger case, and worth heeding, therefore, even if we are not much exercised by the question of how we ought to relate to the angels. Thomas writes:

> As stated above (Q 23, Art. 1), the friendship of charity is founded upon the fellowship of everlasting happiness, in which men share in common with the angels. For it is written (Mt. 22:30) that "in the resurrection . . . men shall be as the angels of God in heaven." It is therefore evident that the friendship of charity extends also to the angels.[11]

Here, Aquinas grounds the appropriateness of love of the angels in the thought that we will one day share with them in "the fellowship of everlasting happiness." And as I have noted, he appeals to the same kind of consideration when asking whether, for example, sinners and non-rational

[10] For the command to love one's neighbor, see Mark 12:31 and parallels.

[11] Aquinas, *Summa Theologiae*, II–II, q. 25, a. 10, ellipsis in the original, trans. Fathers of the English Dominican Province.

creatures are to be loved.[12] From his remarks here, it seems clear that Aquinas is not proposing that I am required to love others (whether the angels or other human beings) as a condition of attaining the beatific vision myself, or as a condition of enabling others to attain that state. Instead, the thought seems to be that the already established truth that we will one day share with them in the beatific vision sets certain constraints on how we are to relate to other human beings here and now, in the present.

On this reading of Aquinas, what makes a particular pattern of life fitting relative to our theological context is not that it helps to bring about, say, our participation in the beatific vision, but the fact that it constitutes an appropriate acknowledgment of an already established theological context, such as the context provided by the fact that we will one day share with other human beings, and with the angels, in the vision of God. For present purposes, I am not going to defend or further examine Aquinas's view, but it is perhaps worth noting the parallel between his position and one very familiar form of moral reasoning. As we all know, the history of our relations to another person can set moral constraints on how we are to relate to the person in the present. And if we follow Aquinas here, then we should say that it is not only the history of our relations to others that can play this role, but also the future (the eschatological future) of those relations. This parallel is enough, I think, to allow us to make some initial sense of Aquinas's proposal.

In sum, we have seen that the spiritual goods that are the object of the infused moral virtues are realized insofar as a person's relationship to created things is properly aligned with his or her theological context. And we have now considered a little more fully what this relationship of "proper alignment" amounts to. In brief, in at least some central cases, proper alignment is to be understood in terms of what we might call existential fittingness, rather than causal efficacy. Although we have been concerned here with just one kind of spiritual good, as understood within one spiritual tradition, it is not too difficult, I think, to find parallels between this general approach and the perspective of a range of other spiritual and religious traditions, including non-Christian traditions.[13] Indeed, I think it reasonable to say, although I cannot argue for the claim here, that spiritual and religious traditions

[12] These matters are treated in Articles 6 and 3, respectively. Aquinas is not a universalist about salvation, so there is a question about how to reconcile his soteriology with his ethics, given that he regards all human beings as properly the objects of neighbor love. But that is not our concern here.

[13] For present purposes, I am assuming that religious traditions typically have a "spiritual," and not only, say, an abstractly creedal dimension, and that there can be secular as well as religious spiritual traditions. Any of a variety of ways of understanding the relationship between spiritual and religious commitment will be compatible with the drift of my case here. For further discussion,

typically provide their adherents with a picture of our metaphysical context, of the kind that will ground a more-than-natural measure of the adequacy of our world-directed thoughts and actions.

We can say of such traditions, as we can say of the spiritual life as Aquinas understands it, that they are directed not simply at otherworldly goods (such as the good of the beatific vision), nor simply at this-worldly goods (such as the good of a diet that is conducive to bodily health), but at hybrid goods, that is, goods that concern our practical and intellectual relationship to the material world, where that relationship is deemed to be good because of its congruence with the beatific vision or some other truth concerning our religious context. So we can say of such traditions, as Aquinas says of infused moral virtue, that they are concerned with our relationship to "created things, as subordinate to God."

Having examined one account of the nature of spiritual goods, I want to move now to our second major theme, by considering the significance of sensory experience for the spiritual life. I shall start by thinking about conversion experience, as it is represented in the work of William James.

Sensory Experience and the Spiritual Life

William James notes that religious converts commonly take themselves to enjoy not only a new relationship to God, but also a newly enlivened appreciation of the everyday sensory world. As he notes in his discussion of conversion experience in his *Varieties of Religious Experience*:

> When we come to study the phenomenon of conversion or religious regeneration, we . . . see that a not infrequent consequence of the change operated in the subject is a transfiguration of the face of nature in his eyes. A new heaven seems to shine upon a new earth.[14]

As James indicates here, a striking feature of conversion reports is that it is not simply the appearance of certain items, or of a localized region, that changes following conversion, but the appearance of the sensory world in general. To put the point in his terms, it is "the face of nature" that changes, so that there is now a "new earth."

see D. McPherson, "*Homo Religiosus*: Does Spirituality Have a Place in Neo-Aristotelian Virtue Ethics?," *Religious Studies*, 51 (2015), 335–46.

[14] W. James, *The Varieties of Religious Experience: A Study in Human Nature* (London: Longmans, Green and Co., [1902] 1910), 151.

James cites various examples of this transformation in the quality of the appearances. Here I'll note just two of these cases. Jonathan Edwards, the American divine, describes his conversion experience in these terms:

> The appearance of everything was altered; there seemed to be, as it were, a calm, sweet cast, or appearance of divine glory, in almost everything. God's excellency, his wisdom, his purity and love, seemed to appear in everything; in the sun, moon, and stars; in the clouds and blue sky; in the grass, flowers, and trees; in the water and all nature; which used greatly to fix my mind.[15]

Edwards is a careful, analytically precise writer, and when he speaks so insistently of the character of the world's "appearance" following his conversion, there is good reason to take his remarks at face value, as a sober description of the phenomena, however hard it may be to make sense of the idea of God's "excellency" "appearing" in the grass and flowers and trees. In a similar vein, another of James's sources remarks that:

> Natural objects were glorified, my spiritual vision was so clarified that I saw beauty in every material object in the universe.[16]

Here again, the convert reports a generalized transformation in the appearance of the sensory world, so that it is now, somehow, transparent to the divine glory.

John of the Cross's description of the "joy" of the "awakened" person, that is, the person who has reached a condition of spiritual maturity, suggests a similar kind of experiential state. John writes:

> Though it is true that the soul here sees that all these things are distinct from God, in that they have a created existence . . . it knows also that God in His own essence is, in an infinitely preeminent way, all these things, so that it understands them better in Him, their first cause, than in themselves. This is the great joy of this awakening, namely to know creatures in God, and not God in His creatures: this is to know effects in their cause, and not the cause by its effects.[17]

This passage is, I take it, a kind of play on Aquinas's comments in the preamble to the Five Ways, when he remarks that a demonstration can move either from knowledge of a cause to a knowledge of its effects, or vice versa, and that proving the existence of God requires a demonstration of the second kind, so that, to put the point in John's terms, we know "the

[15] James, *Varieties*, 248–9. [16] James, *Varieties*, 250.

[17] St. John of the Cross, *The Living Flame of Love by Saint John of the Cross with His Letters, Poems, and Minor Writings*, trans. D. Lewis (London: Thomas Baker, [1585] 1919), Commentary on Stanza IV, 121.

cause by its effects."[18] In this passage, John in effect distinguishes the vantage point that is appropriate for the project of proving the existence of God from the vantage point of the person of spiritual maturity. This person, he is proposing, knows "creatures in God," or "effects in their cause," rather than vice versa.[19]

Since he refers here simply to a knowledge of "creatures" without further specification, we have some reason to suppose that John takes this distinctive knowledge of the person of spiritual maturity to extend to the created order as a whole.[20] If that is right, then in this respect this person is like the converts James describes: in each case, the person has acquired a new appreciation of the sensory world in general. And while John does not explicitly connect this new knowledge to the quality of the person's experience of the world, in light of James's discussion, we have some reason to suppose that such knowledge finds expression in, or perhaps in some measure it takes the form of, a transformation in the appearance of everyday things. If we can read his text in these terms, then we should think of the "joy" to which John refers not as simply a state of bodily feeling, but as extending into the world, so that sensory objects are differently experienced.

So taking into account James's examples, and John of the Cross's understanding of spiritual regeneration, we have good reason to suppose that, at least in some central cases, religious renewal goes along with – and perhaps in part it consists in – a changed perceptual relationship to the everyday world, so that the sensory world in general appears enlivened or inscribed with a new significance. Granted this much, it is natural to ask how we are to understand this shift in the appearances. How could one and the same sensory scene be differently presented to a person at different times, before and after spiritual renewal? Two phenomenological categories will be helpful in giving us at least an initial appreciation of what is involved in this sort of transformation.

Suppose I see a large, fast-approaching, and unfamiliar dog and that I am, reasonably enough, afraid of the dog. In these circumstances, I will be

[18] See Aquinas, *Summa Theologiae*, I, q. 2, a. 2.

[19] In this respect, the "awakened" person's knowledge resembles angelic "morning knowledge." See Aquinas's comment on the varieties of angelic knowledge: "Knowledge of the Creator through creatures, therefore, is evening knowledge, just as, conversely, knowledge of creatures through the Creator is morning knowledge" (St. Thomas Aquinas, *De Veritate*, q. 8, a. 16, ad. 9, trans. R. W. Mulligan [Chicago, IL: Henry Regnery Company, (1256–9) 1952], available here: http://dhspriory.org/thomas/QDdeVer.htm). My thanks to Nathan Lyons for this reference.

[20] This reading is confirmed by the preceding paragraph where John writes of how "the soul sees how all creatures, higher and lower, live, continue, and energise in Him" (121). The phrase "all these things" in our text is a reference back to "all creatures."

focally aware of the dog, while various other features of my environment, such as the color of the linoleum floor on which I am standing, are consigned to the periphery of my awareness. Here, the salience of the object in my perceptual field tracks my affectively toned judgment concerning its significance for me; or we could say that the dog's salience relative to other objects of itself involves a judgment about the worthiness of attention of this particular object, relative to other objects, where the appropriateness of that judgment can be assessed according to the strength of my reasons for thinking the dog a danger.

Let's take a second example. Suppose I discover that the meat I am chewing derives from Shuttlecock, the pet rabbit. In that case, I am likely to become focally aware of the meat. Here again, my developing sense of the significance of an object can be registered in its newly prominent place in the perceptual field. But, of course, in this case, it's not just that the meat will now be newly salient relative to other objects. Its intrinsic phenomenal feel will also have changed: the meat will now be experienced as revolting or disgusting. Let's call this aspect of the appearance of a thing its "hue." So, in this instance, the changed significance of the object for me is recorded both in its heightened salience in the perceptual field and in its changed hue. These developments are, of course, standardly connected: notably, a change in an object's hue is likely to make for a change in its salience relative to other objects.

Following this example, we can understand the relationship between a change in the significance of an object (here, a change in the significance the meat has for me), a change in the appearance of the object (here, a change in the meat's salience and hue), and a change in the quality of one's emotional engagement with the world (here, the shift to a feeling of disgust). This example invites the thought that it is the change in my judgment about the significance of a thing that gives rise to a change in the way it appears to me, and at the same time to a change in its emotional import for me. But these developments might be differently ordered: for example, it may be a change in the appearance of a thing that alerts me to the new significance that it has for me, so that the changed appearance elicits a change in my reflective judgment of the thing's significance, rather than following on from a change in reflective judgment.

Returning to the main thread of our discussion, we can use these categories of hue and salience to understand James's reports of conversion experience. Those reports speak of a generalized shift in the appearance of sensory things, and they represent that change as a matter of objects being newly "glorified," so that their appearance is now somehow brighter or more vivid. As James puts the point, "a new heaven seems to shine upon a new earth." The obverse of this case is evident in James's discussion of depression, where the world appears to the person as grey or colorless, and devoid of life. As he says, in such cases: "The world now looks remote, strange, sinister, uncanny. Its color is gone, its breath is cold, there is no speculation in the eyes it glares with."[21] If we focus on this strand of the experience of religious renewal, whereby everyday objects appear brighter or more vivid, then it is natural to say that it is the color or "hue" of the perceptual field that has changed.

James also notes that to the depressed person, the world can appear "flat." For instance, speaking of Tolstoy's experience of a period of existential crisis, he remarks: "Life had been enchanting, it was now flat sober, more than sober, dead."[22] And writing of another such case, he says:

> The old man, sick with an insidious internal disease, may laugh and quaff his wine at first as well as ever, but he knows his fate now, for the doctors have revealed it; and the knowledge knocks the satisfaction out of all these functions. They are partners of death and the worm is their brother, and they turn to a mere flatness. The lustre of the present hour is always borrowed from the background of possibilities it goes with.[23]

James associates such experiences of "flatness" with a loss of emotional interest in the world. And in the following passage, he invites his reader to apprehend that connection by imagining what it would be like to experience the world independently of any emotional engagement:

> Conceive yourself, if possible, suddenly stripped of all the emotion with which your world now inspires you, and try to imagine it *as it exists*, purely by itself, without your favourable or unfavourable, hopeful or apprehensive comment. It will be almost impossible for you to realize such a condition of negativity and deadness. No one portion of the universe would then have importance beyond another; and the whole collection of its things and series of its events would be without significance, character, expression, or perspective.[24]

Here, James associates a loss of emotional engagement with the world with the loss of any sense of the differentiated significance of things. And this flattening out of the distinctions between objects suggests, in turn, an absence of salience in the perceptual field. So when James's converts speak of the world in general as being invested with a new significance, or as

[21] James, *Varieties*, 151. [22] James, *Varieties*, 152. [23] James, *Varieties*, 141.
[24] James, *Varieties*, 150; James's emphasis.

newly glorified, they may be referring not only to a change in the color or hue of the perceptual field, but also to a change in salience, so that the world no longer appears relatively flat, but as structured according to a clearly defined sense of the relative importance of things. We could distinguish, then, between these two kinds of change: a deepened sense of the significance of the sensory order considered as a whole, which we could take to be recorded in a generalized shift in color or hue; and a deepened sense of the differentiated significance of objects, which we could take to be registered in a sharpening of the patterns of salience that inform the perceptual field.

The Contribution of Perception to the Goods of the Spiritual Life

We have been developing an account of the goods of the spiritual life, here drawing on Thomas Aquinas's discussion of infused moral virtue, and an account of the role of the senses in spiritual change, here following William James. In concluding, I want to bring together these two accounts, to address our initial question: how may the senses contribute to the realization of spiritual goods?

Aquinas's discussion of infused moral virtue suggests a way of representing progress in the spiritual life. Suppose we think of the spiritually mature person as one who understands the significance of material objects according to the relevant divine rule, and of the relatively immature person as one who relates to creatures simply on the basis of a rule of reason, or who has not yet fully assimilated the perspective of the relevant divine rule. As we have seen, so understood, the spiritually mature person does not deny the significance that attaches to things insofar as we relate to them simply on the basis of a rule of reason. For instance, for the spiritually mature person, food retains its significance as a source of bodily nourishment, to be consumed in the measure required for the health of the body. But for this person, food has an additional significance, since it now serves the further goal of relationship to God, or the goal of living congruently with truths about God's nature or activity. Similarly, for the person who practices neighbor love, other human beings will have the significance they would anyway have had when considered from the vantage point of the relevant rule of reason, but they will now have, in addition, a further dimension of significance, one that is relative to the truth that we will one day share with them in the fundamental good of the beatific vision.

Granted this conception of the spiritual life, we can see how spiritual progress involves not simply a new found proximity to God, of the kind that might be realized in a person's prayer life, for example, but also a new sense of the significance of other people, and of everyday objects such as food, once they come to be seen from the perspective of the relevant divine rule. Moreover, it seems to be a consequence of this view that as a person matures in spiritual terms, his or her assessment of the significance of the sensory world will change not just locally, but pervasively: once I recognize the relevant divine rule, it is not just this food before me now that will acquire new significance, but food in general; and indeed, it is not just food in general that will acquire new significance, but sensory things in general, once I see how those things can now be folded into my relationship to God, by reference to the appropriate divine rule. And this new perspective will involve not just a new sense of the significance of things, but a deepened sense of their significance. Why? Because, once again, when viewed from the vantage point of the relevant divine rule, ordinary objects, such as food, will retain all the significance they have relative to the corresponding rule of reason, while bearing, in addition, a further dimension of significance.

So here is one story of the nature of progress in the spiritual life. According to this story, spiritual development requires a deepening appreciation of the significance of the sensory world considered as a whole, and perhaps a deepening appreciation of the significance of objects relative to one another, once they are seen from the vantage point of a divine rule. But as we have seen, a deepening sense of the significance of the world in these respects can also be registered in perceptual experience, as the world comes to seem "brighter" and structured by more clearly defined patterns of salience. And if that is so, then the Thomistic story of spiritual development we have been rehearsing could also be told in an experiential idiom, as a story of the changing appearance of the everyday world. And when told in that idiom, the story will sound, I take it, very like William James's account of conversion, since James's sources also talk of how the world as a whole appears different following conversion, so that sensory things now seem brighter, more sharply in focus, and newly "glorified."

So drawing on these phenomenological categories of hue and salience, there is some reason to think that Aquinas and James have given us two vantage points on one and the same process of spiritual regeneration. Here as elsewhere, Thomas's vantage point is, broadly speaking, metaphysical. On this perspective, we can represent spiritual development in terms of the person's receipt of the "infused" virtues, and his or her capacity to set his or her choices within the relevant theological and metaphysical context. By contrast, James understands spiritual development in terms of a change in the phenomenology of the person's experience of the everyday world. Alongside this difference of vantage point, there is also potentially a difference of chronology: James's converts typically report a relatively sudden transformation in their experience of the world. By contrast, Thomas's account is at least compatible with a much slower process, as the infused moral virtues gradually extend the acquired. But allowing for this difference, each story can be read as an exploration of the relationship between spiritual growth and a deepening appreciation of the significance of the everyday sensory world.

We can use this same Thomistic and Jamesian framework to understand John of the Cross's remarks on the "joy" of the person who comes to know creatures "in God." The person of infused moral virtue understands creatures in light of a divine rule, that is, in terms of their significance for relationship to God. And we could read John's talk of "knowing creatures in God" as a compressed allusion to this same condition. And following our discussion of James, we can think of the understanding of the person of infused moral virtue as having a perceptual dimension. So when John speaks of the "joy" of the "awakened person," we may think of this joy not just as a matter of bodily feeling, but as radiating out into the world, so that the perceptual field is newly colored and newly ordered.[25]

If all of this is so, then we can speak of a kind of religious experience that is not directly of God, but that is instead materially mediated, and that is, more exactly, an experience that registers the import of the everyday world for our relationship to God. On this account, religious understanding is not to be conceived as simply intellectual, or as affectively toned in ways that concern simply the inward state of the person, but also as perceptual: in our experience of the world, so far as that experience is properly ordered and colored, we can register directly, in perceptual terms, the God-directed significance of things. So this is an experience that is not simply of God, nor simply of the world, but of the world and God in combination. In the terms used by Aquinas's translator, we could say that it is an experience of sensory objects as "subordinate to God."

We are now in a position to return to the question with which we began. Following Aquinas's treatment of infused moral virtue, we have

[25] The language of "coloring" may seem to imply that the person is simply projecting his or her feelings onto the material world. But as in our earlier discussion of "hue," the thought is that a certain coloring can be appropriate to, and properly responsive to, the real significance of things. (Compare the discussion of Shuttlecock the rabbit.) Here, that significance concerns, of course, the relationship of the material order to our theological context, as I note in the next paragraph.

noted how our intellectual, affective, and practical relations to everyday objects can be deemed good insofar as those relations are congruent with truths concerning God's nature or activity. And combining Aquinas's discussion of infused moral virtue and William James's account of conversion, we have noted how we can say the same of our experience of the everyday sensory world: depending on its structure and hue, this experience can also be assessed as more or less adequate relative to our ultimate, divine context. And to the extent that our sensory experience does prove congruent with our ultimate context, then our lives as perceivers – and not only as cognizers or doers – will participate in a God-directed significance. On this view, we should suppose that the life of the senses and the life of the spirit are mutually involving, because our senses are capable of realizing hybrid goods, which are neither simply this-worldly, nor simply otherworldly, but which lie, we could say, between heaven and earth.[26]

[26] I am fortunate to have had the opportunity to present versions of this chapter at Heythrop College, London, the University of Exeter, and the 2015 Logos conference on religious experience, held at Notre Dame, and I am grateful for the very helpful comments I received on those occasions. I would also like to thank David McPherson for his insightful remarks on a draft of this chapter.

CHAPTER 7

The Jewish Sabbath as a Spiritual Practice

Samuel Fleischacker

Shabbat (the Jewish sabbath) is the central ritual observance of Jewish life. This much is agreed upon by all streams of Judaism, although they disagree on exactly what observing shabbat involves. Being described as "*shomer shabbat* [shabbat-observant]" was sufficient to mark a person as devout, in former days: the term "Orthodox" was unknown. And keeping shabbat has been regarded by many as essential to Jewish survival. Asher Ginzberg ("Ahad Ha'Am"), the secular founder of cultural Zionism, famously remarked, "More than the Jews have kept the sabbath, has the sabbath kept the Jews." Ginzberg meant this primarily in a sociological sense, but it is equally true of Judaism as a spiritual tradition. I shall try here to explain how shabbat observance functions as a spiritual practice for Jews, and the larger ethical and theological themes it expresses; I'll then turn briefly to the question of what spiritual practices may in general amount to. For the purposes of this investigation, I take as my starting point the *traditional* Jewish sabbath (which I will call, simply, "shabbat"), as described in and mandated by Jewish law codes since the Mishnah,[1] and carried out among Orthodox and traditional Conservative Jews today. I set aside the way shabbat is practiced in progressive Jewish communities. To some extent, that practice draws on the traditional sabbath. To some extent, it varies from that practice for reasons of convenience that I consider unfortunate, from a spiritual point of view. In any case, it is more amorphous and diffuse than the traditional mode of practice, thus harder to sum up. It also often

[1] The Mishnah was codified in the early second century of the Common Era; it is the earliest authoritative source of Jewish oral law, and the first component of the Talmud: the other component is a set of discussions about the Mishnah (or at least, discussions that *begin* with debates over elements of the Mishnah), known as the Gemara. These discussions went on both in Palestine and in Babylon, so there are two Talmuds: a Palestinian one (the "Yerushalmi") and a Babylonian one (the "Bavli"). The law codes that guide traditional Jewish practice begin with Maimonides' attempt to distill the results of the Talmud, in his *Mishneh Torah*, and continue through Joseph Caro's *Shulchan Arukh*, down to volumes on aspects of the law, and of rabbinic responsa to questions about the law, written in the present day.

does not reflect the spiritual reading I will give of the traditional sabbath and hence would obscure or distract from the points I want to make about that.

I will proceed as follows: Section I describes the general contours of the traditional Jewish sabbath, and the phenomenology of living with a commitment to it. Section II draws out some spiritual implications of that structure. In Section III, I tie those implications to central themes in Jewish theology. And Sections IV and V step back from the results of I–III to reflect on what they may show us generally about practices, and about spirituality.

I

Shabbat is defined negatively, in the first instance. "Shabbat" comes from a word that literally means "ceasing" or "refraining" rather than "resting"; it is also known, among both Jews and non-Jews, primarily for what one may *not* do on it rather than what one may do; and the experience of shabbat, while by no means confined to these prohibitions, is pervasively shaped by them. The Mishnah lists thirty-nine tasks that one may not carry out on shabbat, from plowing and shearing sheep to baking and sewing. These are basic tasks needed in an agricultural and pastoral economy, and capture well the sense in which shabbat is meant to relieve us from concern for our material needs. But a later rabbinic tradition understands the list as instead comprising the tasks required to build the Tabernacle in the wilderness: the structure that was supposed to bring God's presence to the people.[2] The interesting implication is that, for the rabbis, even what they regard as *holy* work, *ideal* work, is forbidden on shabbat. We'll return to this point later.

Meanwhile, in practice, the main prohibitions of shabbat are the following: one may not cook, write, use money, manipulate electrical appliances, or use a car or any other vehicle. These prohibitions keep sabbath-observant Jews from their professional work and from everyday leisure activities like watching TV or going to the movies. They also require that one do all shopping and cooking for Friday night and Saturday in advance, set up lights or other electrical appliances so that they don't need to be further manipulated, and make sure that whatever one plans to do on that day takes place at home or within walking distance. Certain kinds of careers are

[2] Babylonian Talmud *Shabbat* 49b; see also *Mekhilta* (a rabbinic commentary to the book of Exodus), "Masechta d'Shabbata," ch. 2.

difficult with these restrictions, and just about everyone observing them needs to make advance arrangements for them with their employers and friends.

It is not unimportant that restrictions are the first and most obvious mark of shabbat, but one misses the feel of the shabbat experience if one stops with these restrictions. For the restrictions make room for a number of activities to fill the time now emptied of chores and professional work. Above all, one can pray, sing, read, have elaborate meals, visit family and friends, take walks, and make love (something that is especially encouraged, between spouses). The Jewish tradition has indeed choreographed, out of these activities, a positive program for shabbat, beginning with an evening prayer service and a melodious prayer over wine to sanctify the day, followed by a rich and expansive meal, accompanied sometimes by traditional songs and attended by the whole family plus, often, friends and other relatives. Saturday morning has a long prayer service, which people usually do at a synagogue if they can, and which includes a lengthy reading of a section from the Torah and a talk on it by the rabbi, followed by another blessing to sanctify the day and another expansive meal, again often with guests and sometimes accompanied by song. After that meal, many people take a walk, talk or play games with family, or attend an afternoon class on a religious topic. At twilight, some partake of a third light meal with a great deal of singing – usually employing quiet tunes suited for the fading of the day – and the sabbath concludes with a final melodious blessing, again over wine, that takes leave of the sacred day and makes room for a new profane week.

It is quite possible to keep shabbat without carrying out the whole of this program; that is the sense in which shabbat is defined by its prohibitions rather than any positive content. Most observant Jews do carry out much of the program, however, and in any case take time on shabbat for reading, elaborate meals, and time with family and friends. And the fact that they all have the same day free for such activities makes it easy to coordinate them with others. One consequence is that shabbat becomes a prime time for parents to spend time with their children, and for friends to see one another. Another is that observant Jews tend to cluster in the same parts of a city, so as to be able to walk to synagogue on shabbat, and to one another's homes. They thereby form communities large enough to share institutions in addition to a synagogue – schools, kosher stores, community centers. That is part of the sociological point Ginzberg was making when he said that "the sabbath has kept the Jews."

Other consequences of the structure of shabbat:

1) If one first starts to keep it as an adult (as this author did), it initially appears as a considerable burden, creating awkward moments in one's relationship to one's boss or professional colleagues, barring one from getting errands done, including ones that seem urgent, and making it impossible to participate in the common Friday night pleasures – going to a movie or concert, or out for dinner – of one's secular and non-Jewish friends. Over time – several months, or even a year or two – it is experienced instead as a great relief, a lifting of the burden of worrying about what one's boss or work colleagues want, of getting errands done, and keeping up with other mundane activities. (It is difficult to convey the joy modern Jews often feel, at the onset of shabbat, at the thought of having twenty-four hours free of cellphones, email, and Facebook, in particular.[3]) One may or may not use the time so freed up to cultivate family relationships and friendships, or one's relationship to God, but the mere fact of *not* being burdened by the wheel of needs that generally rules our lives is a relief. The urge to go out to a movie or concert on Friday night fades – although occasionally one does feel a twinge of disappointment at missing an event of this sort – and the fact that one is separated from the run-of-the-mill secular life becomes, largely, a mark of pride: a mark of one's Jewish identity. In all these ways, keeping shabbat partakes of the meanings associated in ancient times with a "sacrifice."[4] It entails giving something up, but also celebrating one's membership in a community and, ideally, coming closer to God (the word for "sacrifice" in Hebrew – *korban* – derives from a word for "coming close"): experiencing God's presence.

2) Over time, the observance of shabbat structures one's whole life, not just the day on which it occurs. One traditional commentary on the fact that Exodus 20:8 commands Jews to "remember" the sabbath (Deuteronomy 5:12 commands them instead to "keep" it) understands that wording to entail that the thought of shabbat should pervade the rest of one's week.[5] And, to a considerable extent, that is what happens. One's thoughts on Sunday may be preoccupied by something the rabbi said in services the day before, or a conversation with friends over shabbat lunch. On Monday, one may buy a book and think, "I'll get to it next shabbat." On Tuesday or Wednesday, one may pass a bakery or delicatessen and see a cake or cooked dish that would make a nice addition to a shabbat meal.

[3] On this subject, see G. Gorenberg, "An Unvirtual Day": www.hadassahmagazine.org/2015/08/20/an-unvirtual-day/.

[4] On this subject, see M. Halbertal, *On Sacrifice* (Princeton University Press, 2012).

[5] Rashi (the acronym for Rabbi Shlomo Yitzchaki, a tenth-century commentator on the Torah) on Exodus 20:8, quoting the *Mekhilta*.

Thursday is usually the last good day for inviting friends over for a meal on the coming shabbat; most people one knows will be "booked up" after that. And on Friday, if not before, one needs to get all one's shopping and cooking done for that night and the next day; if one is traveling, one needs instead to make sure one has made arrangements for meals in the place where one will spend shabbat. All this is in addition to the arrangements one must make with one's place of work or schooling, to get out of events that take place on Friday night or Saturday, and, in the winter, to leave early so as to be home by sunset. There is thus a "shabbat-consciousness" that runs through one's life. This again serves as a mark of communal and religious identity, and an opportunity to allow the closeness of God one experiences on shabbat to infuse one's mundane experience as well.

The family- and community-building effects of keeping shabbat are, I hope, clear. It should also be clear that the time set aside from mundane activities, by virtue of shabbat observance, can be used, if one wishes, for spiritual exploration of one sort or another: for philosophical contemplation, or meditation, or some other mindful practice. But this is to see shabbat merely as an *instrument* for spirituality. In subsequent sections, I will try to bring out how it can also be a spiritual practice of its own: a discipline that can transform the self.

II

Three ways of understanding the symbolic import of shabbat:

1) As noted earlier, the rabbinic list of the tasks forbidden on shabbat can be read as picking out either need-fulfilling activities, from which it is a relief to be freed, or the highest, most rewarding kind of work, modeled on what we might do to build the Tabernacle: to bring God's presence into the world. The interpretive hook on which the rabbis rely for taking the building of the Tabernacle to provide the model for the work forbidden on shabbat is Exodus 31:13–17, where one version of the command to keep shabbat appears just before the commands about the Tabernacle. A deeper reason for the connection is that building the Tabernacle is presented in the Torah as parallel to God's main act of "work": the creation of the universe. The "spirit of God" (*ruah Elohim*) that hovered over the deep at the beginning of Genesis (Gen. 1:2) is now found in Bezalel, the maker of the Tabernacle (Ex. 35:31). Two cherubim, like the ones that guard the Garden of Eden at the end of the Creation narrative, now appear as guardians of the sacred tablets in the Tabernacle. The Tabernacle is erected

in seven stages (Ex. 40:17–33), each marked by the phrase "as the Lord had commanded Moses," as if to parallel the seven days of creation, with their refrain, "and the Lord saw that it was good." The passage as a whole is also the only extended description of creative work in the Torah, aside from the account of divine creation.

So the kind of work from which Jews refrain on shabbat includes *ideal* work – sacred work, the kind of work in which we imitate God – not just burdensome work.[6] Why might it be good for us to refrain even from ideal, rewarding work: from painting a great picture, say, or writing a philosophical treatise? Well, in the first place, ideal work and burdensome work are often entangled with one another. The artist in the midst of her masterpiece may need to run out and buy more paint; the clarinetist who loves playing Brahms will not necessarily love practicing scales; every artist and philosopher also has to spend time attending meetings, filling out forms, and carrying out other chores that keep her career going. Even building the Tabernacle presumably involved many tasks that were dull or repetitive as well as moments in which its creators could be aware of the "spirit of God." Rewarding work and burdensome work are interwoven, and it is not easy to cease from the latter without ceasing from the former as well.

A second reason to refrain even from ideal work is that it can become obsessive, can take over one's life to the point of addiction or idolatry. I am so immersed in my art or philosophy that I neglect my family, perhaps, or am rude to friends. Or my love for what I do becomes intermingled with a desperate desire for success. In either case, I may lose sight of the *purpose* of creating great art or philosophy – or building a great car or software program, or developing an educational curriculum – and become obsessed with the process of creating these things for its own sake. Ceasing from the work, stopping for a day, can here be a way of breaking addiction, of stepping back from idolatry. However good the things are that we do, we need to recognize that each one is a *limited* good, which must be brought together with other things to make for a decent and healthy life overall.

A third, deeper reason for refraining from ideal work is that only ceasing from work allows one fully to appreciate the value of that work. Shabbat provides a space of stillness from which we can reflect back on what we accomplish, individually and communally, by the world of work. On shabbat we are contemplative beings, but we contemplate what we achieve

[6] On the high value given to work in the Jewish tradition, see A. J. Heschel, *The Sabbath* (New York: Farrar, Straus & Giroux, 1951), 27–8.

as practical beings: shapers of landscapes, material things, communities – creators, in the image of God. The story of creation in the Torah ends with God Himself refraining from work on shabbat (Gen. 2:1–3).[7] This refraining seems itself to be *part* of creation, perhaps a fulfillment of it. So we display the image of God within us – our participation in God's creativity – both in our work and in our refraining from work.

Whatever shabbat signifies is thus intrinsically tied to creativity, not something that stands in opposition to it. Shabbat is a *creative refraining*, not a refraining *from* creation. It is a refraining from creative *work*, but not from creative *rest*: that there is such a thing, and that it is different in kind from passive rest ("relaxation"), is in fact the central teaching of shabbat (we'll consider later what exactly this teaching might mean).[8] Among other things, understanding shabbat this way helps enrich the notion of shabbat as sacrifice introduced earlier. Like the sacrificial offering of a precious lamb or choice bunch of fruits, the refraining from work Jews do on shabbat is a giving up of something one desires as well as a source of joy. We renounce work we love in order to achieve a greater intimacy with our religious community and with God.[9]

2) In the liturgy for Friday night, shabbat is described as *tachlit ma'asei shamayim va'aretz*: "the completion or purpose [*tachlit*] of the making of heaven and earth." *Tachlit* can mean "the last thing" chronologically, but it primarily connotes a purpose. It is thus a close equivalent to the Greek *telos*, or the word "end" in English when it means *telos*. Shabbat, according to the liturgy, is not just the last step in but the telos of creation: the reason for which the heavens and earth were made. In keeping shabbat, then, we are keeping what we were made for: realizing, or approximating, our telos. That is also suggested by a theme that runs through traditional shabbat

7 And presumably God's work does not include burdensome elements, nor would God need to worry about addiction or idolatry. So the point of saying that even *God* rested on shabbat cannot be the two worries I previously described.

8 Heschel notes that we should not assimilate shabbat rest to what Aristotle says about relaxation: that it is "for the sake of activity," a way of restoring oneself so that one can work harder. Shabbat rest, says Heschel, "is not for the purpose of recovering one's lost strength and becoming fit for the forthcoming labour. . . . It is not an interlude but the climax of living" (Heschel, *The Sabbath*, 14). I agree entirely with this, but I think it is more Aristotelian than Heschel implies. We must simply look to Aristotle's account of *contemplation*, not his account of relaxation, for the parallel. Shabbat is *non-needy activity*, just as contemplation is that for Aristotle. See further discussion later.

9 To fully play out the sacrificial analogy, it is worth bearing in mind that many sacrifices were "shared" with God by being consumed in a sacred meal. Here intimacy with God is supposed to result from the very process by which the sacrifice is offered. And that is exactly what happens with the "sacrifice" of beloved work for God: the very process of giving it up makes for a greater closeness with God. The joy of shabbat – *shabbat menucha* – is itself a sacrificial meal. For a deep exploration of the meanings of sacrifice, see Halbertal, *On Sacrifice*.

songs, and appears in the blessing after meals for shabbat: that shabbat is a taste or hint of the world to come, that it gives us a sense of what it would be like to live in a world in which our ends were fulfilled.

If this is right, the famous declaration in the Gospels, that "the sabbath was made for man and not man for the sabbath" (Mark 2:27; cf. Matthew 12:8 and Luke 6:1–11), gets the traditional Jewish understanding of shabbat almost exactly backward. Human beings were made *precisely* for shabbat, on the Jewish view. It represents our highest ideals and aspirations – ideals and aspirations that are beyond everything we ordinarily pursue, that may indeed lie beyond our full grasp. And for that reason it functions – *must* function – through a legal structure that calls on us to suspend our ordinary ends, and the way we ordinarily pursue those ends. So no, we cannot just pick grain when we are hungry, or even cure (non-life-threatening) illness – the subjects of debate in the Gospel story.[10] To do that, for the traditional Jew, is to let ourselves down, to degrade our search for a good beyond our ordinary ends and aspire to less than we could otherwise attain.

This is not to say anything against the Gospel passages as a way of defining a *Christian* sabbath: in which, say, salvation in Christ replaces shabbat as the prime way of achieving the human telos. Jesus is presented in the passages I have cited as having the authority to reinterpret Jewish law ("the Son of Man is lord of the sabbath"), which fits in beautifully with the idea that he comes more generally to redeem humanity from the yoke of legalism. But then we should not expect his view of the sabbath to mesh with how Jews themselves understand it, with their reverence for law as a vehicle of spirituality. We see here an instance of how spiritual practices acquire meaning from a larger cultural context, and therefore differ from

[10] The saying in the Gospels does have a parallel in rabbinic literature: "The sabbath is given unto you, not you unto the sabbath" (*Mekhilta* to 31:13, "Masechta D'Shabbata," ch. 1). But the context of the rabbinic passage is the need to suspend shabbat laws to save life; it is not a general interpretive framework for those laws. From the earliest rabbinic writings up until the present day, it has been built into shabbat law that saving a life (or important bodily functions – saving one's eyesight, for instance) always takes precedence over shabbat restrictions. If there is so much as a *chance* that a wound or illness could be life-threatening, one is required, not merely permitted, to seek medical attention, even where that means one needs to drive, use money and electricity, etc. Possibly, the passage in the Gospels reflects rabbinic debates over the extent of this exemption, or originated in a story that reflected those debates. But as presented in the Gospels, the story suggests a wider and deeper polemic against rabbinic law. It presumably reflects a move away from the traditional Jewish mode of sabbath observance among Jewish Christians who believed that Christ took the place of the rabbis, in interpreting the Torah, and/or that Christ's salvation took the place of shabbat, in realizing God's end for humanity. That certainly seems to be the import of Matthew 12:8 and Luke 6:5. See the notes on these passages, and on Mark 2:27, in A. J. Levine and M. Brettler (eds.), *The Jewish Annotated New Testament* (Oxford University Press, 2011), and D. Boyarin, *The Jewish Gospels* (New York: The New Press, 2012), 59–70.

one culture to another; I'll return to this theme later. For now, the point is just that Jewish law presents shabbat as beyond us, rather than within our control, as something that represents the end or telos we should truly be seeking rather than something that helps us achieve ends that we already have.[11]

3) But what sort of *telos* could shabbat possibly represent? How can a day of *refraining* from activities constitute a fulfillment of who we are? This seems the very opposite of what Aristotle had in mind by a telos: the opposite of an activity that would complete us.

Well, the first thing we might say in response to this objection is that shabbat provides an excellent set of conditions for *inquiry into* what our *telos* might be. Insofar as it provides us with a break from the projects that might otherwise become obsessions, it allows us to put them into question, to think about the place they should properly occupy in our lives, given our other ends. And insofar as it relieves us of mundane responsibilities, errands, and the like, it gives us an opportunity to reflect more generally on where our life is going, and discuss that with others. Shabbat enables us to live for a day in an approximation of the formal conditions that Aristotle set out for anything to be a telos of our lives: conditions that free us as much as possible of the needs that drive most of our activities, and enable us instead to pursue activities that are self-sufficient (compare *Nicomachean Ethics* I.7 and X.7). For Aristotle, these formal conditions entail that philosophical contemplation is our highest good. For a traditional Jew, that need not be the case, but what one does on shabbat similarly has intrinsic rather than instrumental value. Shabbat is typically filled with the sorts of activities that people carry out for no purpose beyond themselves: song and literature, love and friendship, the enjoyment of nature, and the worship of God.

[11] David McPherson has suggested to me an alternative way of describing the differences between Christians and Jews over this issue. He distinguishes among three understandings of the sabbath, and proposes that Jews accept the first while Christians adopt the latter two. The sabbath can be understood, he says, as "(1) the specific requirements of Jewish law (including the specifics of what is not to be done and when), (2) *a day* of restful and grateful enjoyment of the good things of life in an attitude of worship, or (3) *a state* of restful and grateful enjoyment of the good things of life in an attitude of worship, and the fullest realization of this is our ultimate telos" (private correspondence). On this account, it would be a mistake to think that Christians see the sabbath as a *means* to other ends we have; the sabbath in sense (3), especially, just *is* the experience of our highest ends.

To this, I would respond, first, that the traditional Jewish shabbat in fact is supposed to embrace all three meanings McPherson gives to the sabbath, while insisting that (2) and (3) are not attainable, in their highest form at least, except through (1), and second, that for Christians, (3) is not attainable, in its highest form at least, without faith in Christ: which once again displaces the soteriological function that for Jews is performed by shabbat onto the Messiah who is supposed to redeem us from law.

Indeed, if one is not a thoroughgoing Aristotelian, and regards the question of our overall end in life as an open and difficult one, then shabbat provides us with a better response to that question than Aristotle does. For shabbat enables us to walk the fine line between the twin mistakes of supposing that we have found a definitive answer to that question and failing to recognize that we must have *some* idea of how it might be answered, in order to so much as make sense of the question. By providing us with some of the conditions for anything to be a telos for our lives, as well as activities that we think, intuitively, are likely to be part of our overall end, shabbat points us in a plausible direction, for exploring the question about our overall end, while at the same time encouraging in us a laudable humility about achieving any definitive answer to it. If one thinks, as this author does, that our telos is essentially mysterious to us – essentially beyond our full grasp – but that it must at the same time incorporate much of what we take to be intrinsically good, this is just the sort of response one wants to our telic questions.[12]

That said, there is a more substantial way in which shabbat responds to questions about our ends. To see this, consider a third textual source. Genesis 2:2 (recited over the sanctification of shabbat, on Friday night) declares that God completed the work of creation on the seventh day – as if to say that shabbat is *part* of creation. What might it mean that God "creates" shabbat – creates His own refraining from creation?[13] If we look more closely at the verse, it contains an interesting clue. "And God completed on the seventh day His work that He had been doing . . .," it begins. What follows is the first appearance of a form of the word "shabbat": " . . . and God rested/refrained [*vayishbot*] on the seventh day . . . " The rest of the verse tells us that what God rested/refrained from was "all His work that He had been doing." So the verse talks just of "His work" before the word *vayishbot*, but of "*all* His work" after that word: only with the appearance of shabbat does God's work get "completed," become something that can be characterized with the adjective "all."[14] God's

[12] For more on telic questions, see pt. III of Fleischacker, *Divine Teaching and the Way of the World* (Oxford University Press, 2011) or Fleischacker, *The Good and the Good Book* (Oxford University Press, 2015), ch. 3.

[13] For a variety of rabbinic answers to this question, see Heschel, *The Sabbath*, 22–3 and the sources quoted therein (especially *Genesis Rabbah* 10:9). The answer I will give is not quite the same as any of the ones in these midrashim (although I think it is compatible with all of them).

[14] Moreover, in Hebrew "all" (*kol*) is a form of the verb "to complete" (*vayekhal*), which opens the verse. A more literal translation of the verse might run: "And God completed (*vayekhal*) on the seventh day His work that He had been doing and He refrained on the seventh day from the complete work that He had been doing."

work forms a whole only after God refrains from work: God completes the work of creation on the seventh day *by* creating the possibility of resting or refraining. Which is to say: creative work can form a whole only if there is a space between it and its creator. God – *even* God – can see His work as a whole only if He desists from it for a moment, and as it were holds it off from Himself, as something to contemplate.

An ancient truism has it that beauty is located in complete wholes. The very completeness ("perfection") of an artwork, the sense that it contains everything that it needs and nothing more, is essential to its beauty on many views; at the very least, its completeness is a necessary condition for our being able to interpret it, to respond to it aesthetically. Hence the great interest, among aesthetic theorists, in the framing of works: in how a play or novel ends, or what it does to a painting to put a literal frame around it. The wording of Genesis 2:2 suggests that even God needs a "frame" around creation, in order to admire or love it fully. By extension, we need to complete, to frame, what we do if we are to appreciate its value. But we establish that frame only by taking a step back from it, by ceasing to engage in it: by refraining or making shabbat between us and it. Shabbat here becomes a condition for a thing to have an intrinsic value, an inherent beauty. Inter alia, that means that the intrinsic value of our work, the creative activity we carry out during the six days of the workweek, depends on shabbat. We need actively to refrain from work in order to create the space in which we see the value of our work. This, then, is "creative rest." This is what it means for God to create shabbat, and for us to imitate God when we create the rests (*shabbatot*) that punctuate our work lives.[15]

III

The structure of shabbat, as I have depicted it, fits well with central themes in Jewish theology. In the first place, to be told that one needs to refrain for

[15] I focus in this essay just on the creation aspect of shabbat. Shabbat has aspect, however: it is a celebration of freedom. The Exodus version of the Ten Commandments ties shabbat to creation, while the Deuteronomy version of the Ten Commandments ties it to the redemption of the Israelites from Egyptian slavery. In taking a day away from work each week, Jews celebrate freedom: slaves normally do not get a day off. (The liturgy for shabbat marks these two sides of it, celebrating the sabbath of creation on Friday night and the sabbath of freedom on Saturday morning.) In the ideal society, there would be no servitude. And shabbat is supposed to give its observers a taste of the ideal society even as it gives them a taste of a world in which they could realize their highest telos. Indeed, the two things go together: only in an ideal social world, only where there is complete political freedom, could individuals achieve their highest ends. But then the freedom aspect of shabbat is subordinate to its creation aspect: freedom is one *condition* for perceiving and achieving our telos.

a day from professional obligations, artistic commitments, material acquisitions, and the like is to be told not to idolize these things. And in practice, breaking from them for a day indeed helps keep them from becoming idols: goods one regards as absolute, and pursues obsessively. Idolatry has many meanings,[16] but it is frequently associated in the Hebrew Bible with the worship of *oneself*: one's own desires (sexual desires, especially), one's own power (think of Pharaoh), one's own conceptions of God or proper worship (think of the false prophet in Deuteronomy 13), and of course "the work of one's own hands" (see Isaiah 2:8 and Psalm 115:4–9, among many other places). This is also an important meaning the word has had in post-biblical times, among Jews and non-Jews alike. Worshipping ourselves is the deepest betrayal of God, since it prevents us from *perceiving* God: from perceiving a good outside our own desires and beliefs, that can correct and redirect them. But self-worship is also a very common temptation, perhaps built into human nature – we want very strongly to maintain our desires and beliefs intact, and fear losing our identity if we have to change them. Shabbat doesn't require us to change them, exactly, but it does interfere with any blind, unquestioned pursuit of them. Sometimes it demands more than that. Whenever I have faced a strong temptation to set shabbat aside in order to participate in a professional event, or attend a concert or theatrical performance, I have had to ask myself, "Do I worship my profession? Do I worship music or theater?" Sometimes I find, to my discomfort, that I *do* seem to worship these things: it is then that shabbat is particularly effective in reshaping my spiritual priorities, in breaking me of idolatry. At this point in my life, after decades of a professional and personal life structured around shabbat observance, I don't face conflicts of this sort all that often. For other people, they can be frequent and severe. When an actor has to give up on crucial career opportunities, when an artist or writer refrains from continuing work on a painting or novel that has been absorbing all her waking hours, when an athlete doesn't work out or go to practice, they may be making a great sacrifice (here, in the sense that involves loss) for the sake of shabbat. But if they do make that sacrifice, they keep their vocations and avocations from turning into idols: and keep themselves open, thereby, to the worship of a higher good.

In the second place, the negative structure of shabbat fits with the negative theology characteristic of Judaism. As I have noted several times,

[16] See M. Halbertal and A. Margalit, *Idolatry* (Cambridge, MA: Harvard University Press, 1992) for a deep and rich investigation of these, and of how the focus of the prohibition has changed, in the Jewish tradition, over the centuries.

shabbat is marked first and foremost by prohibitions: what one may *not* do on it. Only by way of these prohibitions does it also acquire a positive content. And it offers us a similarly negative path to our telos. First and most directly it marks a space in which we may *seek* our telos – gives us time for that search, clears us of mundane and obsessive concerns that get in the way of that search, etc. Only indirectly does it also contain pointers toward the sorts of activity that may help *constitute* that telos. But all this parallels the way in which, for Jews, *God* is primarily grasped negatively. We know primarily what God is *not* – not the tree or rock in front of us, not a sculpted form, not any human being, no matter how wonderful he or she may seem. We have at best a faint idea of what God *is*. God transcends every thing, every person, and every idea, including the ideas that themselves aim to transcend the finite, to express infinite properties.[17] Even the best things in the world fall short of God; even the projects or goals or experiences that seem ideal are not. God eludes us, remains ever beyond our reach: we find God, if at all, only by realizing what is *not* in a finite thing or idea. In one traditional Jewish image, used widely even by the Jewish mystics who reject Maimonides' extreme doctrine about the impossibility of describing the divine, God secretes himself from us like a flirtatious or furtive beloved from her lover: appearing briefly at the window of her house, on occasion, and then disappearing again.[18] The transcendence rather than the immanence of God is central to Jewish theology: God is always beyond where we think we have located Him or Her.

But finding that God always eludes us induces an experience of the sublime in us,[19] of awe, which is itself regarded by many theologians (Jewish and non-Jewish) as a kind of experience of God.[20] We find God,

[17] Compare Maimonides' account of theological concepts in pt. I, chs. 56–60 of his *Guide for the Perplexed.*

[18] "[T]he Torah resembles a beautiful and stately damsel, who is hidden in a secluded chamber of her palace and who has a secret lover, unknown to all others. For love of her he keeps passing the gate of her house, looking this way and that in search of her. She knows that her lover haunts the gate of her house. What does she do? She opens the door of her hidden chamber ever so little, and for a moment reveals her face to her lover, but hides it again forthwith. Were anyone with her lover, he would see nothing and perceive nothing. He alone sees it and he is drawn to her with his heart and soul and his whole being, and he knows that for love of him she disclosed herself to him for one moment, aflame with love for him. So is it with the word of the Torah . . . " (*Zohar* II, 99a–b, cited in G. Scholem, *On the Kabbalah and Its Symbolism*, trans. R. Manheim [New York: Schocken, 1969], 55).

[19] Kant writes that the prohibition of idolatry – the refusal to see God in any finite thing – is "the most sublime passage in the Jewish law" and the one that "alone can explain the enthusiasm that the Jewish people in its civilized era felt for its religion" (I. Kant, *Critique of Judgment*, trans. W. Pluhar [Indianapolis, IN: Hackett, (1790) 1987], 135 [Ak 5:274]).

[20] Most famously Rudolf Otto, in *The Idea of the Holy*; it is also a running theme in Abraham Joshua Heschel's writings.

to the extent that we do, only by first *emptying* things or moments or ideas of their apparent divinity, and then discovering God's presence in that emptiness.

Shabbat thus seems to be a metaphor for the search for God – we find what is good about it by appreciating what we are *not* doing just as we find God by appreciating what He is not. But in fact shabbat is a synecdoche, not a metaphor, for the search for God. Our highest good is after all a reflection or element of the highest good of the universe. As we search for *our* highest good on shabbat, and catch glimpses of it, we are also searching for *the* highest good – God – and catch glimpses of Him or Her.

As this last sentence indicates, God is not entirely transcendental, for Jews: we have some sense of God as immanent as well. And I think many traditional Jews feel God's immanence most intensely on Friday night, as shabbat comes in. Precisely the *setting aside* of everything else we value makes that possible. Emptying ourselves of even our most wonderful activities and personal projects ushers in a moment in which we glimpse a good beyond all of them: the highest good, perhaps.

IV

I have attributed one set of philosophical and theological meanings to shabbat, but others interpret it in different ways,[21] and there is no creedal insistence, in the Jewish tradition, on any one way of reading it. Practice underlies all these readings. To be plausible, any reading of shabbat must draw on the experience of living shabbat. Simply knowing theoretically that shabbat can be understood in this or that way will not enable one to grasp what it has to teach. The teaching of shabbat belongs to practical wisdom, not theoretical wisdom: one cannot appreciate it by the intellect alone.[22]

In this sense, carrying out shabbat is like the acquisition of an Aristotelian virtue. This should be obvious from my reading of it. We come to see what can be gained by emptying ourselves of our mundane activities, imposing a space between us and our professional, artistic, and other ambitions, only when we actually *do* that: over and over, with all the long-term reshaping of professional and personal habits such discipline requires. We come to see the power of the positive activities

[21] Heschel's *The Sabbath* offers a beautiful alternative, in terms of the sanctification of time.

[22] Compare John Cottingham on the primacy of praxis in religious understanding in J. Cottingham, *The Spiritual Dimension* (Cambridge University Press, 2005), 5–13.

on shabbat, of the friendship and study and play and quiet joy in our environment that can fill it, only by regularly engaging in these things, and developing the relationships that make them possible over time. We come to acquire a shabbat-consciousness, so that we can relax and accept the relief of responsibilities on Friday night, rather than continuing to worry about them, also over time. In all these ways, we come to see the world differently, pick out different elements of it as salient to our decisions – as goods to be pursued or harms to be avoided. Aristotle talks about how temperance and courage and friendship and magnanimity can reshape our perceptions; this is indeed a central theme in the contemporary ethical appropriation of Aristotle. Shabbat is like that: there is a spiritual virtue of shabbat observance, which remakes the perception of people who acquire it. And the new modes of perception they thereby acquire provide them with premises for the peculiarly Jewish ways of understanding God and the human good.

In this respect, shabbat is of course like other religious practices, from the taking of communion to yoga or meditation. It is a discipline that both expresses the teachings of a religion and helps one grasp those teachings. Following that discipline requires a certain humility – a humbling of one's desires and projects, and one's ideas about how to live – which makes room for a source of wisdom outside oneself to show one aspects of the good one has not yet noticed. This is not the same as *moral* humility – people who faithfully practice yoga or meditation or shabbat can be arrogant in interpersonal interactions. It is instead a *cognitive* humility. This can be used to help develop moral humility, but is not always so used. Cognitive humility is, however, necessary if one is to turn outside oneself in exploring goodness, and not suppose that one can determine what is good entirely on one's own. It seems to me that no spiritual commitment is possible without this humility.

To sum up: shabbat, for traditional Jews, both represents and provides a space for exploring our highest end or ends, our telos, and the virtue of shabbat observance inculcates in those who have it both a sense of the importance of that telos and a humility in the search for it. These are qualities we need to appreciate what is good in our lives and to restrain ourselves from thinking that we have full knowledge of that good. Properly developed, these are also qualities that pervade one's life, structuring how one thinks and acts not only on the seventh day, but throughout the weeks that those seventh days complete.

This seems to me as good an example of a "spiritual practice" as one could hope to find.

V

I'd like to close with some general reflections on the phrase "spiritual practice." There are two main reasons, I think, why the word "spiritual" has become popular in recent years as a substitute for the word "religious." First, "spiritual" is meant to cover a concern for or attunement to non-material things that a person may have who does not believe in God. Perhaps she believes in a personal force pervading the universe that does not fit any traditional notion of a god; perhaps she is a pantheist, regarding the entire universe as divine; perhaps she is an atheist who nonetheless thinks there are or may be things of great importance "to the spirit," goals that cannot be reduced to material elements and cannot be achieved by acquiring material things. In any case, she takes seriously the idea that *she* has a spirit with yearnings that go beyond her material desires. The word "spiritual" thus allows people to disavow purely materialistic lives even if they are not religious. It allows them to share many of the attitudes and aspirations of religious people without signing on to any traditional creed.

Second, the word "spiritual" focuses attention on those aspects of traditional religions that concern the yearnings of the spirit: the innermost element of each person's self, or what each person considers to be that. Religions have a lot of business to conduct aside from caring for our spirits. They run organizations, care for the poor and sick, formulate creeds, develop philosophies, and carry out a host of other social, political, and intellectual activities. To be interested in the spiritual side of a religion is thus to be interested in one specific aspect of a religion: although that aspect may seem, to many believers, by far the most important element of their religion, and the one to which everything else ought to be subordinated.

In light of this informal use of the term "spiritual," "spiritual practices" will be those concerned with the innermost self of individuals, and with directing those innermost selves beyond their material desires.

But this definition is terribly vague; practically anything could fit it. Pierre Hadot has provided a more specific conception of "spiritual practices" – or what he calls "spiritual exercises," a phrase he uses to translate the Greek word *askesis.*[23] Hadot says that ancient Greco-Roman

[23] See P. Hadot, *Philosophy as a Way of Life: Spiritual Exercises from Socrates to Foucault*, ed. A. Davidson, trans. M. Chase (Oxford: Basil Blackwell, 1995), ch. 3, and Hadot, *What Is Ancient Philosophy?*, trans. M. Chase (Cambridge, MA: Harvard University Press, 2002), ch. 9. For a thoughtful assessment of Hadot, in relation to traditional Judaism, see C. Fisher, *Contemplative Nation* (Stanford University Press, 2012), 70–8.

schools of philosophy saw their teachings as having to be accompanied by exercises of some sort – a discipline – which could range from a dietary regime (vegetarianism, perhaps, or the moderate athletic diet recommended in Plato's *Republic*) through various modes of concentrating one's attention, to meditations designed to get one to accept the place of disappointment and suffering in life. These exercises were supposed to transform the self – restraining its attachment to its overweening passions and desires, in particular – so that it could both see and achieve its highest good. This orientation toward the self is one reason for calling them "spiritual" – Hadot says they follow from "the individual's entire psychism." Another is that they were supposed to enable people to "rise . . . from a partial and particular vision to a universal perspective": "to raise [themselves] up to the life of the objective Spirit . . . to re-place [themselves] within the perspective of the Whole."[24] There is, then, a Hegelian cast to Hadot's use of the word "spiritual," but that just helps show that the aim of the exercises he describes is to reconcile individuals with the universe as a whole. "Spiritual," in Hadot's sense, is thus closely parallel to what I call a concern with one's telos or overall end.[25]

"Spiritual" in Hadot's sense also fits well enough with the common use of the term today that we may take it as a specification of that usage. Our final two questions may therefore be: Is shabbat a spiritual exercise in Hadot's sense? And if so, what does that tell us about spiritual exercises more generally?

The answer to the first question seems clearly to be "yes." If we fix our attention on the English descendant of *askesis* – "asceticism" – it may sound a bit odd to describe shabbat that way, since it is a day for indulging the pleasures of food and drink and love-making, rather than restricting them. But at the same time shabbat involves a sharp restraint on our desire to pursue our professional and artistic projects and in that sense it is definitely a form of *askesis*; it constrains some of our most important passions. Moreover, Hadot himself is not especially interested in the modern connotations of "asceticism," but simply in the way in which *askesis* functioned to transform the self so that it could perceive,

[24] Hadot, *What Is Ancient Philosophy?*, 190; Hadot, *Philosophy as a Way of Life*, 82.

[25] The editor of this collection, David McPherson, also understands "spirituality" as an orientation toward our end or good; see D. McPherson, "*Homo Religiosus*: Does Spirituality Have a Place in Neo-Aristotelian Virtue Ethics?," *Religious Studies*, 51 (2015), 336–7. And John Cottingham associates "the 'spiritual' dimension of human existence" with "forms of life that put a premium . . . on the search for deeper reflective awareness of the meaning of our lives"; he also sees spirituality as oriented toward practice and the transformation of the self (Cottingham, *The Spiritual Dimension*, 3 and 4–5).

and achieve, its highest end. And that function shabbat is intended to carry out, if my account of it is correct.

Note that in saying this I do not commit myself to any of Hadot's more controversial theses about philosophical discourse, among ancient Greeks, being itself a mode of spiritual practice, or about philosophy having no point, for them, except to promote spiritual transformation. Nor am I taking a stance on the question of whether there is a parallel to philosophy, conceived in this way, in the learning characteristic of rabbinic Judaism. There are clearly passages in rabbinic thought that echo elements of Stoicism,[26] and studying the Torah was regarded as a mode of spiritual transformation among many of the rabbis. My point, however, is that shabbat, which is emphatically *not* an intellectual practice (although it makes room for that), is itself a spiritual exercise in Hadot's sense: helping to transform philosophers and non-philosophers alike, and to give them a mode of attending to themselves and the world that opens them up to the achievement of a higher telos.

The remaining question is what this tells us about spiritual practices generally. I think it tells us one thing of great importance: that spirituality is not a one-size-fits-all phenomenon, but something that varies with culture. Shabbat makes sense as a spiritual practice *for* people who share the Jewish tradition's elusive conception of God, and concomitant open, unsettled approach to the human telos, who are moved by the creation narrative in Genesis, and who have been raised in a community that keeps shabbat, or are drawn to such a community strongly enough to join it: for people, in short, who find *this particular* approach to spiritual transformation inspiring, beautiful, joyous, etc. A person convinced of the centrality of God's self-sacrifice in Christ to human redemption would be likely to find spiritual transformation in other ways, as would a person convinced of the beauty or sacredness of Muhammad's teachings or a person convinced that what we most need to do, to achieve our telos, is merge with a higher world-Self, or abandon the idea of the self. This is not just a matter of traditions *mandating* different spiritual practices, but of different practices *better fitting* the conception of spirituality upheld by those traditions. Meditation directed toward nullification of the self, for instance, makes far better sense for a Buddhist than for most Jews (there are parallel notions of the need for self-nullification in some Hasidic communities). Indeed, the very term "spirituality" – with its suggestion that we have a "spirit" that

[26] See H. A. Fischel, *Rabbinic Literature and Greco-Roman Philosophy* (Leiden: EJ Brill, 1973), especially 70–3 and 93–5.

is higher than our material selves, and that we should, or most deeply want to, satisfy its yearnings – fits some traditions better than it does others.

I don't mean to endorse any strong relativism in saying this. There may well be some general end of all human beings that can be described as involving or consisting in spiritual transformation. But the way to that end and that transformation – the very interpretation of these things – is likely to depend deeply on culture. We might recall the young Schleiermacher's insistence that the feeling of unity with the universe he recommended had to be approached from a multitude of different directions, given the vast differences in our individual religious sensibilities.[27] (I would add, as Schleiermacher does not, that these differences are also shaped by the varying communities in which we are raised.) Shabbat is a powerful spiritual practice *for* people raised in or drawn to the Jewish tradition; different ways of reshaping ourselves so that we can grasp and achieve our highest ends will be appropriate for people raised in other cultures, or whose spiritual sensibilities are for some other reason differently attuned. Spirituality is best seen as a pluriform phenomenon; shabbat is but one way it can manifest itself.

[27] See F. Schleiermacher, *On Religion*, trans. J. Oman (New York: Harper & Row, [1799] 1968), 212–18.

CHAPTER 8

The Power of the Spoken Word

Prayer, Invocation, and Supplication in Islam

Mukhtar H. Ali

> Do you not see how God sets forth a parable likening an excellent word to an excellent tree, its roots firm and its branches in the sky?
>
> (Qur᾿ān 14:24)[1]

The immeasurable expressive power of the Qur᾿ān affords it the highest place in the religion and culture of Islam. Its words form the core of all theological, moral, legal, liturgical, and spiritual practices, as Muslims hold the Qur᾿ān to be the very word of God, revealed to Muḥammad, the last of the Abrahamic prophets. The Qur᾿ān appeared at a time when the Arabic language was blossoming in the deserts of the Arabian Peninsula. It was regarded by the Arabs as the best example of the Arabic language, and for the believers, the perfect fusion of transcendent meaning conveyed in pristine form. Though the Arabs reveled in poetry and rhetoric, Muḥammad was never known to have composed poetry during his lifetime, adding to the wonder of the Qur᾿ān's origin and inimitability. Should the claim to prophethood be accompanied by a miracle, then the Qur᾿ān would be the linguistic miracle of Muḥammad. Precipitated by the effulgence of divine revelation, language, and its mastery became the mainstay of all other branches of learning, particularly philology, lexicography, and grammar.

Islam is essentially defined by the Qur᾿ān, but the words of the prophets and saints, recorded as narrations (hadith), prayers, and supplications have also shaped its message. While some of these prayers inform their followers of the philosophical and ethical underpinnings of the spiritual life, they also focus on a personal relationship with God and how to foster it through open, heartfelt communication. Prayer in Islam not only consists of the five canonical prayers but, as its lexical meaning suggests, includes supplication,

[1] Translations of Qur᾿ān are by the author.

petition, invoking blessing, and seeking forgiveness.[2] Even though Islam deems contemplation, self-reflection, and the pursuit of knowledge as essential forms of worship, this chapter explores the power of the word in three closely related spiritual practices: prayer (*ṣalāt*), invocation (*dhikr*), and supplication (*duʿā*).

God's words, in the real sense, precede the forms of scripture and language. Representing only written or spoken words, sacred texts occupy the last stage of revelation's descent, which have been distilled into human language. Some Islamic metaphysicians argue that the word (*kalima*) refers to Being itself and that it is the nature of Being to effuse every plane of existence before reaching the plane of human language. It is this sacred pedigree that manifests through human speech and intellect and gives rise to the idea that the human being has been created in the image of God.[3] The main argument presented in this chapter is that words are not simply meaningful utterances or symbols on a page, but existential realities that have real effects in the world. "Word" has numerous designations, referring to creation itself, the human being, scripture, or human speech. Thus, we will investigate the ontological roots of the word in the following two sections, "Creation and the Word" and "The Qurʾān as the Word of God," before exploring the nature of its power in human speech, specifically in prayer, invocation, and supplication.

Creation and the Word

Islamic doctrine holds that the very foundation of creation is divine speech; God spoke and there was creation. The greatest mystic of Islam, Muḥyī al-Dīn Ibn al-ʿArabī (638/1240), writes, "He originated all things from the hidden depths of the mystery of this word, 'Be!' (*kun*) . . . for God says, 'Our only word to a thing We desire is to say to it "Be!" and it is.'"[4] When I look at the world and creation, the hidden and the written, I find that the world is but a tree whose original light is from the seed of

[2] The word "prayer" is used in three different ways in the same verse, "God and angels send blessing on the prophet, O believers, send benedictions on him abundantly!" (Qurʾān 33:56). God showers him with mercy, the angels send their blessings, and the believers seek to multiply his reward. See E. Lane, *Arabic-English Lexicon* (London: Williams and Norgate, 1863).

[3] It is interesting to note that Arabic uses the same root letters *n-ṭ-q* to refer to both speech and reason. What makes mankind "noble" is the Islamic concept of the essential goodness of human nature, namely, that it is divine in origin, "And when I have fashioned him and breathed into him of My Spirit . . . " (Qurʾān 38:72). Conversely, human nature also possesses the capacity for evil through the excesses of worldly attachment and the veiling of Spirit's light.

[4] Qurʾān 16:40.

'Be!'"[5] Ibn al-ʿArabī further describes God's creative speech in his encyclopedic work, *Futūḥāt al-Makkiyya*, "Know that existent beings are the words of God which do not cease. . . . Therefore, we say that existent beings are the words of God. God's speech is His knowledge and His knowledge is His Essence."[6] Moreover, the Qurʾān states, "If all the oceans were ink, and all the trees were pens, God's words would not be exhausted."[7] To describe God's infinite power of expression and creativity, the Qurʾān juxtaposes oceans with ink and trees with pens, evoking a parallelism between the macrocosmic words of creation and those produced by conventional ink and pens. The hadith literature adds to the Qurʾānic metaphor and describes the Pen as the first existential reality in the hierarchy of Being. The Prophet is reported to have said, "When God wished to create the creation, he divided Light into four parts and from the first made the Pen, from the second the Tablet, from the third the Throne,[8] then He divided the fourth into four parts . . . "[9] The Pen is the active, creative principle and the Tablet, or as the Qurʾān refers to it, the Guarded Tablet (*al-lawḥ al-maḥfūẓ*), is the passive, receptive principle. Ibn al-ʿArabī further explains, "All scriptures and revealed books proceed from this Presence. From it God dictates to the Highest Pen what it should write upon the Guarded Tablet. The speech of the whole cosmos, both the absent and the witnessed, derives from this Presence – and all is the speech of God – for this is the First Presence."[10] There is a similar idea in the Bible, equating existence with the Word, "In the beginning was the Word, and the Word was with God, and the Word was God."[11]

In the way that words are produced through the breath of a person, God's breath is the fabric of existence and His words (*al-kalimāt al-ilāhiyya*) are the

[5] Ibn al-ʿArabī, *Shajarat al-Kawn* (Bibliotheca Alexandria, 1985), 41–2.

[6] Ibn al-ʿArabī, *Futūhāt al-Makkiyya* (Beirut: Dar al-Kotob al-Ilmiyah, 1999), vol. IV, ch. 198, p. 30. See M. Ebstein, *Mysticism and Philosophy in al-Andalus* (Leiden: Brill 2014), 53.

[7] Qurʾān 31:27.

[8] The Qurʾān refers to the Throne in the verse, "The Merciful is established upon the Throne" (Qurʾān 20:5). The sixth Shi'ite Imām, Jaʿfar al-Ṣādiq, says, "God created the intellect and it was the first creation from the spiritual beings, proceeding from His light from the right side of the divine Throne" (al-Kulaynī, *al-Uṣūl min al-kāfī: Kitāb al-ʿaql wa'l-jahl* [Tehran: Dār al-ʿUswa, 1997], vol. I, no. 1). Maybūdī writes in *Kashf al-asrār wa-ʿuddat al-abrār*, "He is on the Throne; in knowledge (*ʿilm*), everywhere; in communing (*suḥbat*), in the spirit (*jān*); in nearness, in the soul (*nafs*)" (cited in A. Keeler, "Mystical Theology and the Traditionalist Hermeneutics of Maybūdī's *Kashf al-Asrār*," in A. Shihadeh (ed.), *Sufism and Theology* [University of Edinburgh Press, 2007], 15–30).

[9] Zurqānī, *Sharḥ al-mawāhib al-laduniyya* (Beirut: Dār al-Kutub al-ʿIlmiyya, 1990), vol. I, 55–6.

[10] al-ʿArabī, *Futūḥāt al-Makkiyya*, vol. VII, ch. 524, p. 245. See also W. Chittick, *The Self-Disclosure of God* (Albany: State University of New York Press, 1998), 116.

[11] John 1:1 (New International Version).

entities of creation. Ibn al-ʿArabī calls this breath the Breath of the All-merciful (*al-nafas al-raḥmānī*),[12] a term that informs a central idea in Islam, that creation is an outpouring of divine mercy. It was through divine mercy and love that God endowed creation with the blessing of existence, bringing them forth from the hiddenness of nonbeing and enabling them to partake in the beauty and majesty of His Being. When one of the prophets asked God why He created existence, He responded, "I was a hidden treasure and I loved to be known, so I created the creation so that I may become known."[13]

The early Sufi lexicographer ʿAbd al-Razzāq Kāshānī (730/1330), a follower of Ibn al-ʿArabī, writes, "'Word' refers to reality, essence, immutable Archetype[14] or any other individuation of God."[15] The existential words of God, then, are the heavens and the earth, the sun and the moon, and all that exists in creation.

In one of the central books of Shiʿi hadith, we find yet another allegorical description of this creative process:

> God Almighty created the names through letters that do not possess an utterance, through a word that is not spoken, through a figure that is not corporeal, through an allegory that is indescribable, through a color that has no tint, negating all notions of dimension, far removed from limits, veiled from the senses of the imagination, concealed but not hidden. He engendered the Complete Word (*al-kalimat al-tāmma*) simultaneously into four parts, and manifested three divine names without their being attached to creation, and one, He kept hidden; it is the hidden and the reserved [name]. So, these were the names that God, Almighty manifested, who then established for each [name] four pillars, making them twelve in total.[16]

[12] This term is derived from the Prophetic hadith, "I find the Breath of your Lord coming from the direction of Yemen" (Ibn Hanbal, *Musnad* [Beirut: Dar al-Kotob al-Ilmiyya, 2009], vol. II, no. 541). Ibn al-ʿArabī's version is slightly different, using the term "Breath of the All-merciful" (*nafas al-raḥmānī*) instead of "your Lord." He and his followers use this metaphor extensively to describe the creative process and God's engendering of creation.

[13] While not found in the standard hadith collections, Ibn al-ʿArabī states, "This hadith is sound on the basis of unveiling, but not established by way of transmission" (*Futūḥāt* 2:399, line 28; quoted in W. Chittick, *Sufi Path of Knowledge: Ibn Al-Arabi's Metaphysics of Imagination* [Albany: State University of New York Press, 1989], 391, n. 14). See also W. Chittick, *Divine Love: Islamic Literature and the Path to God* (New Haven, CT: Yale University Press, 2013), 18.

[14] "Immutable Archetypes" is a term Ibn al-ʿArabī coined to describe realities in the divine knowledge. In Ibn al-ʿArabī's hierarchy of Being, they are the universal forms of the divine names in the presence of the divine knowledge in their initial individuation. They are the "archetypes" of divine names and "immutable" because His knowledge is identical with the immutable Essence.

[15] Kashānī, *Laṭā'if al-iʿlām fī ishārāt ahl al-ilhām* (Tehran: Miras-e Maktub, 2000), 486.

[16] Kulaynī, *Uṣūl al-kāfī*, vol. I, 166, cited in *Liqā' Allah* of Jawādī Mālikī Tabrīzī (Qum: Āl-e ʿAlī, 2006), 19.

The Word can also refer to the human being, such as prophets Abraham, Moses, Jesus, and Muḥammad, as the Qur'ān states, "The Messiah, son of Mary was only a messenger of God, His Word that He cast into Mary and a spirit from Him."[17] They are words of God because their realities combine every material and spiritual existential plane. The fifteenth-century Persian scholar and mystic 'Abd al-Raḥmān Jāmī (898/1492), commenting on Ibn al-'Arabī's work, *Fuṣūṣ al-ḥikam*,[18] writes, "What is meant by the Word (*kalima*) of each prophet is the path and qualities that God has specified for him and his community. In the mystical tradition, it is the form of the letter arising from the Breath of the All-merciful. As such, every entity is a word of God, as He mentions, 'Say, "If the sea were ink for the words of my Lord, the sea would be exhausted before the words of my Lord were exhausted."'"[19] Thus, the entities are read as the words of God because they resemble words in human speech. The entities acquire determination in the Breath of the All-merciful, which is the expansion of Being and its extension by passing through its degrees, in the same way that [words] acquire form in human breath through its articulations."[20] Each divine book or scripture is the breath of that particular prophet to which it was revealed. On one hand, revelation is God's directive for that prophet and his nation, and on the other, it is the very reality of the prophetic spirit, which is the reason for his receptivity to it, just as lock and key correspond to each other. While the Torah, Bible, and Qur'ān are all the words of God, Muslims hold the Qur'ān to be the culmination of all divine scriptures.

The Qur'ān as the Word of God

Revealed upon the heart of Prophet Muḥammad, the Qur'ān is considered the comprehensive word that contains the knowledge of every reality.[21] It is divine manifestation in the form of speech, as stated by the fourth Caliph and first Shi'i Imam, 'Alī ibn Abī Ṭālib (40/661), "He has manifested

[17] Qur'ān 4:171.

[18] *Fuṣūṣ al-ḥikam*, Ibn al-'Arabī's most famous work, describes the "logos" of twenty-eight prophets, symbolic of the twenty-eight letters of the Arabic alphabet. It is a central work of Sufism for which more than 100 commentaries have been written.

[19] Qur'ān 18:109.

[20] A. Jāmī, *Naqd al-nuṣūṣ fi sharḥ naqsh al-Fuṣūṣ* (Tehran: Iranian Institute of Philosophy, 1977), 83.

[21] The Qur'ān is also called *al-Furqān* (Criterion), *al-Kitāb* (Book), *al-Tanzīl* (Revelation), *al-Ẓikr* (Reminder), terms mentioned in different verses. It is said that the meaning of Qur'ān is derived from the root letters, *qāf, rā'*, and *hamza*, which means to "gather" or "collect," as in water gathering in a pool or the collectivity of the fruits of all the heavenly books.

Himself in His Book but they do not realize it."[22] The Qur'ān is the quintessence of divine manifestation; its letters, words, and verses are symbols for the entities in outward existence, the universe, and inward existence, the spiritual realities within the human being. Just as the comprehensive divine book encompasses both the outward and inward realms, it too possesses an outward and inward dimension. When the Qur'ān mentions the sun and the moon, the heavens and the earth, or relates stories of prophets, there are esoteric aspects that lend themselves to the possibility of multiple readings and interpretations. While the Prophet has stated, "God Almighty has not revealed a verse except that it possesses an outward and inward [dimension]," the Qur'ān itself says, "Therein are determined verses; they are the Mother of the Book, and others symbolic ... And none knows its interpretation save God and those firmly rooted in knowledge."[23] The eponymous founder of the Shi'i jurisprudential school, the sixth Imam, Ja'far al-Ṣādiq (148/765), says, "The book of God Almighty has four aspects: the expression (*'ibāra*), the allusion (*ishāra*), subtleties (*laṭā'if*), and realities (*ḥaqā'iq*). The expression is for the layperson (*'awāmm*), the allusion for the elite (*khawāṣṣ*), the subtlety for the saints (*awliyā'*), and the reality for the prophets (*anbiyā'*)."[24] Among the mysteries of the Qur'ān the reader immediately encounters is the disconnected letters (*al-ḥurūf al-muqatta'a*) occurring at the beginning of certain chapters. While the true meaning of these letters remains a mystery, the underlying principle is that each of the twenty-eight letters of the Arabic language stems from a corresponding cosmic reality. On this premise, early Muslim thinkers developed the mystical science of Letterism (*'ilm al-ḥurūf*) as a corollary of Qur'ānic hermeneutics, to be implemented in certain spiritual practices, healing, and divination.

As for the Qur'ān's relationship to the microcosm, it possesses a direct correspondence to every inward and outward human reality; it is the very blueprint of the human being. In other words, were the realities of the Qur'ān to take physical form, it would be in the form of a human. When the verse states, "The Merciful, taught the Qur'ān, created man, gave him expression,"[25] the order of the verses indicates the creation of man is preceded by the teaching of the Qur'ān. Teaching here is existential, not

[22] *Nahjul Balāgha*, sermon 147; see *Mizān al-ḥikma* (Beirut: Dar Ehia Al-Tourath al-Arabi, 2001), VIII, p. 3326, no. 16417.

[23] Qur'ān 3:7.

[24] M. Majlisī, *Biḥār al-anwār: al-jāmi'a li-durar akhbār al-a'imma al-aṭhār* (Beirut: Mu'assasat al-Wafa', [1403] 1983), vol. 92, p. 95. See F. Mayer, *Spiritual Gems* (Louisville, KY: Fons Vitae, 2011), xxi, and *Sufi Hermeneutics* (Oxford University Press, 2007), 55, citing *'aqā'iq*, ed. Nwyia, "Le tafsīr mystique," 188.

[25] Qur'ān 55:1–3.

intellectual, in the sense that God has fashioned the human being upon Truth, as the verse reads, "So turn your face to religion, in pure faith – with God given nature (*fiṭra*) upon which He has fashioned mankind; There is no altering of God's creation. That is true religion but most people do not know."[26] It is clear from this verse that Islam views human nature as essentially good, identifying true religion with original nature (*fiṭra*), because "God created Adam in His own image,"[27] and as Jaʿfar al-Ṣādiq says:

> The image of man is the greatest proof of God in creation. It is the book that He wrote by His own hand, the edifice that He constructed by His wisdom, and the totality of the forms of the worlds. It is the summation of the Guarded Tablet, the witness of all that is absent, the argument against every denier; it is the straight path to every good, and the bridge spanning Paradise and Hell.[28]

Attainment to God is the return to original nature, as substantiated by the famous hadith, "He who knows himself knows his Lord."[29] Self-knowledge is the realization of Truth on the tablet of the soul, but it is also knowledge of creation, as the verse states, "We will show him Our signs on the horizons and in themselves until it becomes clear that He is the Truth."[30] Alternatively, one who comprehends God's written book fathoms the book of creation, and as a consequence can read the book of his own soul. What he finds in his true self when he arrives at original nature is none other than Truth, Spirit, or God. These three realities, the Qurʾān, creation, and the soul, are mirrors of one another. One who wishes to see his face looks into a mirror, that is, he looks into creation and sees the condition of his soul, as Abraham did. "He cast a glance at the stars and said, 'Lo, I am ill.'"[31] Alternatively, he may look into the mirror of the Qurʾān and gain awareness of himself, recognize his illnesses, then find a cure.

The Qurʾān as a text informs the basis of Islamic devotional thought and practice and every prayer begins with the first verse of the Qurʾān, "In the name of God, the Compassionate, the Merciful." But beyond the text as moral guidance for a spiritual life, there is the aspect of actualization of the

[26] Qurʾān 30:30.
[27] Al-Kulaynī, *al-Uṣūl min al-kāfi* (Tehran: Dar al-Kutub al-Islamiyya, 1973) vol. I, p. 134, no. 4.
[28] F. Kashānī, *Kalimāt al-maknūna* (Qom: Ishraq, 2007), 120.
[29] al-Amūdī, *Ghurar al-ḥikam wa durar al-kalim*, 2 vols. (Tehran: Daftar-e Nashr-e Farhang-e Islami, 2000), no. 7946.
[30] Qurʾān 41:53. "Horizons" refers to outward existence and "selves" refers to the plane of the soul.
[31] Qurʾān 37:88–9.

realities of verses within the soul, which is why many Islamic spiritual thinkers equated the reality of the Qurʾān with the character of the perfected human.

Prayer (*ṣalāt*)

As mentioned earlier, there are three primary forms of Islamic worship: prayer, invocation, and supplication. The first is the prescribed prayer (*ṣalāt*), a daily practice performed throughout the life of the devout, forming one of the cornerstones of Islamic spiritual practice. The Qurʾān reminds on many occasions "Establish the prayer!"[32] while the specifics of its form and content have been laid out separately by Prophet Muḥammad. Regular prayer instills the spirit of gratefulness and humility before God, as the Qurʾān states, "Remember Me and I will remember you, be grateful to me and reject not faith."[33] The purpose of the prescribed prayer is first and foremost the remembrance of God, as announced in the verse, "Verily I am God, there is no god but Me, so worship Me and establish prayer for My remembrance."[34] It is considered the quintessential form of worship for it includes in its standing, bowing, and prostrating along with their accompanying litanies, the best form of God's glorification. Prayer also symbolizes the union of man, God, and creation. The standing posture corresponds to the human plane because the primary orientation of the human being is upright. Bowing corresponds to the animal plane as observed in the quadrupeds, and prostration corresponds to the vegetal and mineral planes, which are connected to the soil. Just as the Islamic calendar is oriented around the lunar cycles, the daily prayer is synchronized by the sun's movement. Such correspondences between the human being and nature indicate that the gnosis of God is attained by being in harmony with His creation. In other words, there is a correspondence between macrocosm, or outward existence, and microcosm, which is the human spiritual plane. By reflecting on God's signs in the natural world one realizes that the outward and inward are mirrors for one another. They are aspects of the same reality, intimating an underlying unity within existence despite the appearance of outward multiplicity. Unifying the inward with the outward is to attain true divine unity, the ultimate purpose of spirituality in Islam.

One may argue that since prayer is a state of the heart, what need is there for one to perform the outward actions of bowing and prostrating? The

[32] Qurʾān 17:78. [33] Qurʾān 2:152. [34] Qurʾān 20:14.

reason is that the human being exists simultaneously in both the outer and inward dimensions. Islamic spirituality is concerned with both aspects and regards one as reflective of the other. Just as virtuous acts are produced by sound intentions, outward actions also produce corresponding inward states and echo within the soul. While there may be various forms of prayer, one may not find a more perfect expression of humility and surrender than prostration. This is because the forehead, which is the loftiest part of the person and the residence of the intellect, is lowered to the dust. It is the intellect that causes hubris in man and thus prostration is symbolic of the effacement of that intellect before God. This annihilation is of the negative ego produced by the shadow-intellect, not of the essential human reality that is the divine intellect, for in the moment of prostration the human spirit attains the greatest proximity to God.[35] Outwardly man returns to his primordial origin, the dust, and inwardly his spirit ascends to God from whence it came.

Invocation (*dhikr*)

Enjoining to the remembrance of God goes beyond the five daily prayers in the form of invocation (*dhikr*). Lexically, the term *dhikr* has many meanings: remembrance, invocation, recollection, memory, mention, reminding, relating, repetition, incantation, recitation, praise, glorification, eminence, and honor.[36] This type of remembrance is keeping the heart[37] engaged in the memory of God through the invocation of a divine name,[38] a Qur'ānic verse or even a single word. While such constant engagement will certainly influence the practitioner, the objective is to fill the heart with spiritual meaning and not simply chant sacred litanies with an empty heart and absent mind. When performed with mindfulness, the heart then becomes receptive to the activity of the tongue and becomes awakened with God's presence, as stated in a well-known hadith, "My earth and My heavens do not embrace

[35] It is said that the worshipper is the most proximate to God during his prostration, therefore one should be abundant in petition, as the verse states, "Prostrate and draw near" (Qur'ān 96:6).

[36] See H. Wehr, *A Dictionary of Modern Written Arabic* (Beirut: Librairie du Liban, 1980) and E. W. Lane, *Arabic-English Lexicon*, 2 Vols. (Cambridge: The Islamic Texts Society, 2003).

[37] In Islamic sources, the heart is a spiritual organ that is the seat of faith, gnosis of God, and perception of divine mysteries. It is symbolically connected to the physical heart insofar as it fluctuates with being filled and emptied, animating the entire body.

[38] The divine names are not the words by which they are described rather the realities through which manifestation takes place. The divine names are existential realities emanating from the divine Essence and are one with the Essence. However, the Essence is singular and the names are multiple. God is one, but He is also the Merciful, the Just, the Wise, etc.

Me but the heart of My believing servant embraces Me."[39] Through the efficacy and power of those utterances God reveals Himself to the creature, thereby forging an awareness of his relationship with Him, as He says in the Qur'ān, "There are those who remember God, standing, sitting or lying on their sides and ponder the creation of the heavens and the earth, [saying], 'Our Lord, You did not create all this in vain; Glory be to You!'"[40]

At every juncture, the Qur'ān reminds mankind to be mindful of God, conscious of His creation, and grateful for His blessings. These are all epitomized in the singular act of *dhikr* as seen in the following verses: "Invoke the name of your Lord and dedicate yourself to Him with a total dedication."[41] "Invoke the name of your Lord, morning and evening."[42] "Surely in the remembrance of God do hearts find serenity."[43] "Has not the time come for the believers to humble their hearts for the remembrance of God?"[44] While contemplation (*fikr*) of God, no doubt, is one of the doors to gnosis, remembrance (*dhikr*) is a stage superior because the former is seeking and the latter is finding.[45] There are many narrations that indicate the primacy of contemplation over all other forms of worship. For example, a sound prophetic hadith states, "An hour of contemplation is better than a year of worship."[46] However, in this context contemplation refers to a preliminary stage of *seeking* knowledge of God, while remembrance is being *present* and mindful of God. Even if the knowledge of God is limitless and the cause of bewilderment, beholding Him by direct witnessing or through one of His manifestations is finding Him; it is remembrance in its truest form and thus a loftier station.

There is ample material in Sufi literature on the need for *dhikr* as an essential spiritual practice. It is the first step in the way of love, for one who loves a thing remembers it often. Sufi Najm al-dīn Kubrā (618/1221) describes clearly the practice of *dhikr* in his treatise on spiritual wayfaring:

> The wayfarer should remember God in the way a lover remembers his beloved, and the remembrance must never leave him. Then he must so much persevere in *dhikr* that *dhikr* gets attached to him, not leaving his heart empty of *dhikr* even for a moment. When he continues in this *dhikr*, it is transformed from human *dhikr* into celestial and holy (*qudsi*) *dhikr*.

39 Quoted by al-Ghazalī, *Iḥyā' 'ulūm al-dīn* (Cairo: Maṭba'at al 'Amirat al-Sharafiyya, 1908–9), vol. III, p. 12. Many authors including Ibn al-'Arabī indicate that "embrace Me" means to embrace the knowledge of God. For an excellent discussion on the Heart, see ch. 10 in S. Murata, *The Tao of Islam* (Albany: State University of New York Press, 1992) and W. Chittick, *The Sufi Path of Knowledge*, 106.

40 Qur'ān 3:191. 41 Qur'ān 73:8. 42 Qur'ān 76:25. 43 Qur'ān 13:28. 44 Qur'ān 57:16.

45 Kāshānī, *Sharḥ manāzil al-sā'irīn*, ed. M. Bidār (Qom: Bidar Press, 1993), 69.

46 al-Amūdī, *Ghurar al-ḥikam*, no. 6537.

> Human *dhikr* is that which is done with the help of sounds, letters and numbers, while holy *dhikr* is that which is free from numbers, letters and sounds. After this stage, the one who performs it (*dhākir*) loses his identity and is submerged within the object *dhikr.* He becomes unaware of his *dhikr* as well as his own being. There are many degrees of *dhikr*, some which are superior to the others, which are hard to begin; but gradually hardship and labor disappears and *dhikr* becomes the nature and habit of the wayfarer.[47]

In her work *Mystical Dimensions of Islam*, Annemarie Schimmel points out an important element of this practice where she writes, "*Dhikr* in its developed forms is usually connected with some sort of breath control."[48] Breath control is a key aspect of meditation practices in many traditions such as Buddhism, Yoga, Qigong, and Chinese medicine.[49] In these disciplines, energy (*Qi*) flows with the breath and allows for focused power, concentration, and will. However, the goal of the mystic is not power for its own sake, but a form of spiritual nourishment as God's name undulates with every breath. Through the breath the mystic is connected to God and his whole being is infused with His attributes. He no longer relies on the world but God alone, who is the source of all power. He becomes one with the divine name that he invokes and embodies its manifestation. Kubrā further adds:

> *Dhikr* flows in the soul of every living creature – even without their will – in the rising and falling of their breaths. In every breath, the [sound of the] letter '*hā*'' of the divine name 'Allah' rises and falls. The '*hā*'' during inhalation resides in the heart and during exhalation resides in the Throne. The letter '*waw*' in *huwa* (He) is the name of the Spirit, because it is one of the servants of the Essence.[50]

In the way that God's Words emanate from the Breath of the All-merciful, *dhikr* infuses every aspect of one's being, not just the breath. It is said that, "*Dhikr* of the tongue is praising (*ḥamd*) and magnifying (*thanā'*), *dhikr* of the soul is striving (*juhd*) and effort (*ʿinā*), *dhikr* of the

[47] N. Kubrā, *Adāb al-sulūk ila ḥadrat Mālik al-Mūluk*, trans. A. N. Baqirshahi, "Adab al-Suluk," in *al-Tawhid Islamic Journal*, 8 (1991), no. 4, 109–25. See also C. Zargar, "The Ten Principles: Theoretical Implications of Volitional Death in Najm al-Dīn Kubrā's *al-Uṣūl al-ʿAshara* (A Study and Translation)," *Muslim World*, 103 (2013), 107–30.

[48] A. Schimmel, *Mystical Dimensions of Islam* (University of North Carolina Press, 1975), 173.

[49] "Heaven within me is Virtue. Earth within me is the Breaths. Virtue flows down, the Breaths expand, and there is life." This is quoted from the *Ling Shu*, one of the canonical Chinese medical texts speaking of the association of Spirits and Breaths, *shen qi.* See C. Larre and E. Rochet de la Vallée, *Rooted in Spirit*, trans. from French (Barrytown, NY: Station Hill Press, 1995), 16.

[50] N. Kubrā, *Fawā'iḥ al-jamāl wa fawātiḥ al-jalāl* (Cairo: Dar Saʿād al-Ṣabaḥ, 1993), 223.

spirit is fear (*khawf*) and hope (*rajāʾ*), *dhikr* of the heart is truthfulness (*ṣidq*) and purity (*ṣafā*), *dhikr* of the intellect is magnifying (*taʿdhīm*) and modesty (*ḥayāʾ*), *dhikr* of gnosis is submission (*taslīm*) and contentment (*riḍā*), *dhikr* of the secret is vision (*ruʾya*) and meeting (*liqāʾ*).[51] Each of these types of *dhikr* pertains to subtleties in the human spiritual landscape and increasing levels of transcendence therein. Even if prayer (*ṣalāt*) is a form of *dhikr*, as in "'Establish prayer for my remembrance (*dhikr*),'"[52] "The remembrance (*dhikr*) of God is greater."[53]

Supplication (*duʿā*)

The most personal and intimate form of Islamic spiritual practice is supplication. Turning to God in supplication forges a personal relationship with the Creator, uplifting our humanity. Whether it is motivated by joy and gratefulness or because of suffering and despair, the need to commune with God sparks a certain spiritual awakening. Islam teaches that mankind was not created for the sake of this ephemeral world, which is only the prism of divine manifestation, but to attain proximity to God through it. Thus, seeking God is rooted in human nature (*fiṭra*) and transcends the forms of religion. To embody the spirit of supplication what is required is not the philosophical mind, but the spiritual intellect. In Qurʾānic terminology, it is called the heart; it is the seat of faith, the place of witnessing, and the wellspring of intention.

While the rituals of prayer are defined by a religious code, supplication is universal. Over the ages, the prophets and saints have guided their followers on the manner of supplication, revealing its mysteries so that people would be able to speak to God directly by means of either a human language or through their condition and state. Language takes on various forms, in speech and writing, gestures of the face and body, or the language of intentions, thoughts, and desires. Intention and will is a subtle energy that can influence the outcome of events as well as others around us. A person may be in pain and exclaim, "Ah!" In spiritual terms, the hadith mentions that "Ah!" is one of the names of God, saying, "We came across some companions with Abu ʿAbdullah and saw a man who kept moaning, 'Ah!' So I said to him, 'Brother, call out to your Lord and seek help from

[51] Al-Ṣadūq, *al-Khiṣāl* (Najaf: Maṭbaʿah al-Ḥaydariah, 1971), 404. See also Schimmel, *Mystical Dimensions of Islam*, 174.

[52] Qurʾān 20:14. [53] Qurʾān 29:45.

Him.' Then Abu ʿAbdullah said, 'Ah! is one of the names of God. So whoever says "Ah!" has indeed petitioned God.'"[54]

There is abundant evidence in the Qurʾān that God is near and receptive to the seeker. "When My servants ask you about Me, [tell them] I am near! I answer the supplication of the supplicant when he supplicates Me."[55] Notice that in this verse, the Arabic root of the word "supplicate" is used three times consecutively for emphasis and to exhort man to call on God. "Supplicate to your Lord humbly and secretly."[56]

Of the various types of address in the Qurʾān some of the most poignant are the verses intended for supplication. In these instances, God prescribes certain words, teaching mankind the manner and etiquette of approaching Him. Beginning with the opening chapter, *al-Fātiḥa*, we find that after praising God and mentioning His attributes, the Beneficent and Merciful, the chapter turns into a prayer, "Guide us on the straight path!" There are many other verses, such as those at the end of the fourth chapter, *Āl-e-Imrān*, "'Our Lord, grant us what You promised us through Your messengers and do not disgrace us on the Day of Resurrection. Indeed, You do not fail in [Your] promise.' And their Lord responded to them, 'Never will I allow the work of any amongst you to be lost, whether male or female; you are of one another.'"[57]

In the early days of Islam, the Prophet supplicated to God on numerous occasions and for various purposes. These words can be considered divine words uttered on the human tongue.[58] There are recorded supplications (*duʿā maʾthūr*) of not just Prophet Muhammad, but also the supplications of Jesus, David, Moses, Noah, and other Prophets mentioned in the Qurʾān and hadith, as well as saints who have reached the station of infallibility. There is indeed a long-standing textual tradition of supplication in Islam. There are supplications that follow each of the five prayers, the days of the week, on special occasions in the Islamic calendar, for an increase in sustenance, for warding off evil, for seeking good outcomes, etc. Then there are those that accompany spiritual states, stations, and

[54] Tabarsī, *Mustadrak al-wasāʾil* (Qum: Muʾassisa Āl al-Bayt li-Iḥyāʾal-Turāth, 1407/1987), ii. no. 1666/15. Kubrā in his *Fawāʾiḥ al-jamāl wa fawātiḥ al-jalāl* (223) relates something similar from the classical Sufi scholar and commentator of the Qurʾān Sahl al-Tustarī.

[55] Qurʾān 2:186. [56] Qurʾān 7:55. [57] Qurʾān 3:194–5.

[58] Various hadith indicate the relationship between a person and their speech: "Speech is the scale of the human being"; "The speech of a man is the scale of his intellect"; "Man is hidden under his tongue"; and "Your speech is the translator of your intellect." These narrations can be found in *Mīzan al-ḥikma*, an encyclopedia of Shiʿi hadith first published in twelve volumes by Dar al-Hadith in Qom, Iran. A condensed bilingual edition entitled *The Scale of Wisdom: A Compendium of Shi'a Hadith* was published by ICAS Press, London, in 2008.

awareness, and those that are simply expressions of love and humility that seek nothing from God save divine proximity. These have all been uttered by either a prophet, saint, or Imam in the Shiʿi tradition, and have been carefully recorded, collected, and passed down through successive generations. These sacred words hold no lesser a place in true Islamic spirituality than the Qurʾān itself. This is because they are not mere words of the uninitiated, but utterances emanating from the pure hearts of prophets and saints. While the Qurʾān holds the highest rank for being the very words of God, the Prophet or Imam is the speaking Qurʾān (*al-qurʾān al-nāṭiq*).[59] Metaphorically speaking, God's word is the "descending" Qurʾān and the Prophet's word is the "ascending" Qurʾān.[60]

In one of the books of hadith, there is a story about Moses: "It is written in the part of the Torah that has not been altered[61] that Moses asked his Lord, 'O Lord, are You near to me that I should whisper [as intimates] or far from me that I should cry out to You.' So, God revealed to him saying, 'O Moses, I am the companion, sitting with one who remembers Me.'"[62] In other words, speak to Me as you would an intimate companion or beloved.

Moses in Islamic tradition has been given the title "the Interlocutor of God" (*Kalīmullah*), since he used to speak to God directly.[63] Yet despite the honorary designation, he sought God's guidance toward the most sublime manner of approach and further asked him, "My Lord, expand for me my breast, ease my task, and untie the knot from my tongue."[64] From historical sources we come to know that Moses suffered a speech impediment, so he asked God to strengthen his speech lest God's message go undelivered to the Pharaoh.[65] This is, however, only the outward meaning of the verse, in the context of particular historical events, but

[59] See M. Amir-Moezzi, *The Spirituality of Shiʿi Islam* (London: I.B. Taurus, 2011), 248; M. Ayoub, "The Speaking Qurʾān and the Silent Qurʾān: A Study of the Principles and Development of Imāmī Tafsīr," in A. Rippin (ed.), *Approaches to the History of the Interpretation of the Qurʾān* (Oxford: Clarendon, 1988), 177–98.

[60] This idea is rooted in the doctrine of prophetic infallibility. If a human being reaches the station of infallibility, then whatever actions, words, or deeds he or she produces, it reflects that degree of perfection. Divine light reflected in a perfect mirror is nothing but that light; it is not admixed with the properties of the mirror.

[61] This is referring to the belief that previous scriptures have been altered whereas the final revelation, the Qurʾān, according to Muslim belief, is protected from emendation.

[62] Al-Kulayni, *al-Kāfī, ii, kitāb al-duʿā*, hadith no. 4.

[63] "He said: O Moses! I have chosen you over other people for my message and by My speaking [to you] so hold to that to which I have given you and be among the thankful" (Qurʾān 7:144).

[64] Qurʾān 20:27.

[65] See also the Bible, Exodus 4:10, when Moses said, "Pardon your servant, Lord. I have never been eloquent, neither in the past nor since you have spoken to your servant. I am slow of speech and tongue" (New International Version).

the Qur'ān's import is more holistic, taking into consideration both the outward and the inward dimensions. His request, in fact, reflected his spiritual state because Moses was tongue-tied when he wanted to express himself to God. He conversed with God with such fervor that it is as if he had exhausted all modes of expression, reaching its endpoint; when a thing reaches its limit, it transforms into its opposite. Certain Sufi scholars say that the inner meaning here is that one must invoke God to the extent that he becomes "mute." That is, he exhausts all words when expressing himself to God and comes to the point of muttering, then reaches silence. Speech comes full circle and transforms into silence. That is why Moses asked God to remove the "knot on his tongue" because it was unable to express these spiritual realities. The true nature of God's Interlocutor is to be bewildered by Him, tongue-tied when speaking to Him, and mute in describing Him.

It may also be said that it is the love of God that made him incapable of expression, as the Sufi saint ʿAbdallah Ansārī (481/1089) writes, "The final stage of love is that which robs one of explicit expression, refines allusion, and cannot be exhaustively described, as it is the pivot of this affair. Anything less is a love proclaimed by the tongues, professed by the creatures, and that which the intellect deems necessary."[66] Thus, Moses was incapable of eloquent expression, a perceived disability on the physical plane and a lofty attribute on the spiritual. It is the very power of speech, awestruck by conversing with the Almighty, that rendered him speechless.

Prayer Manuals

To gain a better appreciation of Islamic spiritual practices, it is necessary to acquaint oneself with the famous supplications collected in various manuals of prayer. The philosophy of supplication is presented here by Imam ʿAlī ibn abī Ṭālib advising his son asan:

> Know that the One who holds in His hands the treasuries of the Dominion of the world and the hereafter has permitted you to supplicate to Him. He has guaranteed its response and has commanded you to ask Him so that He may give you. He is the Merciful, the Generous. He has not placed a veil

[66] Kāshānī, *Sharḥ manāzil al-sā'irīn*, 395. In this state of effacement, the intellect has no capacity to grasp its reality, since the intellect is tied to concepts and ideas that pertain to creation. True expression of love is a matter of the heart and other than what "the intellect deems necessary" since it is neither calculated nor measured.

> between you and Him and has not made anyone an intercessor for you. Then he placed the keys of those treasuries in your hands by way of you asking Him. So, whenever you like you may open the doors of those treasuries by your supplication.[67]

The most famous prayer manual is *al-Ṣaḥīfa al-Sajjādiyya*,[68] by the Prophet's great-grandson and the fourth Shiʿi Imam, ʿAlī Zayn al-ʿĀbidīn (99/717). These magnificent prayers give insight into the depths of the Islamic spiritual tradition, informing fundamental attitudes of the believer toward God, himself, and the world. Although such supplications have filled many volumes and require detailed study, a few examples for the reader are given here. Among the etiquettes of supplication is first to begin with the doxology, "In the name of God, the Beneficent, the Merciful," then after praising God, invoke blessings on the Prophet. Praise and glorification of God occupies the foremost position in these manuals as they are the master key to the other forms of supplication:

> Praise belongs to God, who
> disclosed Himself to hearts through mightiness,
> veiled Himself from eyes through might,
> and exercises power over the things through power!
> Eyes are not firm enough to see Him
> and imaginations reach not the core of His mightiness.[69]

Certain glorifications also give important insights about the nature of the cosmos:

> Glory be to You! You know the weight of the heavens!
> Glory be to You! You know the weight of the earths!
> Glory be to You! You know the weight of the sun and the moon!
> Glory be to You! You know the weight of the darkness and the light!
> Glory be to You! You know the weight of the shadow and the air!
> Glory be to You! You know the weight of the wind,
> how many times it is greater than the weight of a dust mote![70]

Some supplications express states of humility, repentance, confession, need:

> My worn mortal face is prostrate before Your everlasting, ever abiding Face. My face is prostrate, dust-soiled, before its Creator, and meet and right is

[67] M. Majlisī, *Biḥār al-anwār*, vol. 88, p. 204, hadith no. 1.
[68] W. Chittick, *The Psalms of Islam* (London: The Muhammadi Trust, 1988), with emendations.
[69] *The Psalms of Islam*, A Supplication and Magnification, no. 56.
[70] *The Psalms of Islam*, One of His Glorifications of God, no. 55.

> this prostration. My face is prostrate before Him who created and formed it and pierced for it the hearing and the sight. Blessed be God, the Best of Creators. My miserable and lowly face is prostrate before the Mighty and Glorious.[71]

Supplications expressing gratefulness:

My God, the continuous flow of Your graciousness has distracted me from thanking You!
The flood of Your bounty has rendered me incapable of counting Your praises!
The succession of Your kind acts has diverted me from mentioning You in laudation!
The continuous rush of Your benefits has thwarted me from spreading the news of Your gentle favors!

Supplications seeking good outcomes and noble moral traits:

O God, deposit in me no quality for which I will be faulted,
unless You set it right, no flaw for which I will be blamed,
unless You make it beautiful, no deficient noble trait, unless You complete it!
O God, bless Muhammad and his Household
and point me straight to resist him who is dishonest toward me with good counsel,
repay him who separates from me with gentle devotion,
reward him who deprives me with free giving,
recompense him who cuts me off with joining,
oppose him who slanders me with excellent mention,
give thanks for good, and shut my eyes to evil![72]

There are many prayers said for others including the angels, prophets, saints, children, neighbors, friends, and parents:

> And single out my parents, O God,
> for honor with You and blessings from You,
> teach me through inspiration
> knowledge of everything incumbent upon me toward them,
> God, lower before them my voice,
> make agreeable to them my words,
> make mild before them my temper,
> make tender toward them my heart,
> and turn me into their kind companion,
> their loving friend![73]

[71] Translated by C. Padwick in *Muslim Devotions* (Oxford: One World, 1996), 11.
[72] *The Psalms of Islam*, His Supplication on Noble Moral Traits and Acts Pleasing to God, no. 20.
[73] *The Psalms of Islam*, His Supplication for His Parents, no. 24.

Then the whispered prayers (*munājāt*) of the lovers:

> My God, who can have tasted the sweetness of Your love,
> then wanted another in place of You?
> Who can have become intimate with Your nearness,
> then sought removal from You?
> O He the lights of whose holiness
> induce wonder in the eyes of His lovers,
> the glories of whose face arouse the longing of the hearts of His knowers!
> O Furthest Wish of the hearts of the yearners!
> O Utmost Limit of the hopes of the lovers![74]

Or the mystical prayer offered in the month of Shaʿbān called *Munājāt Shaʿbāniyya*:

> My God, grant me total separation from everything but You,
> Illuminate the vision of our hearts by the luminosity of gazing upon You,
> So the heart's vision tears through the veils of light,
> attaining the Fountainhead of Magnificence,
> Our spirits suspended by the Grandeur of Your Sanctity.

Final Words

While these recorded prayers offer supplicants a template to use in their own divine address, some of the teachers of mysticism emphasize the aspects of sincerity and spontaneity in one's prayers. Emulating the prayers of the saints, however perfect they may be, is still one step removed from the unscripted words that come from the heart naturally. This sort of imitation may lead to a pattern of disingenuous performances of litanies and prayers and be the cause of one's spiritual ruin, whereas the true power of the word is with the speaker's intentionality and mindfulness alone. God knows the heart and mind of His creatures and the place from which their words arise, as in the supplication, "You know what is in my heart, and You are aware of my need. You know my mind and are aware of my future and my present, and with what I want to begin my speech, of the request I would utter and the hopes that I have concerning my fate."[75]

Even if the prophets, saints, and sages have taught their followers the best approach to prayer, inculcated in them lofty words and taught their etiquette,

[74] *The Psalms of Islam*, Whispered Prayer of the Lovers, no. 77.

[75] Cited from *Munājāt Shaʿbāniya*, which is a supplication attributed to Imam ʿAli. Sayyid ibn Tawūs and Abbas Qummī have both included it in their prayer manuals, *al-Iqbāl al-aʿmāl* and *Mafātīḥ al-jinān*, respectively. It is also found in Majlisī's hadith collection, *Biḥār al-anwār*, vol. 91, p. 97.

there is yet a more potent type of prayer: the heartfelt personal words with which you address God, directly, without the intermediary of a person, text, or posture. There is a power in these words that has immense efficacy and ensures a response, as a certain spiritual master advises with these precious words:

> Nothing will get you closer to your aim than by speaking to God in a natural way. There is no need to burden yourself with verses or recorded supplications. Speak to Him on your own accord, night and day, sitting, standing, kneeling or walking, during waking hours or before sleep – in any condition. If you make this speech your habit, do not abandon it, because God may seek you out in the places where you habituate conversation with Him and not find you.

CHAPTER 9

Aristotelian Friendship and Ignatian Companionship

Karen Stohr

> This is how you ascertain the truth of spiritual experience: it propels you back toward the world and other people, and not simply more deeply within yourself.[1]

This essay aims to construct a relationship between two accounts of friendship, one with its source in ancient Greece and the other with roots in sixteenth-century Spain. The first account is Aristotle's famous discussion of friendship in the *Nicomachean Ethics*, in which he argues that friendship is an essential part of a flourishing human life. The second account is the less well-known but still highly influential picture of companionship articulated and lived out by St. Ignatius of Loyola. Ignatius was the founder of the Society of Jesus (better known as the Jesuits), the original members of which are commonly called the companions. As part of their efforts to form a new religious community, Ignatius and his companions created a set of structures and practices to govern the lives of the Jesuits as individuals and as members of an order. Those structures and practices formed the basis of a distinctive spirituality, with companionship as a central aspect of it.

On the surface, it may seem as though Aristotelian friendship and Ignatian companionship have little in common, given that the accounts were developed in such different contexts. And yet, there are similarities well worth exploring. Notably, both Aristotle and Ignatius see friendship as an essential part of the human good. They also both emphasize the role of ongoing shared activity and experience in the formation and sustenance of such relationships. My interest in these two accounts, however, is not purely historical or even comparative. Rather, I will argue that exploration of these accounts can help illuminate the good of friendship as we experience it in the current age. In particular, Aristotle and Ignatius provide us with important insights into the challenges of friendship in times of

[1] C. Wiman, *My Bright Abyss: Meditations of a Modern Believer* (New York: Farrar, Straus, and Giroux, 2013), 72.

suffering and grief. Aristotle and Ignatius are surely right that we need friends with whom to walk through our shared human lives, with all their characteristic joys and tragedies. I hope to show that their accounts can help us in our efforts to cultivate and sustain such friendships.

The essay has three parts. In Part I, I set out Aristotle's account of friendship, focusing especially on his claims about shared activity in friendship and the role friends play in times of good and bad fortune. For Aristotle, friends are an essential component of a flourishing human life; we cannot live well without friends. True friends are goods for each other in a variety of ways. Aristotle argued that friends must live together and participate in joint activities as a way of cultivating virtue and doing fine actions. In this kind of closely shared life, friends inevitably end up participating in each other's triumphs and tragedies. I will suggest that even in our dramatically different modern context, Aristotle's account of friendship still has important lessons for how we should think about and undertake the project of sharing in a friend's suffering.

In Part II, I turn to companionship as it appears in both the writings of St. Ignatius and his own life. Although Ignatius is considered the official founder of the Society of Jesus, he did not work alone. Indeed, his companions played a crucial role in developing this novel idea of community and articulating the distinctive spirituality that undergirds it. The early Jesuits had a common aim, but at the outset they had little idea what form that aim would take or what would be needed in order to accomplish it. Ignatius and his companions were spread out across multiple countries and eventually continents, and yet they nevertheless sought to live out a shared spiritual mission. These distinctive (and perhaps surprisingly modern) features of sixteenth-century Ignatian companionship are, I suggest, useful in thinking about friendship as we experience it today. Moreover, Ignatius was well aware of the extent to which we are prone to what he referred to as times of spiritual desolation – interior experiences that take us away from God and subsequently produce a sense of abandonment, loss, and separation. Ignatian spirituality takes it as a given that human life often follows a very rocky and difficult path. The spiritual practices of the Ignatian tradition are designed to help us cultivate the dispositions and habits necessary to sustain us through those experiences of grief, agony, and isolation. Those same dispositions and habits, I will suggest, also enable us to sustain our friends and be good companions during times of both joy and despair.

In Part III, I will draw these two accounts together and consider what friendship on this Aristotelian-Ignatian model might look like today. Here

I will focus on the ways in which friends are companions to each other during the despair and isolation occasioned by serious illness, trauma, and death. Both Aristotle and Ignatius have important insights into the value and function of friendship in these moments, insights that can help us think through the contemporary version of the same problem. How can we be good friends and companions to each other in the darkest times of our lives? How might shared spiritual practices and experiences facilitate this kind of companionship? Taken together, the accounts of Aristotle and Ignatius provide a useful perspective from which to answer these questions.

I

> Further, it is most necessary for our life. For no one would choose to live without friends even if he had all the other goods.[2]

So says Aristotle in his most famous and influential ethical work, the *Nicomachean Ethics.* Indeed, two of the ten books of the *Ethics* are devoted to the topic of friendship, which perhaps is some indication of just how seriously Aristotle took the subject. In Book I of the *Ethics*, Aristotle gives an account of the best, most *eudaimon* life for human beings. That life is one that includes both virtuous activity and external goods. Given how Aristotle portrays friendship, it's plausible to regard it as the most important of the external goods. Friendship, for Aristotle, is good in its own right, but it is also good insofar as our friends (at least, friends of the right kind) help us become more virtuous. We cannot flourish in the absence of such friends.

Aristotle's conviction on this point is due in part to his belief that human beings are by nature social creatures. We do not live by ourselves; we live in communities with others. My good as an individual is, for better or for worse, tied up with the good of the others with whom I share my life. If an account of happiness is to meet his criterion for self-sufficiency, meaning that it is lacking in nothing, it must incorporate the fact that my happiness is tied to the fortunes of my friends. As he puts it in I.7, "what we count as self-sufficient is not what suffices for a solitary person, living an isolated life, but what suffices also for parents, children, wife, and, in general, for friends and fellow citizens, since a human being is a naturally political animal."[3]

[2] Aristotle, *Nicomachean Ethics*, trans. Terence Irwin, 2nd ed. (Indianapolis, IN: Hackett, [ca. 325 BC] 1999), 1155a5–6.

[3] Aristotle, *Nicomachean Ethics*, 1097b9–12.

The implication of this claim is that it makes each person's happiness vulnerable to luck in ways that other accounts of happiness, most notably the Socratic/Platonic account, do not. According to Socrates, a just person with a harmonious soul could be happy even while being stretched on the torture rack. Aristotle appears to find this implausible. Without disagreeing that virtue is the substantial contributor to our happiness (thereby providing happiness with the stability he thinks it needs), he nevertheless expresses skepticism about the idea that a life of torture could be lacking in nothing. The case he offers as support for this view is that of Priam, the ill-fated king of Troy.[4] Clearly Priam's life would have been better if he had not suffered the losses of his family and his kingdom. His seemingly charmed life took a disastrous turn right before its end. No amount of virtue could bring his children back from the dead or recover what Troy had lost. Priam's own virtue undoubtedly helped him cope better with his devastating circumstances than a less virtuous person could have managed to do; still, it is impossible to regard him as anything other than a tragic figure in virtue of his losses.

We need friends because we are fundamentally social, but Aristotle clearly regards some friendships as more worth having than others. He distinguishes among friendships of utility, friendships of pleasure, and friendships of character, or complete friendships. Although Aristotle describes all of them as forms of friendship, it is complete friendship that occupies his attention and that plays a crucial role in his theory. Complete friendships are characterized by the fact that the friends seek not only their own good, but the good of each other as well, and for that other's own sake. In this way, they become goods for each other. As he puts it in VIII.6: "Moreover, in loving their friend they love what is good for themselves; for when a good person becomes a friend he becomes a good for his friend."[5]

For Aristotle, there are multiple senses in which a complete friend is a good for her friend. We enjoy the presence of our friends, but that enjoyment is not what is distinctive about complete friendship. A complete friend takes up the good of her friend as something that is good in its own right, or for its own sake. I want my friend's life to go well not because it means she will be in a better position to help me or because it will make her more fun to be around. I want her life to go well for *her* sake. But Aristotle's

[4] There are scholarly debates over how to interpret Aristotle's use of happy (*eudaimon*) versus blessed (*makarion*) in these passages. It's plausible to interpret him as saying that Priam could be considered happy, but not blessed. On this, see Martha Nussbaum, *The Fragility of Goodness* (Cambridge University Press, 1986), 327–36.

[5] Aristotle, *Nicomachean Ethics*, 1157b34–5.

conception of how we are related to our friends adds a twist to this. For my friend's good is not hers alone; it is also mine. What it means to be a friend is to take up her good as part of my own. When she does well, I do well. When she suffers, I suffer.[6]

Crucially, for Aristotle, caring about my friend's good requires correct judgment about that good. It is her genuine good that matters, and I can be a complete friend only if I am capable of recognizing and promoting what is genuinely good for her. This is part of the reason why Aristotle thought that complete friendship requires virtue, or at least a commitment to virtue. A vicious person is not capable of being a good for another in the relevant way. This is not simply because vicious people are too selfish to care about another person's good for its own sake, in the way that complete friends do. It is also because a vicious person does not have the capacity to recognize or promote someone's good in the first place.

Aristotle thinks that it is impossible to flourish without virtue. Because friends naturally want each other to flourish, this implies that one of the central tasks of friendship is to help each other become more virtuous. On Aristotle's view, we do this primarily by way of shared activities and projects, through which friends cultivate and express virtue together. The centrality of shared activities in the cultivation of virtue is a primary reason why Aristotle insists that friends must live together. It is in the context of that shared life that they develop the habits and practices of virtue, and act in ways that exemplify it. The *eudaimon* life is one conducted together with other people.

Aristotle is attentive to the fact that these shared activities change over the course of human life, in response to alterations in ourselves and our circumstances. Friends are always goods for each other, but the way in which they are goods for each other does not remain static:

> Moreover, the young need friends to keep them from error. The old need friends to care for them and support the actions that fail because of weakness. And those in their prime need friends to do fine actions; for 'when two go together . . . ' they are more capable of understanding and action.[7]

[6] Aristotle's theory is often criticized for being egoistic, insofar as the reasons we have to be virtuous, or pursue friendships, all seem to come back to our own flourishing in some way. This is a very large issue, and I cannot do justice to it here. I will just say that any sense in which Aristotle's theory is egoistic is a very thin sense indeed. Egoism, as we normally think of it, reduces all other concerns to how they impact me. Aristotle's theory, by contrast, expands my own concerns to include the concerns of my family, friends, and community.

[7] Aristotle, *Nicomachean Ethics*, 1155a12–15.

During youth, the primary way in which my friend can be a good for me is to prevent me from making mistakes, the kind of mistakes young people without fully developed practical wisdom are likely to commit. Although Aristotle isn't specific about the kind of error he has in mind, we can imagine from our own experiences the many ways in which friends might help correct the judgments and decisions of each other. If I tend toward recklessness, my more cautious friend may keep me from making dangerous mistakes in my judgments about risk. If instead I am prone to being overcome by fear, my friend may be useful in preventing me from talking myself out of actions that I really should do. Friends serve as crucial correctives to our particular vices and moral failings, and we do the same for them. Together we shape our understanding of what is worthwhile, and we encourage each other in pursuit of what we gradually recognize to be good.

This mutual support in becoming virtuous is perhaps the most important way in which friends are goods for each other. Aristotle also suggests that there is value simply in doing virtuous actions with our friends. This is both because those actions are noble in themselves and also because such shared actions enable us to extend the scope of our own individual agency. Friends working together can achieve far more than each could achieve on his or her own, as Aristotle's remarks about those in their prime suggest. Moreover, older people need friends to help carry out actions they themselves no longer have the strength to do. Friends enable me to act virtuously in ways I could not do by myself, and I do the same for them. In all these different ways, friends reinforce and extend each other's moral capacities.

The importance Aristotle assigns to common experiences and activities explains why he also insists that friends must live together for, as he says, "nothing is as proper to friends as living together."[8] For Aristotle, people who do not live together, however much they wish each other well, cannot be complete friends because there is no way for them to engage in those all-important shared activities. Now, of course, we have other ways of maintaining relationships with friends over distance, but the point about the importance of common experiences still holds. Any Aristotelian account of friendship must provide avenues through which friends can share in each other's lives and experiences in the relevant ways. If they are to be goods for each other, friends who do not live together must still be able to do things together in a way robust enough to count as sharing their lives.

[8] Aristotle, *Nicomachean Ethics*, 1157b20.

(Interestingly, Ignatius did not seem to see great distance as an impediment to companionship. We will return to this in Part II.)

Given that complete friendship requires a deep entrenchment in each other's lives, it is not surprising that Aristotle makes a point of saying that no one person can have many of them. It takes time and energy to cultivate and sustain a complete friendship, and they do not develop immediately. We must know our friends well and come to love them well enough to want their good for its own sake. This latter point is important, because for Aristotle, complete friendships are not just large time commitments. They are also large emotional commitments. Moreover, they are emotional commitments of a distinctive sort. As we have seen, in a complete friendship, my friend's good becomes my own good. It is not simply that I want my friend's life to go well; rather, it is that my friend's life going well is a condition of my own life going well. To be a friend to someone is to bind one's fate to that person. The joys and tragedies of my friend's life are also the joys and tragedies of my own life. This has profound consequences for our day-to-day lives, leaving open the potential for what we might describe as a kind of emotional whiplash. Aristotle notes: "It also becomes difficult for many to share one another's enjoyments and distresses as their own, since you are quite likely to find yourself sharing one friend's pleasure and another friend's grief at the same time."[9] This is, of course, psychologically difficult for the individual, but it is also a challenge for the friendship itself. If I am to be a good for my friend, I must be able and willing to take up the right place in her life, even when that is a very difficult place to be.

Aristotle's brief discussion of friendship in times of trouble points to some of the complexities of friendship in such circumstances. In IX.11, he notes that the presence of friends reduces our burdens, though the mechanism through which this happens is unclear:

> The very presence of friends is also pleasant, in ill fortune as well as good fortune; for we have our pain lightened when our friends share our distress. Indeed, that is why one might be puzzled about whether they take a part of it from us, as though helping us to lift a weight, or, alternatively, their presence is pleasant and our awareness that they share our distress makes the pain smaller.[10]

Aristotle sets the puzzle aside, as he is more interested in noting the phenomenon itself. The presence of friends in times of ill fortune reduces our suffering; that much is clear. This, however, produces a practical

[9] Aristotle, *Nicomachean Ethics*, 1171a6–9. This problem is nicely illustrated by the sometimes jarring nature of a Facebook feed, with posts about tragedies mixed in with cat videos.

[10] Aristotle, *Nicomachean Ethics*, 1171a29–34.

problem for friendship that Aristotle goes on to describe. Complete friends do not want to cause each other pain. They also seek to unburden each other wherever possible. Someone in the midst of a tragedy will want to spare her friends from suffering on her behalf; she will not want them to feel her pain alongside her. She may even try to hide her troubles. And yet, her friend will want to know about her suffering and ameliorate it in any way possible. Although Aristotle puts his point in unfortunately sexist terms, his main observation resonates with common experience. Concern for our friends leads us to want to shield them from the painful turns in our lives. At the same time, their concern for us leads them to seek us out in our pain and share in our burdens.

This may seem inconsistent, but Aristotle is not aiming to write a how-to manual for friendship. We should not expect friendship in complex situations to be straightforward or simple. On Aristotle's view, friendship is a source of both pain and relief from pain. My own suffering is alleviated by the presence of my friends, but it is increased by their suffering. We cannot know in advance how this will work out over the course of a lifetime, dependent as it is on circumstance and fortune. The important point to note is this: the claim that a complete friendship is a good for me does not rule out the possibility that it may put me into very painful circumstances, circumstances I would not otherwise be in.

It is impossible to understand how friendship, taken this way, could contribute to our happiness unless we take seriously the idea that happiness should be understood in the ancient sense of flourishing, rather than in the more modern sense of lengthy periods of warm, fuzzy feelings about the world. What makes my life go better in the first sense may make it go worse in the second sense. This is perhaps most evident when it comes to the virtue of courage. A virtuously courageous person may find herself having to make sacrifices that a less courageous person would not. Aristotle's position is that a courageous person who gives up her life for a noble cause is both losing something genuinely important *and* at the same time living well. In other words, a flourishing human life is not necessarily a pleasant human life.

For Aristotle, friendship always makes our lives better, but it will not always make our lives smoother or more pleasant. The shared activities of friendship are not always enjoyable ones; indeed, many of them are marked by anxiety and pain. Spending time together in an oncologist's waiting room is not what we ordinarily think of when we think of friends getting together. But it is as much a part of the shared life of friends as going to the movies. Friendship can and often does require accompanying our friends into places of deep despair and grief. This is, of course, emotionally draining. But the demands of Aristotelian friendship are not simply demands on my time or emotional energy. They are demands on the deepest part of myself. Moreover, living up to these demands well requires virtue. Virtue, for Aristotle, is an internal state that finds expression in our external choices, attitudes, and actions. In order to be a good friend in times of despair, I must be in the right state myself. I suggest that Ignatian spirituality has much to offer when it comes to describing that state and helping us learn to cultivate it.

II

> I call desolation all the contrary of the third rule, such as darkness of soul, disturbance in it, movement of things low and earthly, the unquiet of different agitations and temptations, moving to want of confidence, without hope, without love, when one finds oneself all lazy, tepid, sad, and as if separated from his Creator and Lord.[11]

The legacy of St. Ignatius is characterized by his unique and enduring perspective on human spiritual experience, in both its interior and its exterior manifestations. The focus of Ignatian spirituality is on the ways in which we experience God's presence and absence in our lives and in the world. But Ignatian spiritual practice is not something conducted in isolation from other people. Companionship is a central component of it, and indeed, an essential part of Ignatius's own life and work. His vision of companionship is expressed, in different ways, in his two most influential books – the *Spiritual Exercises* and the *Constitutions*. The *Spiritual Exercises* provide a framework for individual spiritual development and practice, whereas the *Constitutions* are the foundational governing documents for the new society he was in the process of forming. Both works express his view that even individual spiritual formation takes place within a community. Spiritual formation, like the cultivation of Aristotelian virtue, aims to produce an inner state with an outward focus. And like Aristotelian virtue, that inner state is cultivated, sustained, and expressed through the common activities and practices of companions sharing their lives with each other.

[11] St. Ignatius of Loyola, "Rules for Perceiving and Knowing in Some Manner the Different Movements which Are Caused in the Soul," *The Spiritual Exercises*, trans. Elder Mullan (Chicago, IL: Acheron Press, [ca. 1525] 2012).

The foundation of Ignatian spirituality is a set of loosely structured Exercises, originally spelled out by Ignatius in the *Spiritual Exercises* and subsequently modified in various ways. That practice of formation, referred to in Ignatian circles as the Exercises, is organized as a four-"week" retreat of prayer, reading, and reflection. A person making the Exercises works with a spiritual director, who serves as a companion and guide to the process. As we will see, this relationship between the retreatant and the spiritual director provides useful insight into the Ignatian vision of companionship. The *Constitutions*, which were written six years after the publication of the *Spiritual Exercises*, set out Ignatius's vision for his fledgling Society of Jesus. The primary aim of the *Constitutions* is to spell out how such a community should be formed and administered so as to foster the spiritual growth and work of its members. Ignatius recognized that even seemingly minor details were essential to the ability of the new Jesuits to live and work in harmony. It sets out a collaborative model for a community seeking to live out a shared mission, but remaining responsive to the ever-changing needs of its members and the broader community. Together, the *Spiritual Exercises* and the *Constitutions* illuminate the spiritual life Ignatius sought for himself and his companions. They also make apparent the unusually adaptive and open structure of the Society itself and its understanding of its own work in the world. It is the adaptiveness and openness characteristic of the Ignatian approach to companionship that makes it such a useful source of insight about friendship in difficult circumstances.

Ignatius was born into a privileged family and led what can only be described as an eventful and exciting life, but he also faced his share of challenges and difficulties. A soldier in his younger days, he was badly injured in battle and suffered through a prolonged and arduous recovery. During that time period, he underwent the spiritual awakening that eventually led him to form the Jesuit order. Importantly, his conversion did not present him with any sort of fully articulated plan of action. Indeed, he had little idea about what exactly he was called to do, other than to "help souls," as he was fond of saying. The road toward the Society of Jesus was circuitous, and involved what we might describe as some wrong turns. What Ignatius did have was confidence that he was doing God's will and the companionship of other like-minded people. Some of these companions came and went; others stayed and joined Ignatius as the original members of the Society. It is clear, however, that the presence of these companions was enormously influential on Ignatius himself and on the eventual shape of the Society.

Biographical accounts of Ignatius during the years leading up to the founding of the order, as well as the years afterward, show just how much he relied on the wisdom and judgment of his companions, and the divine guidance he believed it reflected.[12] Ignatian spiritual practice focuses on discerning God's will for oneself and one's life, and Ignatius took very seriously the results of such discernment in his colleagues. This led to what might seem like a somewhat disjointed and scattershot way of proceeding, especially during the earliest years of the Society. Although the companions had their initial base in Paris, they often went in separate directions (with Francis Xavier heading to India and later Japan and China). They also engaged in constant discernment and readjustment of their plans, based on their varying experiences and abruptly changing circumstances. Ignatius had the idea that he and his companions would become missionaries to the Holy Land; instead, they found themselves setting up schools, first in Messina, and then gradually spreading throughout other parts of Italy and eventually other parts of the world. Although most people now associate the Jesuits with their highly respected secondary schools and universities, it was certainly not what they set out to do or initially saw as the defining mission of their order.

What drew them into education? The short answer is that they saw a need within the new order and in the surrounding communities, and they responded to that need.[13] The foundational principle for the Jesuits is to free themselves to discern and do God's will as it presents itself in the world. Their aim, in the words of Ignatius, is simply to help souls, and the mission of the Society is to help souls in whatever way that prayerful discernment directs. Since the founding of the Jesuit order, that capacity for prayerful discernment has been shaped and cultivated in crucial ways by the practice of the Exercises. The Exercises seek to help a person become the kind of person who is capable of doing what she is called to do in the world.

The Exercises, as Ignatius conceived of them, consist of a progressive set of imaginative reflections, meditations, and contemplative activities. The division into four weeks is mostly metaphorical. Although Jesuits and some laypeople do in fact spend a month in retreat doing the Exercises, the weeks

[12] For a comprehensive account of the early Jesuit companions, see J. W. O'Malley, SJ, *The First Jesuits* (Cambridge, MA: Harvard University Press, 1993).

[13] For the longer answer, see J. W. O'Malley, SJ, "How the First Jesuits Became Involved in Education," in G. Traub, SJ (ed.), *A Jesuit Education Reader* (Chicago, IL: Loyola Press, 2008), 43–62.

aren't necessarily to be taken as literal time periods.[14] They are more like landscapes through which a person travels, stopping for rest or nourishment at certain points along the way. The aim of the Exercises is to cultivate in the retreatant a state of interior openness to God and God's activity in that person's life. That requires that the person acquire awareness of his or her own passions, attachments, and motivations and become free of anything that takes the person away from God.

Given how focused the Exercises are on the interior experience of the person undertaking them, it may seem strange to look to them for illumination about friendship. But as we have already seen, Ignatius himself relied heavily on his companions and their own processes of discernment when making decisions about the future of the order. Ignatian spirituality is at once personal and collaborative. The collaboration is necessary not simply because we live and work with others, but because we need the insight of those others to help us complete the interior work of the Exercises. In the Ignatian tradition, the Exercises are undertaken with a director, an experienced companion whose task is to discern the needs and desires of the retreatant and provide gentle, careful guidance at each step. The job of the director is not to set an agenda, but to accompany the retreatant on his or her movement through each of the four weeks. This means that Ignatian spiritual direction is a dynamic process with no defined set of procedures or rules. It is, rather, a deeply personal relationship aimed at the retreatant's own spiritual growth as she understands it. The process cannot work unless both the retreatant and the director are prepared to be receptive to insights and experiences that might produce unexpected alterations in the plan. The director does not know where the retreat will lead any more than the retreatant. The Exercises are a shared journey along a path that is different every time.

I will return to this idea of accompanying someone on an unclear path in Part III. First, however, I want to expand on three themes from the Exercises, themes that help us understand what friendship characterized by Ignatian ideals and principles might be like in general and specifically in times of despair. These themes are: 1) the interior experience of consolation and desolation; 2) the state of being present to someone or some experience; 3) the process of discernment about courses of action. I should note that by highlighting these three themes, I am addressing only a small part of the Exercises, which are rich with material for reflection. I am also taking

[14] Ignatius himself made provisions for people to do the Exercises in other timeframes, with the 19th Annotation being widely practiced among laypeople.

up a single angle on the themes, and there are certainly many others. My aim is to show how these themes can help us think better about the specific challenges suffering poses to friendship.

One of the central insights of Ignatian spirituality is that the human experience is characterized by periods of what Ignatius called desolation and consolation. Desolation, as described in the quote from the *Spiritual Exercises* that opened Part II of this chapter, is fundamentally an experience of isolation or separation from God, although the subject of the experience may not think about it that way. Consolation, by contrast, is a feeling of drawing closer to God, and of feeling God's loving embrace. The Exercises encourage introspection and self-awareness about one's inner state, with a particular emphasis on what kinds of prayers, activities, and thoughts produce feelings of consolation and desolation. As Ignatius describes them, consolation and desolation are primarily a matter of a person's inner experience and reactions, but it seems plausible to think that in at least some cases, these states arise as a result of external events and circumstances that catapult us into joy or anguish. It is not always predictable how this will occur; the death of a child can strengthen the faith of one parent while destroying every shred of it in another. What *is* predictable is that every human life will include these periods of consolation and desolation. The Exercises certainly aim at helping retreatants identify and cultivate sources of consolation, but Ignatius was under no illusions that the Exercises would provide any kind of easy cure for despair and suffering.[15]

Let me now turn to the second theme, which is that of presence. Ignatian spirituality is in many ways most deeply about presence – being present in contemplative prayer and feeling the presence of God in one's surroundings and in daily activities. The Exercises encourage presence in a variety of ways, including contemplation, meditation, and imaginative reflection. A crucial aspect of the Exercises is that it is not a purely, or even primarily, rational endeavor. The prayers and activities of the Exercises engage the emotions, in part by harnessing the retreatant's imaginative capacities. Retreatants may be asked to imagine themselves in various circumstances or settings, including Gospel stories. The idea is to cultivate the capacity to enter more fully and purposefully into some particular moment or experience.

[15] This point is well illustrated in the letters of Mother Teresa, who herself struggled through long periods of what Ignatius describes as desolation. See *Come Be My Light: The Private Writings of the Saint of Calcutta*, ed. B. Kolodiejchuk, MC (New York: Doubleday, 2007).

In an influential essay on Ignatian spirituality, Howard Gray gives an account of Ignatian engagement with other persons that is helpful for understanding this idea of presence. He distinguishes among three elements: attention, reverence, and devotion.[16] Gray defines attention as "allowing the reality of the other to be present to you in all its integrity." This is harder than it seems, as it requires that we be capable of setting aside our own ideas, plans, and frameworks in order to see what is in front of us more fully, more openly, and more accurately. It is a receptivity to what is there, taking the time and trouble to see it properly. Attentiveness must be followed by reverence. As Gray puts it, "reverence means that what one has been attentive to must now be accepted as it is, in its own terms."[17] Like attentiveness, reverence requires that we set aside ourselves and our own wishes and desires and simply acknowledge the reality we perceive, without necessarily trying to alter it to suit our own desires.[18] Finally, there is devotion, which Gray describes as a "moment when the heart is touched, drawing the person to greater love or deeper faith."[19] It is through fully attending to another person that we can come to value them and love them for who and what they already are. In order to do this, we must cultivate certain dispositions in ourselves, dispositions that enable us to engage with the world receptively and lovingly, open to whatever it is we might perceive and where it might take us. Ignatian spiritual practice aims at producing not a particular outcome, but a particular approach to the world.

The third and final theme is that of discernment, which we might describe as the art of wise decision making. Ignatian spirituality hardly has a monopoly on this concept, but Ignatian discernment does have distinctive elements. The idea is that the disposition of open, loving attention to the world makes it possible to see better what God wills for the world and for the person undertaking the discernment. Ignatius made a point of saying that big decisions should not be made in times of either desolation or consolation, believing that these might produce distortions in our perceptions. The appropriate state of mind for Ignatian discernment is one of robust self-awareness. The person must be attentive to the various patterns of emotion and response into which she tends to fall, so that she is able to reflect honestly and openly about what is pulling her in

[16] H. Gray, SJ, "Ignatian Spirituality," in G. Traub, SJ (ed.), *An Ignatian Spirituality Reader* (Chicago: Loyola Press, 2008), 64.

[17] Gray, "Ignatian Spirituality," 65.

[18] For a slightly different, but largely compatible account of reverence, see P. Woodruff, *Reverence: Renewing a Forgotten Virtue*, 2nd ed. (Oxford University Press, 2014).

[19] Gray, "Ignatian Spirituality," 66.

certain directions or making certain courses of action seem particularly salient or appealing. She must also be sufficiently receptive to new possibilities and challenges that make themselves visible to her during the process of discernment. Just as Ignatius had to be open to the idea of creating schools, despite that not being the original plan, so the person engaging in Ignatian discernment has to be open to the idea that she may be called to do things or take on tasks that never occurred to her or that she may think herself unequipped to take on.

These three themes – consolation and desolation, presence, and discernment – are important to understanding not just Ignatian spirituality, but also distinctively Ignatian companionship. Consider, again, the role of the spiritual director in the Exercises. The director has the task of guiding the person's reflections in such a way as to cultivate the relevant dispositions in that person. She must be able to recognize indications of desolation and help the person become aware of them himself – no small task. It requires that the director be fully present to the retreatant and his experiences, both those he can articulate and those he cannot. The director's role is a dynamic one, always shifting in response to the individual retreatant's needs. Judging how to respond to those needs requires skills of discernment on the part of the director. The goal is to point the retreatant in directions that will be beneficial while remaining in a fundamentally background role. Her job is not to lead the person to God directly; rather, her role is better described as clearing away the brush so that the person can see her own way forward.

The Ignatian spiritual director is, in many ways, a complete friend in Aristotle's sense.[20] She takes up the good of the retreatant as her own and becoming a good for the retreatant. One of her primary tasks is to help the retreatment identify moments and experiences of consolation in her life. But there is another sense in which she herself is a kind of consolation, insofar as her activity has the effect of making it easier for the person to find her way to God. This happens as much through her presence as through anything that she says or does. The point of spiritual direction is not instruction; it is accompaniment. The director cannot accompany someone well unless she is prepared to follow the same uncertain path the early Jesuits did. The same is true for the retreatant. Neither knows in advance how the Exercises will turn out, but they are committed to heading into it together.

[20] David McPherson has pointed out to me that many relationships of spiritual direction lack the persistence and pervasiveness of Aristotelian friendship. They may also be closer to relationships of unequals in Aristotle's terminology.

I suggest that the model exemplified in this relationship between the spiritual director and the retreatant is useful in helping us think about friendship in times of despair. The habits and dispositions cultivated through the Exercises and exemplified in the spiritual director's work are the habits and dispositions of a friend in a more general sense. To be a good friend to someone in a time of desolation is to be the face of God for that person, a living, instantiated reminder of God and God's presence. In the Ignatian tradition, it matters little whether the sufferer would describe it in those terms. The point is to help the sufferer feel embraced by love itself, even in the midst of that suffering. This is how an Ignatian companion is consolation to another, and this is how such companions are goods for each other.

III

> Come sit beside me on my mourning bench.[21]

In this last section of this essay, I will draw together these two accounts of friendship in the context of friendship in times of despair. There are, of course, many forms of despair, but I will focus on situations in which one of the friends is going through a personal tragedy of some kind, such as her own grave illness or impending death, or that of a loved one. Such events are common occurrences in any human life, but they pose a significant challenge to friendship. My goal in this last section of this essay is to consider how the Aristotelian and Ignatian pictures of Parts I and II shed some light on what it takes to share another's suffering well.

The quote that opens this section is from *Lament for a Son* by philosopher and theologian Nicholas Wolterstorff, whose twenty-five-year-old son died in a mountain climbing accident. *Lament for a Son* is a reflection on grief, both as an abstract concept and as a personal experience. Wolterstorff notes that there is a tendency for people to minimize or explain away suffering, with the effect of creating distance between themselves and the sufferer:

> But please: Don't say it's not really so bad. Because it is. Death is awful, demonic. If you think your task as comforter is to tell me that really, all things considered, it's not so bad, you do not sit with me in my grief but place yourself off in the distance away from me. Over there, you are of no help. What I need to hear from you is that you recognize how painful

[21] N. Wolterstorff, *Lament for a Son* (Grand Rapids, MI: Wm. B. Eerdsman Publishing, 1987), 34.

> it is. I need to hear from you that you are with me in my desperation. To comfort me, you have to come close. Come sit beside me on my mourning bench.[22]

Friendship in times of despair is a matter of coming close. This, however, is a challenging thing to do well. As we will see, it requires what we can describe as the cultivation of a specific disposition or virtue.

Wolterstorff describes his experience of grief as deeply isolating and alienating. In his grief, he no longer sees the world as he did before, and he is unable to engage with it as he did before and as other people still do: "I walked into a store. The ordinariness of what I saw repelled me: people putting onions into baskets, squeezing melons, hoisting gallons of milk, clerks ringing up sales."[23] The result is that he feels alone in the world, out of step with it, even when among fellow grievers:

> Though united in that we are grieving, we grieve differently. As each death has its own character, so too each grief over a death has its own character – its own inscape. The dynamics of each person's sorrow must be allowed to work themselves out without judgment. I may find it strange that you should be tearful today but dry-eyed yesterday when my tears were yesterday. But my sorrow is not your sorrow. There's something more: I must struggle so hard to regain life that I cannot reach out to you. Nor you to me. The one not grieving must touch us both.[24]

Here we see both the presence of desolation and an opening for consolation. But the individuality, the solitude of the grief is a challenge. It is not enough to know that we should try to help a grieving friend; we must figure out how we come close enough to sit beside her on her mourning bench. It calls for a certain interior awareness that enables us to be fully present to the suffering friend and succeed in being a good to her.

One of Wolterstorff's striking insights is that even words intending to be comforting can have the effect of making the sufferer feel even more alone. He experienced attempts at consolation that minimized his loss not as comfort, but as distancing. The people who told him that death wasn't really demonic were, from Wolterstorff's standpoint, putting themselves further away from him and his suffering. In his book *A Grief Observed*, C. S. Lewis describes his own similar reaction to people who tried to use Christian theology (or at least certain platitudinous versions of it) to comfort him during the painful death of his wife:

[22] Wolterstorff, *Lament for a Son*, 34. [23] Wolterstorff, *Lament for a Son*, 52.
[24] Wolterstorff, *Lament for a Son*, 56.

> Talk to me about the truth of religion and I'll listen gladly. Talk to me about the duty of religion and I'll listen submissively. But don't come talking to me about the consolations of religion or I shall suspect that you don't understand. . . . If a mother is mourning not for what she has lost but for what her dead child has lost, it is a comfort to believe that the child has not lost the end for which it was created. And it is a comfort to believe that she herself, in losing her chief or only natural happiness, has not lost a greater thing, that she may still hope to "glorify God and enjoy Him forever." A comfort to the God-aimed, eternal spirit within her. But not to her motherhood. The specifically maternal happiness must be written off. Never, in any place or time, will she have her son on her knees, or bathe him, or tell him a story, or plan for his future, or see her grandchild.[25]

Lewis found no solace in his faith during certain periods of his grief. When he sought out God in his desperation, he experienced this response, which is an apt description of desolation: "A door slammed in your face, and a sound of bolting and double bolting on the inside. After that, silence. You may as well turn away."[26] Lewis was not inclined to doubt God's existence in his grief, although many people are. His desolation was mostly expressed as anger at God and doubts about God's ultimate goodness:

> Not that I am (I think) in much danger of ceasing to believe in God. The real danger is of coming to believe such dreadful things about Him. The conclusion I dread is not, "So there's no God after all," but "So this is what God's really like. Deceive yourself no longer."[27]

It seems unlikely that Lewis, at that particular point in his life, would have found consolation in any attempts at theodicy. There could be no comfort for him in a defense of God's ultimate goodness or a description of a happy reunion in heaven. The loss he mourned was the loss of the living, breathing human being who was his wife, and no theological abstraction was capable of reaching that part of his pain. Even direct personal appeals to God left him feeling abandoned and alone in his suffering.

The idea that religion may be unable to console a religious believer may seem unnerving. What Wolterstorff and Lewis found so alienating, however, was not religion itself, but rather a particular use of religion. Consider how common it is for people who have suffered through the death of a child to be told that it is part of God's plan, or that God had a reason for it, or that their precious child is now an angel. Although some people might find such remarks consoling, others do not. Not all grieving parents are

[25] C. S. Lewis, *A Grief Observed* (San Francisco, CA: HarperCollins, 1961), 25–7.
[26] Lewis, *A Grief Observed*, 6. [27] Lewis, *A Grief Observed*, 6–7.

theists, of course, but even theists may hear such remarks as a dismissal of their loss as unimportant or even good in the broad scheme of things. As Lewis points out, this fails to acknowledge the reality of the loss for those parents and its shattering effects on their lives.

We might think, then, that the lesson is simply to avoid making platitudinous remarks. And yet, the problem isn't really with the remarks, annoying as they may be. Such misplaced attempts at consolation often fail not because of the words chosen, but because of the person choosing the words. Some people respond to the tragedies of friends by simply drifting away. This kind of distancing is familiar enough, but there is a more subtle form of distancing that can happen even when the would-be-consoler stays nearby, trying to help. It arises from our own fears and anxieties, and can deceive us into thinking that words that comfort us will also comfort the sufferer. When it comes to death and dying, we are prone to engaging in a great deal of magical thinking, as Joan Didion has so aptly put it.[28] If we can chalk up the other person's circumstances to some fault, some misstep, some past sin, then we can rest in the illusion that we ourselves are not vulnerable to the same suffering. Likewise, if we can minimize the badness of the person's loss, we can shield ourselves from the possibility of having to face such pain ourselves. In other words, we make the other person's suffering about ourselves, not about them. To some extent, that is because their suffering *is* our suffering, as we saw in Aristotle's account of complete friends. It really is terrible to draw close to a suffering friend and see the landscape as they see it. But that is precisely what friends must do.

In her memoir about the death of her infant son from Tay-Sachs disease, Emily Rapp suggests that mothers of dying children are simply too frightening for many people to face:

> Our grief is primal and unwieldy and it embarrasses people. Talking about end-of-life care decisions for our babies to a bunch of parents with typically developing kids is tantamount to breathing fire at a dinner party or on the playground. Nobody wants to see what we see so clearly. Nobody wants to know the truth about their children, about themselves: that none of it is forever.[29]

For Rapp, this is as much about the unwillingness to see as the inability to see. We fail to come close to suffering people not because we can't imagine their pain, but because we don't *want* to imagine it.

[28] J. Didion, *The Year of Magical Thinking* (New York: Alfred Knopf, 2005).

[29] E. Rapp, *The Still Point of a Turning World* (New York: Penguin, 2013), 18.

When we are faced with someone else's suffering, there is a strong temptation to deal with it by taking it into our own hands and shaping it into something we find more palatable. But if I recast my friend's experience to make it fit with what I would prefer it to be, I render myself unable to be a good for her. As Wolterstorff says, I place myself away from her when she needs me to come close. Coming close, though, requires that I first become aware of myself and my own motivations. I have to be able to recognize the difference between joining my friend in her grief and taking it over to make it more bearable for me. This is possible only by cultivating a disposition that is at once focused inward on myself and outward on my friend. I have to know myself before I can place myself next to her.

As I said in Part II, the individual reflections and prayers of the Exercises often ask the retreatant to engage in imaginative activities. Many of these activities involve imagining oneself in a scene from the Gospels, taking up the perspective of the people in it and how they experience what is happening. In the context of the Exercises, these reflections seek to bring the person closer to the person of Jesus, but they also help cultivate a sense of what it means to be present in a particular moment as it is occurring. It is not about writing a new story; it is about using one's imagination to put oneself in a story that is not one's own.

The early Jesuits set out with each other on a path that at many points was quite uncertain. They did not know where they would be going, what they would be doing, or how they would manage it. Ignatian spiritual practice is, in many ways, about cultivating one's own ability to walk into such uncertainty with faith and hope. The spiritual director needs this disposition in order to be a companion to retreatants making the Exercises, where they will cultivate it themselves. And friends need this disposition in order to accompany each other into the abyss of illness and death.

The disposition is one that we might describe as a kind of selfless self-awareness. We need to be able to see when our own needs and anxieties are intruding on the other's experience in such a way that we are not really sharing it. Employing Gray's framework, we might say that to console a suffering friend, we need attention, reverence, and devotion. We have to acknowledge the reality of the suffering and our friend's experience of it without trying to recast or alter it to suit our own desires. If I am insisting that everything will turn out all right because I need to believe that in order to alleviate my own anxiety, then I am not being fully present to my friend as her companion. I may think that I am diminishing her pain, in the way that Aristotle says friends do, but that would be a mistake. Rather, I am just attempting to change it so that it becomes less terrifying for me. Sitting beside a friend on her mourning bench requires that I be open to seeing the view from where she is, even when the view is bleak. This is not to say that we should deceive ourselves into thinking we understand just how our friend feels or what the loss means to her. That would just be another way of reshaping her experience to suit me. The goal is not to try to make sense of her loss, either for her or for myself. It is simply to be present in it with her, to share the activity of grief and mourning with her.

This kind of presence demands a great deal from us in some ways, but not in others. It does not demand that we offer explanations, defenses, or reasons for what has happened. It does not demand that the consoler herself even believe that there is an explanation for what has happened. The consoler need not be a believer herself, and she certainly doesn't need the kind of religious certainty we think spiritual consolation requires. Ignatian consolation requires that we *be* the presence of God for another, but it does not ask us to make sense of God or the suffering. It asks only that we witness it with our friend and stay with her. Rapp is not a theist in any traditional sense, but she describes her experience of accompanying her son Ronan through his short life in quintessentially Ignatian terms: "My plan was simple and yet impossible: to go with him as far as I could along this journey that we call life, to be with him as deeply as I could from moment to moment, and then to let him go."[30]

Rapp's simple, impossible plan is not very specific, but it is hard to imagine how it could be. As she knows, her only real job is to love her son through it all. She does not know, and could not know, what that will entail for her. Her love for Ronan is expressed through her commitment to go with him and be with him, wherever that takes her. She declines to think of this as brave, since, as she says, she has no other real choice. That is of course true, but we might rightly consider her brave in virtue of her willingness to face her own despair and commit to loving Ronan fully through it all.

In the face of a grim diagnosis, the path ahead for both the sufferer and her friends is often a very uncertain one. This is true of both the outcome and the experiences they will face along the way. Friendship commits us to walking along that uncertain path with the sufferer, without knowing where it will go or what it will require of us. We have to be prepared to take up new tasks, including profoundly challenging ones, if that is what our friend needs from us. Most importantly, we must be willing to confront our own darkest fears so that we can be present to our friend and share in the difficult activities that now characterize her life.

[30] Rapp, *The Still Point of a Turning World*, 114.

In this section, I have been describing the disposition needed to serve as true consolation for suffering friends. It requires that we reflect on our own inner tendencies, fears, and desires so that we can recognize when we are using them as self-protection. I can only be a good to my friend if I can come close to her; if I cannot free myself from my own fear and despair, I will distance myself instead. I must be open to her despair and love her well enough to accompany her on a path about which we know nothing, except that it will be painful for both of us. Although Aristotle's complete friends wish to spare each other pain, they also wish to face it together.

Aristotle and Ignatius share the view that friendship is an essential component of a good human life, making us better and making our lives better. We are goods for our friends and they are goods for us. This is true even when our shared activities are painful ones. In such circumstances, virtuous friends are genuine consolation to each other simply through their presence. Ignatian spirituality gives us insight into what such consolation looks like and what it requires from us. The Exercises also give us tools with which to cultivate it. The challenge of friendship in times of despair is to do what seems impossible to help each other bear what seems unbearable. In this way, we somehow make the experience both possible and bearable. Friends extend our capacities in moments of desolation, enabling us to face well what we cannot at any rate avoid. The shared activities of virtuous friends are not always enjoyable, but they are no less noble for that. As Aristotle put it, "anyone who is to be happy, then, must have excellent friends."[31, 32]

[31] Aristotle, *Nicomachean Ethics*, 1170b18.

[32] I have been exceptionally lucky to be surrounded with good companions. When it comes to understanding Ignatius himself and Ignatian spirituality, I am especially indebted to Tony Moore, Howard Gray, SJ, Phil Burroughs, SJ, Kevin O'Brien, SJ, and John O'Malley, SJ. I am also grateful to David McPherson for his helpful comments on this chapter, and to the friends who have allowed me the grace of sharing in their suffering.

CHAPTER 10

Starting with Compassion

Richard White

There is a view, widespread among different spiritual traditions, that authentic spiritual life really begins with the death of the ego and our need to hold on to a separate, self-centered existence: as Rumi says frequently, "You must die before you die!" In Christianity (or Islam), we must subordinate our own will to the will of God; in Stoicism, we should think of our reason as a fragment of the divine Logos and accept whatever happens as the will of the cosmos itself. For Buddhist thinkers, the achievement of compassion is a kind of ego death, and in this respect, it can also be viewed as the true starting point of spiritual life. The seventh-century writer Śāntideva puts it this way:

> Whoever longs to rescue quickly both himself and others should practice the supreme mystery: exchange of self and other.[1]

Compassion – "the supreme mystery" – is based on the equivalence of self and other. In a sense, we are all the same because we all suffer, and so:

> I should dispel the suffering of others because it is suffering like my own suffering. I should help others too because of their nature as beings, which is like my own being.[2]

Without compassion, I remain separate and fixed, and I treat whatever is outside of me like an object to be used or known. But with compassion, the well-being of others becomes a significant part of my own well-being. The experience of compassion opens me up to the lives of others, and it takes me beyond my own selfish horizons. And by undermining a strong sense of my own separate self, it puts me in touch with a spiritual reality that would otherwise be unknown to me.

[1] Śāntideva, *The Bodhicaryāvatāra*, trans. K. Crosby and A. Skilton (Oxford University Press, [ca. 725] 2008), 99.

[2] Śāntideva, *The Bodhicaryāvatāra*, 96.

None of this is self-evident, of course, and philosophers in the Western tradition have routinely condemned compassion as a sign of weakness or a refusal to be oneself. Kant does not consider compassion a real virtue; Nietzsche views compassion as "the last temptation of Zarathustra," or the ultimate impediment to personal sovereignty; and even the Stoics, who have a lot in common with Buddhists in other respects, seem to deride compassion as a serious failing. I think we have to ask ourselves, what is going on here? Am I really in danger of losing myself if I follow my compassionate impulses? And how do Western philosophers, like the Stoics, Kant, or Nietzsche, think that we should deal with the problem of suffering?

This chapter considers the important insight that compassion is the everyday origin of spiritual life and so we must start with compassion. It is not intended as a defense of Buddhism or any other view, although I think that the Buddhist emphasis on compassion (and the Christian emphasis on love) is correct. I begin with a discussion of what compassion is, focusing mainly on Buddhism and Western thought. Then I consider the value of compassion and its criticism by Western philosophers, as well as possible responses. Does anyone really think that there is too much compassion? This seems unlikely, given everything else that's going on in the world, and so in the final part of this chapter, I think in more practical terms about how to *enhance* compassion as a virtue. For as Aristotle says, the whole point of studying ethics is to make us better people.

I

We can begin with basic concepts: compassion, pity, empathy, and the relationship between them. First, the English word "compassion" is derived from the Greek *pathein*, meaning to suffer or experience, and *com* or with, which means that compassion involves suffering *with* someone else. But what exactly does this mean? I think that we are typically afraid of someone else's suffering, let alone our own, and part of us wants to run away from another's misery just because it is difficult to deal with, and we fear the contagion of suffering. In this respect, compassion can be viewed as a form of strength, because it involves *staying open to suffering*, and not avoiding it by one ruse or another. Compassion involves being on the same level as the one who is suffering, for it signifies that I take her misfortune seriously and it is also a source of sadness for me. Compassion, we could say, is a *horizontal* relationship in which the subject, the one who experiences compassion, exchanges himself for the one who is in distress by putting himself in her situation and "feeling for her," at the same time that he tries to bring relief. In this way, compassion involves identification with others, and experiencing the common reality of suffering, which is a part of the human condition.

Looking at things the other way, when *we* are suffering, we feel a kind of alienation from the world around us. Suffering isolates us, and so we respond positively to another's compassion because it brings us back in to the world. We are grateful for compassion; even if it is only a few words of commiseration or just a smile or a nod, it can mean a lot because it shows that in spite of everything we are still cared for and held in some esteem. This is in contrast to pity. Pity is a *vertical* relationship in which I look down on someone. "I pity you," I say with contempt; or else we insist that we don't *want* someone else's pity. But I don't think we mind compassion, because compassion involves identification and acceptance.

Compassion is related to empathy: empathy implies putting yourself in someone else's place to the extent that you can feel what he or she is feeling. And so if you lose all your money or suffer a terrible setback, I can feel your pain because this may be something that has happened to me, and I know exactly what it's like. Empathy seems to involve a blurring of the boundaries between the self and the other person: when I say, "I feel your pain," I mean what I am saying, and I may remember all the anguish I felt when I was in your situation. – But then the problem is that it's still about me! In compassion, on the other hand, I respond to the other person as a separate being that I respect, just because he or she is the one who is suffering at this moment. I don't lose myself in compassion, but when I experience compassion, I put my own selfish projects to one side, and I focus my attention on the other person as the one who must be cared for. As Thich Nhat Hanh puts it: "Compassion contains deep concern. You know the other person is suffering, so you sit close to her. You look and listen deeply to her to be able to touch her pain. You are in deep communication, deep communion with her, and that alone brings some relief."[3] From all of this, we may conclude that compassion involves being affected by the suffering of another *and* having the desire to respond or help. On the face of it, it sounds like compassion involves being passive and we might be tempted to think of it as nothing more than feeling sorry for someone else. But compassion is more than this: it involves respect and caring, and it is active as well as passive because it includes the impulse to help or give comfort to another (which may or may not be stronger

[3] T. Nhat Hanh, *Teachings on Love* (Berkeley, CA: Parallax Press, 2007), 6.

than other impulses like repulsion or fear). In this respect, it implies a fundamental movement away from our usual self-involvement.

In Buddhism, *karuna* is listed among the Four Immeasurables, or sublime attitudes, along with *maitri* (loving-kindness), *upeksha* (equanimity), and *mudita* (sympathetic joy).[4] *Karuna* is usually translated as "compassion," and there is no question that it is among the most important of all the Buddhist virtues, especially when it is informed by wisdom. It is the wish for all beings to be free from suffering; by cultivating this attitude through meditation, and thereby transforming ourselves, we may benefit an innumerable number of beings. But is *karuna* the same thing as compassion? And is it a "virtue" in the same sense as courage, generosity, and all the other recognizable virtues in the Western tradition? In his discussion of *karuna*, Thich Nhat Hanh comments as follows:

> *Karuna* is both a Sanskrit and a Pali word and it is usually translated as "compassion," but that is not exactly correct. "Compassion" is composed of com ("together with") and passion ("to suffer"). But we do not need to suffer to remove suffering from another person. Doctors, for instance, can relieve their patients' suffering without experiencing the same disease in themselves. If we suffer too much, we may be crushed and unable to help. Still, until we find a better word, let us use "compassion" to translate *karuna*.[5]

This is an important qualification, and we certainly oversimplify matters by presenting *karuna* as the chief Buddhist virtue, and the same thing as "compassion," that we must cultivate if we want to become better persons. In Western ethics, the ideal of self-cultivation is supposed to lead to personal happiness or fulfillment as its goal. From the Buddhist perspective, however, the goal cannot simply be one of personal happiness, because it is ultimately impossible to separate my own well-being from the well-being of all sentient beings. On this view, I am not a separate being, but a part of the stream of life. It would also be a mistake to think of the ego's achievement of virtue as a spiritual goal; such an attitude would manifest spiritual pride, and it would only affirm the ego that should be overcome. In his book *Cutting Through Spiritual Materialism*, Chögyam Trungpa underlines this point when he notes that compassion is not to be understood as a personal achievement since this is ultimately self-regarding. On the contrary, compassion is an impersonal force – one of the immeasurables – that opens us up to all of the energies of life. As he puts it:

[4] See, for example, Thich Nhat Hanh's discussion in *Teachings on Love*, 3–9.
[5] Nhat Hanh, *Teachings on Love*, 6.

> Compassion has nothing to do with achievement at all. It is spacious and very generous. When a person develops real compassion, he is uncertain whether he is being generous to others or to himself because compassion is environmental generosity, without direction, without "for me" and without "for them." It is filled with joy, spontaneously existing joy, constant joy in the sense of trust, in the sense that joy contains tremendous wealth, richness.[6]

On this reading, true compassion (*karuna*) is not a limited personal capacity, or a sorrowful state of mind, but a real force in the universe that involves responsiveness and receptivity to suffering wherever it occurs. It is not based on our own projections but on the pure responsiveness to need, and regardless of whether we are dealing with an "enemy" or a "friend." According to Trungpa, compassion is a kind of "crazy wisdom": "It is totally wise, but it is crazy as well, because it does not relate to ego's literal and simple-minded attempts to secure its own comfort."[7]

From this it follows that the highest kind of compassion is much more than an emotional response. For Trungpa and other Buddhists, compassion – or *karuna* – is also a form of wisdom because it reflects the (Buddhist) view that everything is impermanent; there is no substantial or underlying self; and everything is interdependent and connected through dependent origination. In compassion (as *karuna*), I grasp this fundamental reality since I am beyond any absolute distinction between myself and others; and this makes compassion the most appropriate response. But does this mean that "compassion" and "*karuna*" are only loosely related to each other, insofar as both of them involve responding to the needs of others? In the end, it might be argued that they are ultimately incommensurable because the Buddhist concept of *karuna* presupposes a particular kind of metaphysics (no-self, impermanence, dependent origination, etc.), whereas the Western view regards compassion as an ethical achievement or a personal virtue that inspires and enhances the life of the community. Or is there some way in which we can bring these two different concepts together, to show how compassion and *karuna* are related ideals that can illuminate each other?

On this point, the Dalai Lama's work is helpful. The Dalai Lama is a relevant thinker because he comes from the Tibetan Buddhist tradition in which these kinds of spiritual issues have been discussed in more depth and more detail than probably anywhere else. But at the same time, the Dalai Lama is very much aware of the Western concept of compassion, and in his

6 C. Trungpa, *Cutting Through Spiritual Materialism* (Boston, MA: Shambhala, 2002), 98–9.
7 Trungpa, *Cutting Through Spiritual Materialism*, 210.

more popular books he has sought to build a bridge between the Buddhist view and the traditional Western mode of understanding. In books like *How to Expand Love* and *An Open Heart*, for example, he asks us to think of compassion as a kind of process or continuum that leads from basic empathy to the highest level of compassion, which is called (in Tibetan) *nying je chenmo*, or the "great compassion."[8] To begin with, think about how you would teach compassion to a child. Perhaps the first thing would be to get the child to identify with someone else who is going through a difficult time, by asking her, "How would you feel if that happened to you?" In thinking about this, the child might begin to feel what someone else feels. This is empathy, but empathy is only the beginning of fully-fledged compassion, which can gradually be cultivated within ourselves.

In the next stage, we actively cultivate compassion. Compassion is "the wish that others be free of suffering," and it is grounded in feeling and in reason.[9] It goes beyond caring only for those whom we know and love, while it is wary of all emotional states that can undermine it or cause it to burn out. The Dalai Lama comments that putting our altruistic intentions into practice requires much effort and it can be disheartening:

> In the middle stages, when putting altruistic intentions into practice, you discover that it is not easy to help even one sentient being overcome the manifest form of even one type of problem, not to mention overcoming its latent predispositions in the mind. Such improvement requires continuous effort. You might become tired and discouraged, but if you continue to develop compassion you will not lose the altruistic dedication that you generated earlier. If you keep your compassion strong when you encounter difficult circumstances, your commitment will increase naturally. This is the importance of compassion in the middle stages; it is like water nurturing spiritual qualities that will in turn nurture others toward enlightenment.[10]

In other words, compassion inspires more compassion; and every compassionate act will have a kind of ripple effect, inspiring and enhancing the spiritual lives of others.

Finally, at the end of this continuum, one achieves the "great compassion" (*nying je chenmo*), where one is profoundly sensitive to the suffering of others, to such an extent that one's compassion becomes unconditional,

[8] Dalai Lama, *How to Expand Love* (New York: Simon and Schuster, 2005); Dalai Lama, *An Open Heart: Practicing Compassion in Everyday Life* (Boston, MA: Little, Brown, 2001).

[9] See Dalai Lama, *An Open Heart*, 91–106; elsewhere he comments: "True compassion is not just an emotional response but a firm commitment founded on reason" (Dalai Lama, *The Compassionate Life* [Somerville, MA: Wisdom Publications, 2003], 21).

[10] Dalai Lama, *How to Expand Love*, 135.

unlimited, and universal in scope.[11] In the West, probably more often than not, we are told that we should not feel compassion for a criminal or for a truly evil person like Hitler; we are also told that compassion for an animal may be inappropriate because animals are not like us – and this is what Aristotle maintains in his *Rhetoric*.[12] But at the level of the "great compassion," which is also the bodhisattva ideal, compassion has become second nature to us, and responding to the suffering of others has become a basic part of who we are. In fact, we identify so completely with this ideal that we don't see any conflict in following it, even if it goes against what seem to be our own best interests. The point is our center has now shifted from preoccupation with ourselves to a preoccupation with life itself. Hence the vow of the bodhisattva, at the very end of Śāntideva's work, which gives a sense of this possibility – the great compassion as an empowering spiritual ideal:

> As long as space abides and as long as the world abides, so long may I abide destroying the sufferings of the world.
>
> Whatever suffering is in store for the world, may it all ripen in me. May the world find happiness through all the pure deeds of the Bodhisattvas.[13]

From the Western perspective, this may be what Kant and others have called a "regulative ideal" that is meant to guide individual behavior even though we know we may never reach the ultimate goal. But the Buddhist view is that through continual reflection and meditation on this theme, the practitioner may eventually incorporate it at the deepest level of his or her being. Indeed, the practitioner will come to identify so completely with the value of compassion that he or she may eventually become a bodhisattva.

Thus, we can posit a kind of continuum beginning with empathy or feeling sorry or sad for someone. Next comes compassion as a more developed kind of virtuous response. Finally, after this, comes the "great compassion." The Western view of compassion is a part of this continuum along with *karuna* and the bodhisattva ideal, so that the two perspectives can be related to each other. Even so, compassion remains a difficult theme to articulate because from one standpoint, it is an achievement of the self (according to the Western virtue tradition), while from another standpoint (the Buddhist one), it is the *overcoming* of the self – or the separate ego – that allows the bodhisattva to be with others in a way that is completely present or

11 For an extended discussion of *nying je chenmo*, see Dalai Lama, *Ethics for the New Millennium* (New York: Riverhead, 1999), 124.

12 See Aristotle, *Rhetoric* [ca. 325 BC], in *The Basic Works of Aristotle*, ed. R. McKeown (New York: Random House, 1941), 1385b12ff.

13 Śāntideva, *The Bodhicaryāvatāra*, 143.

mindful. All of which may suggest that our spiritual and ethical responses are ultimately tied to our metaphysical beliefs. This is problematic and we will return to this point later, for it is by no means obvious that metaphysics determines the nature of spiritual life. In fact, the opposite may also be true, in the sense that sometimes spirituality helps to shape metaphysical beliefs.

II

What is the value of compassion? In Plato's *Republic*, describing the ideal city is another way of thinking about justice, which is clearly considered the supreme virtue. In Buddhism, a strong case can be made for the priority of compassion as the highest virtue of all. Among his other names, the Buddha is known as "the compassionate one"; and Śāntideva expresses a common Buddhist view in *The Bodhicaryavatara* that compassion must be fostered even if it means assuming the pain of others:

> You may argue: compassion causes us so much suffering, why force it to arise? Yet when one sees how much the world suffers, how can this suffering from compassion be considered great?
>
> If the suffering of one ends the suffering of many, then one who has compassion for others and himself must cause that suffering to arise.[14]

Now we might expect disagreement between Greek and Buddhist philosophers about the ranking of the different virtues. What is more surprising is that compassion is often viewed with real suspicion by Western thinkers, and some philosophers have argued that compassion is actually a vice! This is a striking point, but it's not just a philosophical matter: philosophers reflect and rationalize the values of their communities just as often as they challenge those values; by undervaluing or even rejecting compassion, they seem to confirm a popular prejudice. But why do we have this prejudice against compassion? Why do we often think of compassion as just feeling sorry for someone, or as a kind of weakness that undermines responsible action? In this section, I want to consider the arguments for and against compassion, looking first at Western philosophy, and then at Mahayana Buddhism as the two basic perspectives.[15] How *do* we measure the value of

[14] Śāntideva, *The Bodhicaryāvatāra*, 97.

[15] I do not talk about Christian or Jewish views. The ideal of compassion is celebrated in stories like the Good Samaritan and that of Joseph who forgives his brothers, but the announcement of a final judgment of souls seems to challenge compassion as an ultimate ideal, and this makes things very complicated. But there are also those who think that a belief that "God is love" requires universal salvation or at least God working ceaselessly toward it.

compassion? In this chapter, I am arguing that compassion can be viewed very positively as the basic condition of a spiritual life. But if it could be shown that compassion is a spurious ideal, then we would not be entitled to make any such claims about it.

First, the Stoics point out that we cannot control fame and fortune, health, or any of the vicissitudes of life. But we can control how we respond to whatever happens to us: we can be angry because we didn't get our way, we can be grief stricken about our loss, or we can accept whatever happens without complaint – or even excitement – as the will of the cosmos itself. As Marcus Aurelius says: "Do not be aggrieved, then, if things are not always to your liking. As long as they are in accord with nature, be glad of them, and do not make difficulties."[16] In this regard, the Stoic writings are full of spiritual exercises that help us to focus on our own existence and to strengthen our sense of self. We must anticipate future threats to our spiritual well-being, and we can undermine the sting of loss by reflecting on the death of others before it actually happens. Anything that challenges self-sufficiency or self-control must be rejected as the greatest danger. And this includes compassion, which means abandoning *self*-determination in response to another's distress. Seneca talks about compassion with scorn; it is an unmanly response that leads to the very worst outcomes: "There are women, senile or silly, so affected by the tears of the nastiest criminals that, if they could, they would break open the prison."[17] This suggests a strong distinction between following one's reason, which Stoics view as a fragment of the reason that rules the universe, and not being true to oneself. Many other examples could be given, but the basic point is that Stoics view compassion as a kind of weakness or emotional self-abandonment which goes against the requirements of reason.

Both Kant and Nietzsche are heirs to this tendency, because both of them affirm the priority of personal autonomy in opposition to all the distractions of the world, which could include the suffering and distress of others. Kant is not quite so extreme. In his ethical philosophy, he argues that morality presupposes the autonomy of the individual, which means following the moral law – the rules of reason – that we are bound to respect because *we* are rational beings ourselves. In his writings on virtue, Kant talks about visiting debtors' prisons and sickrooms so that we can cultivate sympathy for others, but he is usually suspicious of emotional responses,

[16] M. Aurelius, *Meditations*, trans. M. Staniforth (London: Penguin [ca. 170–80], 1964), bk. XI, sec. 16.

[17] Seneca, "On Mercy" [ca. 55], in *Seneca's Moral and Political Essays*, ed. J. Cooper and J. Procope (Cambridge University Press, 1995), 161.

and he explicitly affirms the "cold-hearted" benefactor in preference to those who are motivated only by generous or compassionate impulses.[18] His thinking is that emotions come and go, and we cannot base an ethics on something so inconstant. Like the Stoics, Kant argues that the most important thing is to follow the rule of reason and we should not let ourselves be distracted by our emotional responses, which may or may not be in accordance with duty. At one point, Kant offers an argument that even utilitarians would probably embrace: since compassion involves suffering over another's suffering, it cannot be justified because it cannot be right to increase the amount of suffering in the world without good reason: "When another suffers and, although I cannot help him, I let myself be infected by his pain (through my imagination), then two of us suffer, though the evil really (in nature) affects only one. But there cannot be a duty to increase the evil in the world and so to do good from compassion. That would be an insulting kind of beneficence."[19] For the most part, though, Kant seems to insist on the moral irrelevance of our emotional responses, and so compassion is neither good nor bad in any ultimate sense.[20]

By contrast, Nietzsche has the greatest contempt for compassion [*Mitleid*], and in various passages, he reflects the Stoic view that compassion is a kind of self-abandonment. In *Thus Spoke Zarathustra*, for example, he argues that compassion or pity is an offense to the one who is suffering – he should be left alone – while it also diminishes the one who shows compassion, because it is a weakness of the will that distracts one from his own path.[21] We can focus our attention on the following passage, which condenses much of Nietzsche's hostility to compassion, including compassion for oneself. Here, compassion is contrasted with "hardness," which is taken as the preferred disposition. You must become hard, Nietzsche says, for anything gentle is a sign of weakness:

> The Hammer Speaks:
>
> "Why so hard?" The kitchen coal once said to the diamond. "After all, are we not close kin?"

[18] See, for example, I. Kant, *Foundations of the Metaphysics of Morals*, trans. L. W. Beck, 2nd ed. (London: Pearson, [1785] 1989), 14–15 [398–9].

[19] I. Kant, *The Metaphysics of Morals*, trans. M. Gregor (Cambridge University Press, [1797] 1991), 250.

[20] For a discussion of Kant's views on compassion, see D. Cartwright, "Kant's View of the Moral Significance of Kindhearted Emotions and the Moral Insignificance of Kant's View," *Journal of Value Inquiry*, 21 (1987), 291–304.

[21] See F. Nietzsche, *Thus Spoke Zarathustra* [1883–5], in *The Portable Nietzsche*, trans. W. Kaufmann (London: Chatto, 1971), 200–2.

> Why so soft? O my brothers, thus I ask you: are you not after all my brothers?
>
> Why so soft, so pliant and yielding? Why is there so much denial, self-denial, in your hearts? So little destiny in your eyes?
>
> And if you do not want to become destinies and inexorable ones, how can you one day triumph with me?
>
> And if you're hardness does not want to flash and cut and cut through, how can you one day create with me?
>
> For all creators are hard. And it must seem blessedness to you to impress your hand on millennia as on wax.
>
> Blessedness to write on the will of millennia as on bronze – harder than bronze, nobler than bronze. Only the noblest is altogether hard.
>
> This new tablet, O my brothers, I place over you: become hard![22]

For some people, the best response to suffering is just to tough it out, which means becoming hard and impervious to sorrow. But this is not a good response because in hardening ourselves – or becoming fixed and stony – we separate ourselves from all that is gentle and good inside of us. And in becoming hard or oblivious to our own suffering we become oblivious to the suffering of other people. We even become capable of inflicting great suffering on them because we cannot feel our own pain. Of course, there are many difficult life situations where the temptation is just to shut down so that we don't have to experience our own anguish or the suffering of others. But this is a kind of spiritual death that closes us off to the source of life and spiritual renewal.

Much the same can be said about the other arguments against compassion that we have already considered: is compassion a distraction and a sign of personal weakness, or should we think of it as a kind of inner strength? Now certainly, we all have different motivations for what we do, and sometimes the motivation can be avoidance. But at the same time, shutting oneself down, refusing to stay open to suffering, or running away from suffering wherever it occurs is typically a sign of weakness rather than strength, since it derives from an inability to deal with whatever lies outside of our own personal concerns. The Good Samaritan didn't have to stop and help the man who lay beaten on the side of the road, but he stopped just because here was someone who needed help. The Good Samaritan felt compassion for the man, and he acted on this feeling, which probably saved the man's life. This seems an obvious example of compassion as an expression of inner strength. We are not told about any selfish reasons

[22] Nietzsche, *Twilight of the Idols* [1888], in *The Portable Nietzsche*, 563. This passage also appears in *Thus Spoke Zarathustra.*

for his action – like reward or glory or the avoidance of guilt – but even so, the story makes sense because it is possible to care about the well-being of another person even if you have never met them before, just because he or she is someone in distress. And to be capable of putting aside one's own needs, like this, is a sign of strength rather than weakness. As the Dalai Lama says:

> If you have a sense of caring for others, you will manifest a kind of inner strength in spite of your own difficulties and problems. With this strength, your own problems will seem less significant and bothersome to you. By going beyond your own problems and taking care of others, you gain inner strength, self-confidence, courage, and a greater sense of calm. This is a clear example of how one's way of thinking can really make a difference.[23]

So in responding to the other with compassion or love, we actually enhance our sense of who we are. And – *pace* Stoicism – this will never happen if we remain self-contained. Compassion involves opening up to others and responding to their needs, but even though it is based on an emotion, it is also a kind of wisdom – perhaps a *crazy* wisdom – in knowing how to take care of a particular situation. The truth is, through compassion, I come to know myself and I grasp the full extent of what I am really capable of. In this respect, it requires self-overcoming or self-loss as the condition for returning to an enlarged sense of self.

Kant complains that compassion only produces more suffering in the world. He insists that the only thing that's really important is action: you should do the right thing, you should help, but feeling the anguish of another's situation is to create even more pain. But Kant misses the motivational force of compassion. Without compassion, we might have no reason to do the right thing apart from the intellectual recognition of our duty or fear of censure if we acted otherwise. But in compassion, I experience a sense of identification with others, and it motivates me to act for them. On this point, the Dalai Lama notes that there is a qualitative difference between your own suffering and the suffering you feel because another is suffering. For one thing, your own suffering is never freely chosen; you are pinned down by suffering and you cannot escape it just by thinking of something else. In the case of compassion, however, the assumption of suffering is at least in part a voluntary act, and this means that it is not experienced as an intolerable burden, but as something we are capable of affirming for ourselves.[24]

[23] Dalai Lama, *The Compassionate Life*, 13–14.

[24] See the Dalai Lama's discussion in *The Compassionate Life*, 32–3.

We can briefly return to Nietzsche's claim that we should become hard. This may be a part of his polemical attack on Schopenhauer and the "decadent" morality of pity.[25] But the imperative to become hard is also the least spiritual response. By refusing to stay open to suffering – whether our own or anybody else's – we are limiting ourselves to our narrow horizon of existence. Compassion is a much more affirmative possibility since it opens us up to the spiritual dimension of life. Many examples could be given to show the dangers of hardness and the refusal of compassion: the perpetrators of the Holocaust were not afraid to dehumanize the Jews in the way they treated them, and this encouraged others to contribute to their extermination, or just to stand by and watch it happen. Nazi leaders encouraged soldiers to become hard and suppress their natural feelings for the sake of the war and the triumph of the Third Reich.[26]

Now that we have considered the basic objections to compassion, what reasons can there be for embracing compassion as a virtue? In some of his writings, the Dalai Lama argues that compassion is not equivalent to pure altruism, since individuals can benefit themselves by acting with compassion. As he notes:

> Another thing that is quite clear to me is that the moment you think only of yourself, the focus of your whole reality narrows, and because of this narrow focus, uncomfortable things can appear huge and bring you fear and discomfort and a sense of feeling overwhelmed by misery. The moment you think of others with a sense of caring, however your view widens. Within that wider perspective, your own problems appear to be of little significance, and this makes a big difference.[27]

This makes compassion into a kind of "wise selfishness," for when we focus on the difficulties of others, we no longer experience the weight of our own distress, and at the same time we gain a kind of inner strength by assisting other people. I wonder, however, if this way of presenting things – in terms of the difference between my own interests and the interests of others – isn't part of the problem. The Dalai Lama wants to appeal to his Western readers by emphasizing that a life of compassion is of great benefit to whoever pursues it, and that we shouldn't think of such a life as a sacrifice or a loss. But once we start thinking along these lines, we are back to Socrates' dilemma in Book 2 of the *Republic* – for why *should* I pursue a life of virtue?

[25] See Martha Nussbaum's discussion in "Pity and Mercy: Nietzsche's Stoicism," in R. Schacht (ed.), *Nietzsche, Genealogy, Morality* (Berkeley: University of California Press, 1994), 139–67.

[26] See J. Glover, *Humanity: A Moral History of the Twentieth Century* (New Haven, CT: Yale University Press, 2001) for many examples and a much fuller discussion of this point.

[27] Dalai Lama, *The Compassionate Life*, 13.

It is not clear that even Socrates can show that a life devoted to justice is always going to be "happier" than a life devoted to injustice, for many unjust people are apparently successful and happy, while many just people are punished for speaking out, and they may suffer an early demise just for being good. But if this is the case, then presumably we would need to argue against the Dalai Lama that a compassionate life isn't always a happy one. Indeed, the more suffering we are exposed to and the more we try to help others who may not appreciate our efforts, the more we may experience personal distress and compassion burnout. We have to protect ourselves in order to do the greatest good in the long run. But then it seems that compassion becomes a more limited or conditional value, and a personal virtue that depends on our strength of will at any given time.

As I suggested earlier, one way of getting around this issue might be to say that the validity of compassion as a basic virtue is linked to the metaphysics that supports it. In the West, personal identity is usually accepted as a kind of given. We don't necessarily know what it means to be a self, but I think there is a basic belief – both in philosophy and in common life – that we are at least a "self-in-process" or an individual who exists over an extended period of time as a separate being. From the perspective of Western ethical thought, it follows that individuals should try to excel and be accomplished in the virtues that would make them better people. These virtues include wisdom, courage, temperance, justice (for we are social beings), and compassion; but compassion is ambivalent because it seems to undermine our essential autonomy, or self-reliance, insofar as it involves an emotional response rather than an act of reason.

By contrast, the Buddhist metaphysical view emphasizes no-self, impermanence, and "dependent origination" or the ultimate interdependence of everything. And with this kind of metaphysical orientation, compassion seems like the most appropriate response, since it doesn't prioritize self over others. It recognizes suffering as the basic condition of all sentient creatures; it emphasizes "moral luck" as a determining factor – the fact that none of us chooses where we are born, who our parents were, or the values of our society – and so we are dependent on others. And all of *this* leads to a sense of community rather than separation. From this point of view, compassion puts us in touch with the fact that at a deeper level, we are basically alike: we all have the desire to be happy and to live a full life. We want good things for those we care about. And like everyone else, we want love, good health, and some kind of success in whatever we choose to do with our lives. Compassion allows us to become aware of this, and so it puts us in touch with our humanity. Now this is not a straightforward deduction where Buddhist metaphysical beliefs like no-self, karma, and Nirvana serve to justify Buddhist values, including compassion. But the value of compassion is *confirmed* by this background Buddhist metaphysics. In a similar way, the presuppositions of Western metaphysics – primarily religious and philosophical ideas including the self or the idea of an immortal soul – emphasize individualism and produce ambivalence concerning compassion and other emotional responses.

So there probably is a deep connection between our virtues and our metaphysics, and our metaphysical beliefs can shape how we think about our ethical and spiritual lives. But at the same time, the reverse is also true, for ethical and spiritual realities can help to shape our metaphysical beliefs to a considerable extent. Thus, we may respond with compassion to another person or an animal in distress, and because of this natural responsiveness, we may also feel very strongly about the absolute reality of human rights or animal rights. Because of feeling empathy, we may be predisposed to think that the idea of the "self" as a sovereign self-contained existence is basically a fiction. In Buddhism especially, the practical is given priority over the theoretical, which means that Buddhist metaphysical ideas are a kind of "ladder" that can help us toward enlightenment. They are not intended as absolute dogma, and there is a problem if we make a fetish out of specific doctrines or theories. In *The Bodhicaryāvatāra*, for example, Śāntideva encourages us to think of ourselves from the point of view of others. As we have seen, from a Buddhist standpoint, the absolute distinction between self and others is questionable; but at this point in the text, the self–other distinction can help us to cultivate compassion, and this is important since it can ultimately lead to enlightenment. In this way, as with Stoicism, Epicureanism, and other schools, Buddhist philosophy can be thought of as a kind of medicine that helps us to live in the best way – but this is not the same thing as a strict deduction of the truth from a prior metaphysical framework. Instead, theory and practice seem to implicate and enhance each other until we reach the point of a "reflective equilibrium."[28]

In the end, I think that the arguments against compassion fall short, while the arguments in favor of compassion confirm its value both as a

[28] I have benefited from two recent essays that also explore the relationship between the theoretical and the practical aspects of Buddhism: L. E. Patrik, "A Buddhist 'Good Life' Theory: Śāntideva's *Bodhicaryāvatāra*," in W. Sweet (ed.), *Migrating Texts and Traditions* (University of Ottawa Press, 2012), 189–200; and O. Flanagan, "It Takes a Metaphysics: Raising Virtuous Buddhists," in N. E. Snow (ed.), *Cultivating Virtue: Perspectives from Philosophy, Theology, and Psychology* (Oxford University Press, 2015), 171–95.

spiritual and as an ethical virtue. Compassion is a spiritual virtue in the sense that it seems to express the openness or the generosity of the universe itself. It may seem strange to say that in caring for someone else we are only losing ourselves. But perhaps in another sense, this is the right way of thinking because the experience of compassion involves the rejection or the overcoming of our separate ego, and without such a movement spiritual life is impossible. The Dalai Lama puts it this way:

> Compassion enables us to refrain from thinking in a self-centered way. We experience great joy and never fall to the extreme of simply seeking our own personal happiness and salvation. We continually strive to develop and perfect our virtue and wisdom. With such compassion, we shall eventually possess all the necessary conditions for obtaining enlightenment. *We must therefore cultivate compassion from the very start of our spiritual practice.*[29]

III

To conclude this chapter, I want to remember Aristotle's claim that the purpose of studying ethics is not to learn about all the different ethical theories, but to become a better person. I think the same can be said about compassion and the study of spirituality: intellectual reflection on spiritual themes is important, but we cannot leave things at the level of mere understanding. Spiritual practices should not be neglected because the primary goal of studying spirituality should be one of spiritual transformation or spiritual growth toward enlightenment. Pierre Hadot and others have shown us that the earliest philosophers saw philosophy as a way of life and not just as an intellectual achievement.[30] And this is why the works of the Stoics, Epicureans, and others are full of spiritual exercises that help us to incorporate the intellectual truths that are being put forward at the deepest level of who we are. So let us briefly review some of the tentative conclusions of this chapter, and then turn to a more practical question concerning compassion: for if compassion really is a "starting point" and a fundamental spiritual virtue, we should think about how we can cultivate compassion.

In this chapter, I have argued that compassion is the true opening of spiritual life. For the most part, we are self-contained and we enjoy our existence. But what wrenches us out of this pleasant condition is suffering,

[29] Dalai Lama, *An Open Heart*, 106; my italics.
[30] See, for example, P. Hadot, *Philosophy as a Way of Life*, trans. M. Chase (Oxford: Basil Blackwell, 1995).

and this can be our own suffering or the suffering of others. Because of suffering, life becomes profoundly problematic, and the question is how to deal with this. Many religious believers talk about the will of God, which justifies everything that happens as a good thing because it must be in accordance with His will. As we have seen, Stoics and other philosophers urge us to remain indifferent to whatever happens to us; Nietzsche said we should become hard. I believe that compassion is the most authentic response because it involves staying open to suffering, and in so doing we embrace a deeper reality that lies beyond the horizon of our private existence. In this respect, compassion is the most original form of spiritual response, and it is the basis of other spiritual virtues like forgiveness and love, as well as the starting point for ethics itself. Compassion involves accepting suffering and change, and leaning into it instead of pulling away from it. It puts us in touch with the reality of other lives and it gives us a sense of *belonging* in the cosmos. It is the starting point of spiritual life, and without it we would remain self-absorbed and indifferent to spiritual values. Compassion is an ethical and a spiritual virtue, and I have shown how some of the key arguments against compassion are invalid. Given the importance of compassion, however, the next question is, how can we cultivate compassion within ourselves and others? In what follows, I will suggest a few of the ways.

First, I want to emphasize the relevance of art, literature, and music as spiritual possibilities that refine and cultivate the soul. In her work, Martha Nussbaum argues persuasively that one of the most important reasons to study literature is that it helps to inspire compassion by presenting us with the lived experience of another person, which is something that we could never achieve by ourselves.[31] By reading *The Narrative of Frederick Douglass*, for example, we may begin to understand what it is like to be a slave and someone else's property; by reading a story like *The Book of Job* – or watching a play like *King Lear* – we are witness to the terrible anguish people endure, whether this is deserved or undeserved, and we come to feel for them because we are just like them, damaged and fallible, and there's no reason why something like this couldn't also happen to us. In this way, the play or the story enhances our sense of compassion by letting us leave our everyday selves – if only for a while – to imagine what it would be like to live a life completely different from our own. So art and literature have a spiritual value, because they open us up to spiritual possibilities of life that might

[31] See, for example, M. Nussbaum, "Compassion: The Basic Social Emotion," *Social Philosophy and Policy*, 13 (1996), 27–58.

otherwise remain unavailable. Nussbaum argues that literature enhances our moral understanding by promoting compassion. I would add that all art is capable of enhancing spiritual life by putting us in touch with different spiritual possibilities that enlarge our sense of who we are, so that we are capable of responding to others with openness and compassion.

Next, Buddhist philosophies have never forgotten the unity of theory and practice, and in the works of authors like the Dalai Lama, Śāntideva, and others, real attention is paid to spiritual exercises that can increase compassion within the practitioner's heart. One spiritual practice involves the cultivation of empathy. In ancient Buddhist writings or more contemporary works, we are asked to imagine our loved ones in profound despair or torment.[32] Try to visualize this situation, and dwell on it. How terrible! Next we must imagine someone we don't know going through the same distress. Think about it: this is also very hard to bear. But finally, imagine your enemy or someone you don't like going through the same terrible anguish. Put aside all negative thoughts, explanations, or storylines that would draw you away from the reality of the suffering itself. At each level, you should say to yourself: "Like me, this person desires happiness, but she is stricken with pain. May this person be free from suffering and the causes of suffering!" In each case, suffering is a bad thing, and by imaginatively extending sympathy to others, we can become more sensitive to suffering wherever it occurs. In *The Bodhicaryāvatāra*, we are asked to imagine how people who are superior to us, inferior to us, or equal to us must think about who we are, and how the inevitable comparisons that people make, when self and other are distinguished, only lead to enmity and ill-feeling:

> Creating a sense of self in respect of inferiors and others, and a sense of other in oneself, imagine envy and pride with a mind free from false notions![33]

Ironically then, as we noted earlier, we can use the very idea of selfhood to undermine our affection for the self. Over several stanzas we are asked to meditate on the imagined responses of others who possess a different station in life than we do, and in this way, through the practice of sympathetic imagination, the resolution to abandon the ego and affirm compassion is ultimately strengthened:

> Acting as the other person, take away from this body every useful thing you see in it, and use that to benefit others.[34]

[32] See, for example, Dalai Lama, *How to Expand Love*, 140–5.

[33] Śāntideva, *The Bodhicaryāvatāra*, 100.

[34] Śāntideva, *The Bodhicaryāvatāra*, 102.

I have argued that such responses are enhanced by a background metaphysics that affirms impermanence, interdependence, and the unreality of the self. But I think the spiritual exercises are helpful even if you don't accept basic Buddhist beliefs about life, death, and karma. In fact, continual meditative absorption on the way of the bodhisattva can be transformative as one opens oneself to the compassionate ideal. That's because none of this depends on deductive reasoning, but on spiritual practices that work along the same lines as those of the Stoics, Epicureans, and others.

For example, *tonglen* is a spiritual practice associated with Tibetan Buddhism that can be used to enhance our compassionate involvement with others.[35] Basically it involves visualizing the suffering of another as a thick black smoke. Then we imagine ourselves breathing in that smoke and exhaling our own breath as a pure light that will bring the person happiness and relief from pain. At the same time we say to ourselves, "May this person be released from suffering, and may *all* people in this situation also experience relief." Although it is less widely known in the West, *tonglen* has been used for centuries as a way of experiencing our compassionate connection to other people; it undermines the boundary between self and other, and in this way, it keeps us *open*, even though another person's suffering is something we typically turn away from. Once again, this is something we can choose to cultivate for ourselves. The fact is, our moral personalities and our spiritual virtues are not "fixed" once and for all, because we can choose to enhance these things through focusing prayer and meditation, or through practices like *tonglen*.

Finally, you could also make an effort to stay open to your own suffering. Not by rehashing all the wrongs you have experienced in your life, and fixing on who is to blame for all this – yourself, your parents, God, etc. – but instead, focusing on the suffering itself, as a physical and emotional sensation, detached from every rationalization and storyline. You may not be able to do this for long, but invite the pain in, contemplate it as something that is passing through you, and then let it go. Such a practice can be deeply transformative because it cuts away all the fear and anguish that we usually associate with the suffering itself.

Compassion is not just a strategy for personal wellness and spiritual well-being. It *is* that, but at the same time, it is also a way of promoting the spiritual and ethical good of humankind. And given the general state of the world, staying open to suffering by cultivating a compassionate response

[35] This discussion of *tonglen* follows Pema Chödrön's account in *The Places That Scare You* (Boston, MA: Shambhala, 2001), 55–60.

may be the only way in which we can save ourselves as a species. But this is something that must begin with individual acts of compassion and kindness, for the habit of compassion has a ripple effect where those who experience it pay it back or pay it forward to others. In this way, the spiritual life of everyone can be enhanced. Today, we worry about ourselves, our children, and our grandchildren. But we are also concerned about future generations of people who are as yet unborn. Largely because of social and environmental factors, like pollution, overdevelopment, terrorism, and the threat of nuclear war, we are beginning to realize that we have responsibilities to those who will come after us. Probably, this shows that we are capable of taking a bigger view of things, which goes beyond our own selfish perspective or even that of our family and friends. But this is the same viewpoint Śāntideva sought to inculcate in *The Bodhicaryāvatāra* more than a thousand years ago:

> In the same way that the hands and other limbs are loved because they form part of the body, why are embodied creatures not likewise loved because they form part of the universe?
>
> In the same way that, with practice, the idea of a self arose towards this, one's own body, though it is without a self, with practice will not the same idea of a self develop towards others too?

And he concludes this line of thought:

> Therefore, in the same way that one desires to protect oneself from affliction, grief and the like, so an attitude of protectiveness and of compassion should be practiced towards the world.[36]

In compassion, we care about the suffering of others, and we feel motivated to do something about their suffering because we identify with them. But suffering will continue to exist, and we must remain open to it, instead of hardening ourselves against it. In this respect, compassion is the most basic spiritual response; in the end, it may be the only way we can save ourselves and the world we belong to.

[36] Śāntideva, *The Bodhicaryāvatāra*, 98.

CHAPTER 11

Identifying with the Confucian Heaven
Immanent and Transcendent Dao

May Sim

Confucianism: Moral Philosophy or Religion?

Whether Confucianism is a religion is in dispute despite its being included as one of the great world religions, first by Max Müller in his 1888 Gifford Lectures, and in textbooks, best-selling books, courses, and surveys about world religion since then.[1] One reason for the skepticism, according to Anna Sun, is that it is not regarded as a religion by most mainland Chinese, including the Chinese government.[2] Even those who advocated the Confucian religion movement in the late nineteenth and early twentieth centuries, such as Kang Youwei and his student Chen Huanzhong, did so by emphasizing the ethical significance of religion. As Yong Chen explains it in *Confucianism as Religion: Controversies and Consequences*, Kang maintains that "The essential significance of any *jiao* [Kang equivocates *jiao*, which could mean 'teaching' and also 'religion'] consists in making men avoid evil and do good,"[3] and offers an evolutionary interpretation of Confucianism in abnegating divine authority, saying, "Confucius loathed divine authority for its excessive influence [on men] and swept it away... As a founder of religion Confucius represented an advanced stage in cultural progress... Now as men's intelligence gradually develops, divine authority gradually loses its hold on them. Confucianism therefore suits the present world best."[4] Similarly, Chen quotes Chen Huanzhong's evolutionary take on Confucianism:

> There are all kinds of *jiao* (religions). Some instruct people by means of the divine way, some others by means of the human way. Although they take

[1] See A. Sun, *Confucianism as a World Religion: Contested Histories and Contemporary Realities* (Princeton University Press, 2013), xi; Y. Chen, *Confucianism as Religion: Controversies and Consequences* (Leiden: Brill, 2013), 85–6.

[2] Sun, *Confucianism as a World Religion*, 1.

[3] Chen, *Confucianism as Religion*, 48.

[4] Chen, *Confucianism as Religion*, 50.

> different paths, they are the same in the sense that they are all *jiao*. . . Now some claim that *jiao* of the "human way" is not *jiao*. Is this different from claiming that a winter coat is not clothing, dinner is not a meal? . . . In the age of mythology, *jiao*-founders of the savage world always appealed to ghosts and spirits [to set forth doctrines]; in the age of humanity, *jiao*-founders of the civilized world always emphasized moral values. This is the principle of evolution.[5]

Not surprisingly, in the face of the May 4th hundred days of reform, Chen reports that another student of Kang, Liang Qichao, who used to support the Confucian religion movement, opposed his master by saying:

> So-called religion specifically refers to belief in superstition. The authority of religion resides beyond the physical body. It takes soul as its lodging place, worship as its ritual, transcendence as its purpose, heaven as its destination, and benediction in the next life as its conviction. Although there are different kinds of religions, they all share the basic features.[6]

What is clear from both Anna Sun's and Yong Chen's discussions of Confucianism as religion is that how "religion" is defined is contested. This is already evident from the difference between Kang's and Liang's respective definitions. Whereas Kang emphasizes the moral purpose of religion, Liang stresses superstition and the afterlife of the soul in his definition of religion. Others who don't regard Confucianism as a religion because of its lack of concern with an afterlife include Matteo Ricci and Max Weber.[7] Chen explains that Weber's view is that "Confucianism lacked an eschatology and doctrine of salvation, any transcendental values, the concepts of ecstasy and asceticism, and individual prayer. Nor was there any sense of sin or grace existent in the tradition."[8]

Despite the different definitions of religion we have considered so far by the proponents of the Confucian religion movement and their rivals who deny that Confucianism is a religion, these authors are agreed that Confucianism is concerned about cultivating social and moral values in this life, rather than adhering to a divinity who is transcendent and dictates values that are not bound up with existence in this social world. However, before giving in to the apparent consensus among the aforementioned rivals who hold that Confucianism is just a moral philosophy, we should examine if it possesses the resources for offering the sort of transcendent values called for by those who dispute its status as a religion. I aim to show that Confucianism does have the resources for offering such transcendent

[5] Chen, *Confucianism as Religion*, 52. [6] Chen, *Confucianism as Religion*, 53.
[7] See Chen, *Confucianism as Religion*, 72, 76. [8] Chen, *Confucianism as Religion*, 76.

values and thus would qualify as a religion for those who insist that a religion must have *some* form of transcendent values. I consider some different appeals to transcendent values in the next section.

Alternative Definitions of Religion

Consider those who point to talk of Heaven (*tian* 天) and the high God (*shangti* 上帝) in the five classics that make up the Confucian canonical texts. For instance, Chen says that in the *Book of Poetry* (*Shijing* 詩 經), *shangti* was mentioned twenty-four times and *tian* was mentioned more than 150 times.[9] Opponents of such a defense attempt to drive a wedge between a Confucian conception of Heaven and that of theism by saying that the Confucian Heaven is more cosmological and naturalistic in contrast to the more personal and theological understanding of theism. However, defenders of Confucianism as religion point to the kinship between these traditions and argue that the Christian God, for instance, is more than a personal God, being the ultimate source of everything.[10] As such, a Christian God is comparable to the Confucian Heaven that is also the source from which "all things stem."[11]

Another way of approaching the issue of religion in Confucianism is to include the subject who engages in the practice of religion rather than rely solely on the object of transcendence. For instance, Rodney L. Taylor defends Confucianism as a religion by following Frederick Streng's account that religion is a "means of ultimate transformation."[12] Applying this definition to Confucianism, Taylor maintains that Confucianism is a religion because it engages in "1) the search for ultimate meaning and 2) the identification of an absolute with *tian* (天 Heaven) in the classical tradition and *tianli* (天理 Principle of Heaven) in the Neo-Confucian tradition."[13] Further, Taylor maintains that 3) the process of transformation leads to the identification of the individual with the absolute, and to 4) the cultivation of sagehood as identical with the religious way of life.[14]

[9] Chen, *Confucianism as Religion*, 22.

[10] See Chen, *Confucianism as Religion*, 70; M. Sim, "A Natural Law Approach to Law: Are the Confucians and the Thomists Commensurable?," *Journal of Comparative Law: Studies in Comparative Law*, 12, ed. R. Wilcox and A. Carty (London: Wildy, Simmonds & Hill Publishing, 2015), 87–8.

[11] Chen, *Confucianism as Religion*, 69.

[12] R. L. Taylor, "Confucian Spirituality and Qing Thought," in T. Weiming and M. E. Tucker (eds.), *Confucian Spirituality*, 2 vols. (New York: The Crossroad Publishing Co. 2004), vol. II, 163.

[13] Taylor, "Confucian Spirituality," 164.

[14] Taylor, "Confucian Spirituality," 163–4.

Taylor's emphasis on the subject's activities in the practice of religion also resonates with an analysis of how religion relates to spirituality. For example, Ralph W. Hood reports a distinction between being religious and being spiritual in Roof's 1993 sociological study of 1,599 people in which those who identify themselves as "highly active seekers" also identify themselves as "spiritual" instead of "religious."[15] Referring to Roof's study, Hood says, "Most important for our present purposes is the consistent finding that for almost all of the persons interviewed, distinctions could be made between being religious and being spiritual. Religion conveyed some institutional connotation, sometimes negative; spiritual connoted something deeply subjective and individual."[16] More elaborately, one difference between religion and spirituality is the presence of institutional support in the former and its lack or a greater emphasis on the subject's personal experience in the latter, according to Hood.[17] Another difference is that some subjects find religion negative in comparison to spirituality because they feel constrained by the objects of transcendence, dogmas, and rituals integral to religious institutions, whereas spirituality is free from such constraints.[18] Some proponents of spirituality criticize religion by maintaining that people can attend church services, for instance, and perform the rituals without experiencing any spiritual emotions.[19] In spite of Roof's study, which seems to support a sharp distinction between those who identify themselves as spiritual and those who identify themselves as religious, Hood reports traditional empirical research initiated by Ken Pargament (the 1997 president of the American Psychological Association) to the effect that for most Americans who participated in his study, being religious and being spiritual are intertwined.[20]

Having outlined some disagreements between interpreters of Confucianism as regards its being a religion because of its emphasis on social and moral values, lack of a personal God, as well as its lack of concern for an afterlife, I've sketched in addition various definitions of religion that scholars have proposed. For example, we have looked at definitions that focus on the divine as the ultimate source of all things rather than as a

[15] R. W. Hood Jr., "The Relationship Between Religion and Spirituality," in A. L. Greil and D. G. Bromley (eds.), *Defining Religion: Investigating the Boundaries Between the Sacred and Secular* (Bingley, UK: Emerald, 2003) 245–6.

[16] Hood, "The Relationship Between Religion and Spirituality," 246.

[17] Hood, "The Relationship Between Religion and Spirituality," 244.

[18] Hood, "The Relationship Between Religion and Spirituality," 242, 244, 249.

[19] Hood, "The Relationship Between Religion and Spirituality," 247.

[20] Hood, "The Relationship Between Religion and Spirituality," 250–1.

personal God, and those that focus on the subjective experience and transformation of the practitioner instead of a transcendent God. By examining the philosophical texts of classical Confucians such as Confucius and Mencius, I shall show that these alternative definitions enable us to identify the resources in Confucianism for addressing questions as to whether it is a religion according to some definitions of religion, and whether it could offer a spiritual way of life.

Confucius

At first blush, it would seem that Confucius's *Analects* does not offer us a religion. Analect 5.13 asserts, "We can learn from the Master's cultural refinements, but do not hear him discourse on subjects such as our nature (*xing* 性) and the way of *tian* (*tiandao* 天道)" (see also 7.21).[21] Since the appeal to *tian* (天 Heaven) is one way of showing that Confucianism offers a functional equivalent of a transcendent object, lacking any talk of *tiandao* or the way prescribed by Heaven, makes it doubtful if Confucius offers a religion. Moreover, lack of any talk of human nature (*xing* 性), which is the subject that is to relate to the transcendent object, would also seem to prevent one from defending a Confucian view of religion from the transformative perspective as Taylor has proposed, or from the religious-spiritual perspective Hood has discussed. Consider, for instance, Thomas Aquinas's discussion of natural law – that human reason by nature pursues the good and shuns evil because of its participation in eternal law.[22] Such a discussion would explain why human beings are bound up with God and the norms of what is ethical for them. Lacking any talk of both *tian* (Heaven) and *xing* (human nature), Confucius seems to be without resources from both the transcendent object and self-transformation perspectives for being a religion. This conclusion seems to be reinforced by Confucius's remark to the effect that *tian* does not speak. He says, "Does *tian* speak? The four seasons proceed and the ten thousand things are produced. Does *tian* speak?" (17.19, my trans.). This remark could be

[21] Unless stated otherwise, all parenthetical references to and quotations from Confucius's *Analects* are from *The Analects of Confucius: A Philosophical Translation*, trans. R. T. Ames and H. Rosemont Jr. (New York: Ballantine Books, [ca. 500–250 BC] 1998).

[22] As I have put it in "A Natural Law Approach to Law" (85), Aquinas holds that natural law is the rational creature's participation in the eternal law, which imprint accounts for his natural inclination toward his proper act and end. Aquinas says, "the light of natural reason, whereby we discern what is good and what is evil, which is the function of the natural law, is nothing else than an imprint on us of the Divine light. It is therefore evident that the natural law is nothing else than the rational creature's participation of the eternal law" (*Summa Theologiae*, q. 91, a. 2).

interpreted to mean that *tian* is a source of everything in the world, thus supporting a naturalistic and cosmic entity rather than a divinity with a special relation, e.g., through speech, to human beings.

On the contrary, that the *Analects* offers an account of *tian* and its mandate (*tianming* 天命) can be seen in Confucius's assertions to the effect that *tian* is the source of his virtue (7.23), as well as the preserver of culture (9.5) and the determination of the *dao* (道 14.36). Confucius is so confident in the purposefulness and activity of *tian* in controlling the presence or absence of goodness in the world that he thinks that there's nothing that his political opponents can do to him despite their threats. The *Analects* offers an account of an occasion when Confucius was surrounded in Kuang by political opponents and he says, "With King Wen 文 long dead, does not our cultural heritage (*wen* 文) reside here in us? If *tian* were going to destroy this legacy, we latecomers would not have had access to it. If *tian* is not going to destroy this culture, what can the people of Kuang do to me!" (9.5). Again, when bemoaning the fact that no one appreciates him to Zigong, one of his disciples, Confucius says that he does not blame *tian* or people and adds that *tian* knows him (14.35).

Crediting *tian* for his virtues and the preservation of culture, which for Confucius is key to the cultivation of virtues, not only shows that there is a transcendent source for him, but one that is also providential. These two characteristics of *tian*, as a transcendent and providential source, strengthen Confucianism's candidacy as a religion. Moreover, for Confucius to say that *tian* knows him even when no one knows or appreciates him could even be interpreted to mean that *tian* is more than a transcendent absolute source of the natural world; it seems to be akin to the personal God espoused by the Abrahamic religions.

Before rushing to the conclusion that the Confucian *tian* is closer to the personal God of the Abrahamic religions, we need to examine more closely other remarks in the *Analects* that challenge this view. Consider Confucius's views of sacrifice and prayer. Once, when Confucius was very ill, he refused Zilu's (one of his disciple's) request to pray for him, and asked if that is an accepted ritual. Zilu explained that it is and that he will pray to the spirits in the Heaven above and the earth below. Upon hearing this, Confucius responded, "Then I have already been praying for myself for a long time now" (7.35). Confucius's response is puzzling because it could mean that he, like Zilu, believes in praying to the spirits in Heaven and earth to intercede in his affairs so that things will go his way. If so, why should he stop Zilu from praying for his recovery?

A more likely interpretation of Confucius's refusal of Zilu's offer of prayers for him is that despite Confucius's self-professed long-standing prayers to the spirits in Heaven and earth, they are not for the purpose of benefiting himself. That this sort of prayer, regardless of its effects on Heaven, seems to be a more plausible interpretation of Confucius's own prayers is supported by other passages about spirits in the *Analects*. For example, Confucius responded to Fan Chi's inquiry about knowledge by saying that he should "do his utmost for the people by being appropriate (*yi* 義, sometimes translated as "righteous") in his actions and respect ghosts and spirits and keep away from them" (6.22, my trans.). Another passage that seems to convey Confucius's disinterest in influencing spirits is this: "Sacrifice as if present [is interpreted as] sacrifice to the spirit as if the spirit is present. But if 'I' am not acting in accord with the sacrifice, it is as if I am not sacrificing" (3.12, my trans.). Here, as in other passages in which Confucius emphasizes the importance of one's attitudes and emotions in performing ritual actions (*li* 禮), what is significant to him is the personal investment of oneself in the ritual of offering sacrifices, or the sincerity in performing the ritual, rather than the presence of the spirits. Ritual propriety (*li* 禮) prescribes the proper sorts of behavior toward various relations, e.g., toward one's elder and younger relations in the home, as well as toward one's superiors or subordinates outside the home. Filial piety (*xiao* 孝), for instance, is the ritual propriety that calls for obedience to and respect for one's parents and elders in the home. When responding to Ziyou's inquiry about being filial (*xiao* 孝), Confucius says: "Those today who are filial are considered so because they are able to provide for their parents. But even dogs and horses are given that much care. If you don't respect your parents, what is the difference?" (2.7; see also 2.8 in which Confucius emphasizes having the proper countenance when serving the elders).[23] Taken with 6.22 about keeping away from spirits, and 7.35 about how Confucius has been praying for himself for a long time, in conjunction with his assertions about how *tian* preserves culture and the *dao*, Confucius's view in 3.12 is more likely one of self-reliance instead of reliance on the spirits to answer one's prayers. This interpretation is also plausible if we consider how he stresses *tian* as the sole determinant of culture and the *dao*, thus making it doubtful that anyone could persuade

[23] See also Confucius's response to Lin Fang's question about the basis of ritual propriety: "In observing ritual propriety, it is better to be modest than extravagant; in mourning, it is better to express real grief than to worry over formal details" (3.4).

Heaven to do otherwise, even through sacrifices to spirits.[24] That *tian* does not even always seem to side with the good can be seen when Yan Hui, one of Confucius's favorite disciples, credited for being able to retain the humane (*ren* 仁) heart/mind for months, in contrast with others who would only engage in such a heart/mind on rare occasions (6.7), died young. In response to his premature death, Confucius cried repeatedly, "*Tian* is the ruin of me!" (11.9). Again, this shows that *tian* is not something that can be influenced by human beings, even those who are virtuous. Nevertheless, that *tian* is the ultimate norm of what is right for Confucius is clear when someone asked about the meaning of the saying, "It is better to pay homage to the spirit of the stove than to the spirits of the household shrine" (3.13). To this inquiry, Confucius responded, "It is not so. A person who offends against *tian* has nowhere else to pray" (3.13). This reply reveals that Confucius, much like Plato and Aristotle, is against the religious convention of his day, which maintains that *tian* (correspondingly, the gods for the Greeks) could be bribed to favor one regardless of one's lack of morality.

Other commentators also support the claim that the performance of the rituals for Confucius is for the sake of self-transformation rather than to obtain the benefits from Heaven. P. J. Ivanhoe says Confucius "dismissed sacrifice or prayer that was carried out with the intent of inducing Heaven to provide one with specific benefits ... Sacrifice was an occasion for the cultivation of proper attitude and the expression of ideals – not the satisfaction of appetites."[25] Michael Puett too would agree that talk of sacrifice in 3.12 emphasizes self-transformation of the subject performing the ritual. He explains that Confucius's remark is a "critique of contemporary sacrificial practice, in which one engaged a ritual specialist to perform sacrifices properly ... to transform the spirits so that they would act on behalf of humanity."[26] Instead of persuading the spirits, Puett says that Confucius argues for how "one should focus instead on the human realm ... to transform the human performing the ritual. Accordingly, one must perform the act oneself."[27] As I have emphasized, what is key

[24] Mencius would agree with such an interpretation in which *tian* is the sole determinant of what occurs. Consider his anecdote regarding how Emperor Yao could not have given the rulership to Shun, but only *tian* could have done so, and how *tian* reveals its mandate (*ming* 命) through actions and affairs (*Mencius* 5A 5.1).

[25] P. J. Ivanhoe, "Heaven as a Source for Ethical Warrant in Early Confucianism," *Dao: A Journal of Comparative Philosophy*, 6 (2007), 215.

[26] M. Puett, *To Become a God: Cosmology, Sacrifice and Self-Divinization in Early China* (Cambridge, MA: Harvard University Press, 2002), 98.

[27] Puett, *To Become a God*, 98.

in the performance of ritual is not just the action, but the emotions and attitudes, especially the sincerity, that accompany the ritual action. The appropriate feelings and attitudes are the essential characteristics without which one does not have the specific virtues of filial piety, appropriateness, humaneness, etc.[28]

Despite the fact that Confucius does not advocate the performance of sacrifices to spirits to obtain specific favors from Heaven, he nevertheless maintains that proper respect is due to the spirits because cultivating such respect is continuous with that of cultivating respect for human beings. In fact, respect for spirits presupposes respect for human beings. This is clear when Confucius replies to Zilu's inquiry about how one should serve ghosts and spirits by saying, "Not yet being able to serve other people, how would you be able to serve the spirits?" (11.12). Continuing to respond to Zilu's query about death, Confucius says, "Not yet understanding life, how could you understand death?" (11.12). We have seen that even though Heaven is the source of virtue and preserves the *dao* and culture for Confucius, our relation to it is not one of supplication. Rather, we are to adhere to the *dao*,[29] which existence depends on *tian*. Consequently, knowing *tian's* decree (*tianming* 天命) is key to achieving the virtues and becoming an exemplary person for Confucius. He says, "Not knowing Heaven's mandate (*tianming* 天命), there's no means to become an exemplary person (*junzi* 君子)" (20.3). Since one cannot become an exemplary person without having *ren* (humaneness, the highest Confucian virtue exercised by the graduated extension of love for one's own family to the rest of the community), which is in turn impossible without loving persons and knowing them (12.22), requiring years of cultivation through ritual actions, it is not surprising that Confucius says that he himself did not know *tianming* until he was fifty. In reference to Rodney Taylor's analysis, it looks like Confucianism, as expressed in the *Analects*, satisfies his first two conditions for being a religion in that it not only identifies *tian* as an absolute, but also depicts a progression toward knowing *tian* by knowing how to relate to others and to perfect one's virtues toward other people in this world, which provide ultimate meaning to one's life.

[28] For an account of the requirements of the appropriate emotions and attitudes for virtues in Confucianism, see my "Why Confucius's Ethics Is a Virtue Ethics," in M. Slote and L. Besser-Jones (eds.), *The Routledge Companion to Virtue Ethics* (New York: Routledge, 2015), and "Confucian and Daoist Virtue Ethics," in D. Carr, K. Kristjánsson, and J. Arthur (eds.), *Varieties of Virtue Ethics* (London: Palgrave-Macmillan, 2016).

[29] For passages in the *Analects* discussing the significance of the *dao*, see 7.6, 4.8, 4.5, 4.20, and 8.13.

At this point, a skeptic of Confucianism's being a religion might object by insisting that what Confucius offers, in requiring knowledge of *tian* or *tianming* for the perfection of human virtues, lacks religiousness or spirituality. More elaborately, a skeptic might say that we are still dealing with secular relationships in this natural world without any emphasis on what transcends this concrete world, for even the culture and *dao* that are preserved by *tian* are about this world. In response to such an objection, one might ask about what one expects in leading a religious life, to see if such a goal or its functional equivalent is accessible in Confucianism. A glance at a few religions, such as Hinduism, Buddhism, and Christianity, will reveal an apparent consensus amongst them regarding an ultimate goal such as happiness, or some sort of flourishing life within which one is free from suffering. Is such a goal possible for Confucius?

To begin, we could consider Confucius's remark, "Persons who are not humane (*ren*) cannot be committed for long, nor can they be happy for long. The humane person is content in being humane, and the one who has knowledge benefits the humane" (4.2, my trans.). This shows that Confucius's view is that one with the highest virtue of humaneness is not only capable of having enduring happiness, but can be trusted in his commitments. What is significant in this passage is Confucius's remark about how one with knowledge is enabled to be humane. This assertion about requiring knowledge to have the virtue of humaneness is consistent with his claim that an exemplary person knows Heaven's mandate (*tianming* 天命) (20.3). But how is such knowledge acquired if *tian* does not speak?

Recall that Confucius thinks that *tian* determines (*ming* 命, mandate) if the *dao* continues to exist, and is also the preserver of culture. In addition, for anyone else to acquire knowledge of *tian* and be an exemplary person, the prerequisite of there being concrete embodiments of culture or the *dao* in the community must be met. This is expressed when Confucius says about Zijian, "He is truly an exemplary person (*junzi* 君子). If Lu had no other exemplary persons, where could he have gotten his character from?" (5.3). In general, Confucius holds that the former sage kings were exemplary persons and their success was due to their character virtues. Praising King Yao, Confucius says:

> How great indeed was Yao as ruler! How majestic! Only *tian* is truly great, and only Yao took it as his model. How expansive was he – the people could not find the words adequate to praise him. How majestic was he in his accomplishments, and how brilliant was he in his cultural achievements. (8.19)

The impact exemplary rulers have on the people is reiterated in Confucius's assertion about Yao and Shun, "How majestic they were – Yao and Shun reigned over the world but did not rule it" (8.18). What enables these sage rulers to successfully govern the world and have the majestic effect on people comes from the cultural ritual they embody by modeling after *tian*. Recall Confucius's earlier claim that *tian* does not speak and yet ten thousand things are produced and the seasons proceed. What is connoted in that passage is the effortlessness with which *tian* accomplishes its work. Likewise, the power that such exemplary sage rulers have over people, allowing them to govern so easily, is based on the cultural ritual that *tian* preserves in the *dao*. Thus, the ease and effectiveness with which sage kings rule can be traced to their being like *tian* in enacting the rituals it decreed.

More elaborately, the performance of ritual actions by the sage king expresses a unity with *tian* because it actualizes the *dao* or culture that *tian* decrees and preserves. Herbert Fingarette illustrates the significance of the cultural contexts as follows:

> There is no power of *li* [ritual action] if there is no learned and accepted convention, or if we utter the words and involve the power of convention in an inappropriate setting, or if the ceremony is not fully carried out, or if the persons carrying out the ceremonial roles are not those properly authorized... In short, the peculiarly moral yet binding power of ceremonial gesture and word cannot be abstracted from or used in isolation from ceremony. It is not a distinct power we happen to use in ceremony; it is the power *of* ceremony.[30]

This emphasis on the accepted convention or culture also fits Taylor's third condition of a religion regarding the identification of the subject with the absolute, especially if the Confucian sage king's action is *tian*-like, and the culture within which he acts is caused by *tian*. An example of the *tian*-like and thus magical effect that an exemplary person exerts on the people is Confucius's response to a query if effective government can be achieved by killing those who are without the *dao*. Confucius says,

> What need is there for killing? If you want to be truly good, the people will be good. The virtue of the *junzi* (君子 exemplary person) is like the wind, and the petty person is like the grass. When the wind blows on the grass, it must bend. (12.19, my trans.)

[30] Herbert Fingarette, *Confucius: The Secular as Sacred* (New York: Harper & Row, 1972), 12.

Confucius's answer shows how natural, powerful, and easy it is to govern by virtue. The impact of the ruler on the people is as sure and swift as the wind's effect on grass. Fingarette explains the magical power of the proper exercise of rituals for Confucius when he says:

> By 'magic' I mean the power of a specific person to accomplish his will directly and effortlessly through ritual, gesture and incantation. The user of magic does not work by strategies and devices as a means toward an end; he does not use coercion or physical forces. There are no pragmatically developed and tested strategies or tactics. He simply wills the end in the proper ritual setting and with the proper ritual gesture and word, without further effort on his part, the deed is accomplished.[31]

Again, Confucius explains the effectiveness of governing by virtue and rituals:

> Lead the people with administrative injunctions (*zheng* 政) and keep them orderly with penal law (*xing* 刑), and they will avoid punishments but will be without a sense of shame. Lead them with excellence (*de* 德) and keep them orderly through observing ritual propriety (*li* 禮) and they will develop a sense of shame, and moreover, will order themselves. (2.3)

What this passage shows is that ruling by punitive measures is not as effective as governing people by being a model of virtue expressed through the ruler's observance of ritual propriety. Whereas the former way requires the ruler to be constantly on the lookout for transgressions and administer punishments in response to them, the latter way just takes the virtuous ruler to be himself, and relate to others in the way that is mandated by *tian*, i.e., through the rituals practiced in the culture.[32] As Confucius puts it, "Governing with virtue (*de* 德) is comparable to the North Star, it remains in place and the multitude of stars pay tribute" (2.1, my trans.).

More concretely, consider Confucius's example of how Zichan (Duke of Zheng) exhibits the *dao* of the *junzi* "in four respects: he was gracious in deporting himself, he was deferential in serving his superiors, he was generous in attending to needs of the common people, and he was appropriate (*yi* 義) in employing their services" (5.16). These characteristics of respecting his superiors and caring for the people, as well as being appropriate in employing the people, are virtues acquired through cultivating the rituals of filial and fraternal piety in the home. As Master You puts it,

[31] Fingarette, *Confucius*, 3.

[32] In Fingarette's words, "The force of coercion is manifest and tangible, whereas the vast (and sacred) forces at work in *li* are invisible and intangible. *Li* works through spontaneous coordination rooted in reverent dignity. The perfection in Holy Rite is esthetic as well as spiritual" (*Confucius*, 8–9).

"Having filial and fraternal piety is the root for being *ren*" (1.2, my trans.; see also 1.6). Since filial and fraternal piety are about love and respect for one's parents and elder brothers, respectively, Confucius's view is that these rituals harmonize our relations with the elder and younger relatives in the home, which harmony is in turn extended to our relations to superiors and subordinates outside the home. It is important to realize that in Confucianism, despite the emphasis on the role of the exemplary ruler who inspires the people to be orderly through his performance of rituals, the same effect of harmonious relations with everyone is open to each and every person, since everyone is to relate to his family members through filial and fraternal piety and extend such relations to those outside the family.[33] Again, that harmony results from ritual actions is evident when Master You says, "Achieving harmony is the most valuable function of observing ritual propriety (*li* 禮). In the ways of the Former Kings, this achievement of harmony made them elegant, and was a guiding standard in all things large and small" (1.12). Cultivating the virtues of sagehood and exercising them in one's relations, as exemplified in Confucius's discussions of sage kings, can be seen as satisfying Taylor's fourth condition of the identity between the cultivation of sagehood and the religious way of life. Consider the similarity between the cultivation of sagehood in Confucianism and someone's following the eightfold path in Buddhism, or practicing meditation in Hinduism; each exemplifies a religious way of life.

In sum, knowledge of what's decreed by *tian* (i.e., the *dao*) is transmitted through the performance of ritual proprieties, which is the means by which one acquires the power of virtue to harmonize with everyone in the community. The ability to harmonize with everyone by doing what's humane and appropriate is a source of happiness because such virtue is not only the *dao* of *tian*, and thus one is being *tian*-like when exercising virtue, but one's action is also effortless and sustainable. Thus, Confucianism, like other religions, does provide a flourishing life by offering a life of self-transformation, which eliminates conflict and pain in how we relate to others. Despite the fact that the virtues are practiced in the human world, the effectiveness of an exemplary person's actions in transforming everyone around is akin to the transcendent power of *tian* without requiring speech.[34]

[33] For the continuity between the family and the state, so that the state is just the family writ large, see my *Remastering Morals with Aristotle and Confucius* (Cambridge University Press, 2007), ch. 6.

[34] As Tu Weiming puts it, "For the Confucian literatus, this shore and the other shore, the sacred and the secular, and the mundane world on earth and the Kingdom of God yet to come are inseparable" ("Confucian Spirituality in Contemporary China," in F. Yang and J. B. Tamney [eds.], *Confucianism and Spiritual Traditions in Modern China and Beyond* [Leiden: Brill, 2012], 85).

Mencius

Confucius claims that *ren* (仁 humaneness) is near, saying, "How could *ren* be at all remote? No sooner do I seek it than it has arrived" (7.30). His remark sounds as if anyone can achieve this highest virtue by himself. Yet we cannot help but notice that several prerequisites involving the community must be met before one can become *ren*. As we have seen for Confucius, not only must the right culture and *dao* be in place, there must be exemplary individuals, preferably in the roles of government, to inspire us to be virtuous. One major contribution that Mencius made to Confucianism is an account of human nature that makes it possible for individuals to become *ren* regardless of being in a well-governed state that has the *dao*, or being ruled by exemplary rulers. More elaborately, Mencius downplays the role of the community and ritual practices by maintaining that human nature, like everything else's nature, is produced by Heaven, and as such, already has virtue as its norm. Since the norm of human nature is to be virtuous, human beings are naturally good and incline toward virtue. Mencius quotes one of the *Odes* expressing this direct relation between Heaven and human beings:

> Heaven gives birth to the teeming people.
> If there is a thing, there is a norm.
> This is the constant people cleave to.
> They are fond of this beautiful virtue. (6A 6.8)[35]

The norm in human beings is human nature endowed by Heaven for Mencius. More specifically, Mencius explains that human nature necessarily comes with four feelings: compassion, disdain or shame, deference, and the preference for what is right as opposed to what is wrong, which he claims are like four sprouts. To prove that human beings by nature possess compassion, Mencius asks that we consider a child who is about to fall into a well. He says that anyone in such a situation would feel alarm and anxiety for the child, regardless of whether one is related to the child. Compassion, for Mencius, and the other three feelings, are incipient virtues, which like sprouts, will mature into four full virtues. Mencius says,

> If one is without the feeling of compassion, one is not human. If one is without the feeling of disdain, one is not human. If one is without the feeling of deference, one is not human. If one is without *the preference for what is right as opposed to what is wrong*, one is not human. (2A 6.4, my mod.)

[35] Unless otherwise stated, all translations of Mencius are from *The Essential Mengzi* (*Mengzi* hereafter), trans. B. W. Van Norden (Indianapolis, IN: Hackett, [ca. 350–300 BC] 2009).

He continues to explain, "the feeling of compassion is the sprout of benevolence" (*ren* 仁, humaneness) (2A 6.5), that of shame/disdain is the incipient virtue of righteousness (*yi* 義, appropriateness), that of deference is the incipient virtue of ritual propriety (*li* 禮) and finally, the preference for what is right over what is wrong is the incipient virtue of wisdom (*zhi* 智) (2A 6.5). In 6A 6.7, he even identifies each of these feelings with its respective virtue, e.g., saying, "The feeling of compassion is benevolence." What Mencius wishes to emphasize is that these virtues are innate in us and hence, human beings are by nature good. Rather than rely on a well-governed state and the presence of exemplary rulers like Confucius did, without which one is prohibited from becoming virtuous, Mencius maintains that Heaven has endowed each and every one of us with the virtues so that "We and the sage are of the same kind" (6A 7.4).[36] Thus, just as mouths have the same preference for flavors, ears have the same preference for music and eyes for beauty, he holds that our hearts/minds (*xin* 心) have the same preference for orderliness (*li* 理, principle) and righteousness (*yi* 義, appropriateness). Mencius asserts, "order and righteousness delight our hearts like meat delights our mouths" (6A 7.8). Just as the presence of *dao* in a state is decreed by *tian* for Confucius, which way of life is one of cultivating the virtues of sagehood, by moving these virtues into human nature, Mencius is making *dao* immanent, thus offering an identity between the absolute and the individual from the beginning, or at least, offering a direct path to *tian* independently of mediation through the cultural rituals.

Upon closer examination however, Mencius's account of human nature does not preclude the necessity of cultivation, for *most* human beings. This is evident from the fact that there are vicious people and one of the four sprouts is deference (for our parents and elders in the home), which implies that cultivating the virtue of ritual propriety, and the resulting effect of harmonious relations with others, is part and parcel of our lives. How then does Mencius explain the phenomenon that the four sprouts of virtue do not develop into complete virtues? His answer is that ordinary people become corrupt when they lose their Heaven-given heart (*xin* 心, 6A 15.2), which function is to reflect on their nature, and grasp their innate virtues.[37] Discussing how by nature all human beings would desire righteousness more than life in their hearts and hate being unrighteous more than death, Mencius explains that what distinguishes ordinary people from the sage is not that only the sage has such a moral

[36] For a detailed discussion of Mencius's view of the sage, see my "The *Phronimos* and the Sage," in N. E. Snow (ed.), *Oxford Handbook of Virtue* (Oxford University Press, forthcoming).

[37] 心 *xin*, though translated as "heart," always refers to the "heart" and "mind" in Chinese. It does not separate the emotional from the rational faculties.

heart. Rather, the distinction lies in how the sage never loses his human heart (6A 10.5). Mencius thinks that as long as one has not lost one's heart, using it to reflect will enable one to "get it" ("it" refers to how humans are by nature good and have as their goal the realization of virtues): "If it does not reflect, then it will not get it" (6A 15.2). And those who "get it" go on to become great human beings; those who do not become petty persons.

Mencius's account differs from Confucius's in not requiring a community in which the ritual proprieties exhibiting the *dao* is in place, nor exemplary persons to inspire someone else to become virtuous, *if* that person is a sage. Instead of these institutional prerequisites, Mencius relies on the sage's innately good heart to know and practice the virtues. Even if the sage requires a reminder, it is extremely minor, as Mencius explains in the following anecdote about the sage king Shun:

> When he was young and lived deep in the mountain wilds, Shun lived among trees and rocks and traveled with deer and pigs. He differed only slightly from the wild people of the deep mountains. But as soon as he heard one good saying or saw one good deed, it was like a river overflowing its banks, torrential, so that nothing could stop it. (7A 16.1)

As is clear from this passage, instead of a state that has the *dao*, all that Shun needed was one instance of a good saying or action to remind him of his innate goodness. For the ordinary people however, Mencius requires more or less the same communal prerequisites as Confucius. Thus, he attempts to advise several rulers about effective governance, just like Confucius.[38] For instance, advising King Xuan of Qi about how to govern effectively, Mencius says, "Treat your elders as elders, and extend it to the elders of others; treat your young ones as young ones, and extend it to the young ones of others, and you can turn the world in the palm of your hand" (1A 7.12). This remark shows his agreement with Confucius about how filial and fraternal piety in the home is the root of *ren*, which virtue is essential for harmonizing all relationships inside and outside the home so effortlessly that governing is as easy as turning the world over in one's palm. In another passage, Mencius advised King Xuan to regulate the state's economic goods so that people would not only have enough to care for their parents, and their wives and children in good times, but also in times of adversity, such as famine. Over and above such considerations, Mencius also maintains that the king should make sure that the people have enough leisure to cultivate the virtues of appropriateness (*yi* 義) and ritual propriety (*li* 禮). Unlike Confucius, who thought that the

[38] For a detailed discussion regarding the degree of self-determination that Mencius's view offers, see my "Self-Determination and the Metaphysics of Human Nature in Aristotle and Mencius," in Yang Xiao (ed.), *Dao Companion to the Philosophy of Mencius* (Dordrecht: Springer, forthcoming).

cultivation of virtues can be accomplished in the home, Mencius thinks that one of the ruler's jobs is to ensure that the virtues of righteousness and ritual propriety, such as filiality, are taught at schools. Accomplishing this goal of teaching righteousness and filiality in the schools would result in a state in which old people wear clothes made of silk and eat meat, and the younger people are fed and sheltered. Under such circumstances, Mencius says that the person who accomplished this goal is sure to become a king (1A 7.24).

The differences between Mencius and Confucius, about offering an account of human nature, the degree to which a community is required for cultivation, and where the cultivation of filiality is to occur notwithstanding, they are agreed that the highest virtue of humaneness is the *dao* of *tian*. And when one exercises this virtue, which presupposes the other virtues, one's effects on others is *tian*-like. More elaborately, Mencius, like Confucius, asserts that the *dao* is near: "The Way lies in what is near, but people seek it in what is distant; one's task lies in what is easy, but people seek it in what is difficult. If everyone treat their parents and their elders as elders, the world would be at peace" (4A 11.1). We have seen that Mencius's account seems to offer a better justification for the nearness of the *dao* given that the virtues to be perfected are innate in human beings. One could imagine that knowing that we are to treat parents and elders as elders might be problematic for Confucius if we do not live in a well-governed state, or in functional families. Though problematic too for ordinary people in Mencius's account, his discussion of sagehood allows a path to this ideal of filiality since the sage never loses his Heaven-endowed heart. Maintaining that filiality and righteousness are to be taught in schools also enables Mencius to overcome the challenge of dysfunctional families.

More helpful than Mencius's account of the four sprouts of human nature for understanding Heaven's *dao* and our relation to it is his discussion of Heaven's way as sincerity (*cheng* 誠, genuineness) (4A 12.1). For instance, while explaining how someone in a subordinate position could gain his superior's confidence, that will in turn enable him to order the people, Mencius asserts that he needs to gain the trust of his friends. To gain the trust of one's friends, one would in turn need to serve one's parents in a way that will make them happy. To make one's parents' happy, Mencius maintains that one should, upon self-examination, find oneself to be sincere. Finally, sincerity is achieved by being enlightened about the good (*shan* 善). Accordingly, Mencius says, "Sincerity is Heaven's way. Reflecting upon sincerity is the human way. There has never been a case of one reaching the ultimate of sincerity yet not inspiring others. There has never been a case of one not being sincere yet being able to inspire others"

(4A 12.2–12.3). Examining the radicals that make up the character of sincerity, *cheng* 誠, would clarify the significance of this term. The left radical is *yan* 言, meaning speech; the right is *cheng* 成, meaning complete. Someone who is sincere then, is one who says something and brings to completion what one has said. This analysis also makes clear why sincerity is Heaven's way and being enlightened about the good is key to being sincere. Even though *tian* does not speak, the culture (which includes language) is decreed and preserved by *tian*. Since *tian* is the source of goodness in everything, creating a norm with everything it produces (6A 6.8), which norm of human beings is virtue, it follows that human behavior is most *tian*-like when we know what is good and enact the good. This means that we are to act in such a way that we only say things that we can bring to completion, just as *tian* produces everything and mandates each thing's norm. That neither speech nor action is arbitrary, but each is guided by the good that unites everyone (because the virtues are innate in every human being), offers the identity between Heaven and human beings for Mencius. Because one cannot be sincere without being enlightened about the good, what is called for in Confucianism is an identity with everything else in the cosmos, since that too is the realm of goodness created by *tian*.[39]

In conclusion, whether what we are seeking in a spiritual or religious life is an absolute, or self-transformation in a way that identifies the human and the absolute, it seems that Confucianism, which at first blush seems to be no more than a secular moral philosophy, can offer resources for such a life. Beginning with Confucius's discourse on *tian* that is so absolute that it cannot be swayed by human sacrifices or spiritual intervention, Mencius's contribution is to reconcile this transcendent *tian* with the immanent realm by offering an account of human nature that is innately good. The goodness of sincerity, as both Heaven's way and the human way, ultimately enables human beings to identify not only with Heaven but also with its cosmic creations. Identifying with Heaven and all of its creations enables a human being to harmonize with everything and lead a life that is both spiritual and flourishing.

[39] As Tu Weiming puts it, "Confucian humanism, unlike secular humanism in the modern West, is a comprehensive and integrated vision of the human condition. It seeks to integrate four dimensions of the human experience: self, community, nature, and Heaven. . . . A human being so conceived is an observer, appreciator, partner, and co-creator of the evolutionary, indeed the cosmic, process. Human responsibility must be expanded from the self, family, community, nation, world, nature, and ultimately to the 'great transformation' of the cosmos" ("Confucian Spirituality in Contemporary China," 89).

CHAPTER 12

Agnostic Spirituality

John Houston

A Reply on Behalf of the Agnostic

The Benedictine monk and contemporary interlocutor of Anselm, who we know as Gaunilo, is famous for having penned his "Reply on Behalf of the Fool." In that essay, Gaunilo took great pains to show that perhaps Anselm was mistaken to claim that only an empty-headed fool could say of God that He does not exist. Whether Gaunilo's reply on behalf of the fool was successful is irrelevant to the purposes of this essay. What is relevant is that he spoke on behalf of one who might find himself ostracized by the faith community. Similarly, in this essay, I wish to write on behalf of one who might find himself alienated in certain respects from the faith community. I am referring to the agnostic. The agnostic is one whose epistemic attitudes toward God's existence fail to rise to belief, or confident intellectual assent. Such a person might find it hard to find a home spiritually in the world, let alone in the Church, as the Church frequently makes belief the first of its necessary conditions for full communion or fellowship of its members. In the course of this essay, I draw upon the scriptures, Socrates, and William James to identify the plight of the agnostic and the live options he or she might face when grappling with "belief" in God. My focus will be on the Christian community because it identifies itself as a creedal community – such that full membership entails being able to affirm not only that God exists, but several aspects of how God exists and who God is. But what I have to say might extend relevantly to other areas of monotheism about which I know less. I leave that for the reader to decide.

Let us begin our journey with a famous recent Christian. The twentieth-century Oxford don C. S. Lewis famously described himself at the point of his conversion to Christianity as "the most dejected and reluctant convert in all England," as a prodigal "brought in kicking, struggling, resentful, and darting his eyes in every direction for a chance of escape."[1] In other words, he was eventually overwhelmed, and even compelled, by the conviction

[1] C. S. Lewis, *Surprised by Joy: The Shape of My Early Life* (Orlando, FL: Harcourt, 1955), 229.

that theism, and Christianity in particular, is true. His was a journey from unbelief to belief, from skepticism about God to the conviction that God exists and is a particular sort of being. As a result of this conversion, he was able to embrace a life of faith and deep spiritual significance to himself, and to embrace the spiritual practices of a rich tradition from which he never departed. Unfortunately, it rarely occurs to many believers that the road Lewis traveled is a two-way street: many people are, through no fault of their own, dragged kicking and screaming away from the life of belief and faith that they loved and cherished, and that permeated every part of their understanding of reality. Very little attention is paid to this phenomenon by believers, and almost no attention is paid to the moral, psychological, and spiritual implications it has in the lives of those who experience it. Insofar as such people's experiences are discussed or acknowledged by the faithful, they are often acknowledged with pity. Or worse, those who have lost the power to believe are met with ostracism by those who have never endured the vertigo and nausea of this experience. Insofar as it is acknowledged by unbelievers, it is often met with a smug "congratulations" for one's being purged of a pernicious fantasy.

Both believers and unbelievers take for granted that the loss of belief must entail the loss of any form of faith. For some people, the loss of belief (and therefore faith) is a liberating experience. For others, it is nothing short of crushing. But for almost all, it is, at least for some period of time, deeply disorienting. There are many reasons for this, but perhaps one of the most significant concerns the fact that losing one's belief, and consequently one's faith in God, almost invariably entails the loss of one's practical life-orientation – hence the experience of vertigo. This is unsurprising, since for many believers, their belief in God and subsequent faith practices lie at the very center of the way in which they value and relate to the world. Indeed, for devout believers, belief in God is the alpha and omega of their inspiration for living and acting in the world, and in some cases, for even living at all. For the earnest and sincere believer, belief in God's existence is the background against which he or she conceives and interprets the ethical and metaphysical dimensions of everyday life: belief in God is not some ornamental finishing touch on a painting; it is the canvas on which the painting is done, the very thing that provides the conditions of possibility for rendering reality meaningful and intelligible. Consequently, it is no surprise that for devout believers, the loss of belief in God means the upheaval of the very center and foundation of their values, sometimes bringing them to ask whether life is worth living at all. But here a question is in order: Must finding oneself with the inability to believe God exists necessarily entail the loss of faith and the faith practices that define the believer's life? I will argue that the answer to this question is no.

My focus concerns a fairly specific sort of person, viz., the person who actually cares about the question from an existential (as opposed to a merely academic) perspective. This is not, so far as I can see, a rare or idiosyncratic person. But it is a person whose personal challenges are rarely discussed in public contexts of believers, except maybe insofar as believers distance themselves from such persons, or unbelievers regard them as persons who kindle the fires of childish fantasies. I am speaking of persons who, for whatever reason and through no fault of their own, have either lost or never quite had the confidence required to affirm the central articles of the faith of their fathers, the first of which is belief that God exists.[2] Notice that I'm referring not to the avowed atheist, but to the agnostic. And this agnostic is of a particular stripe. She is one for whom the question of God's existence is open-ended, and for whom there might persist the desire or will to believe or to engage and live out the practical life-orientation of faith, but who nonetheless finds herself incapable of acquiring the epistemic attitude of belief.

The agnostic on whose behalf I write is one who sees the beauty of faith, hope, and love, but who, in spite of herself, lacks the epistemic confidence of both the ardent believer and the ardent unbeliever. She stands in the gap of the middle ground with a disposition of open agnosticism. Whether she has striven for belief in God and failed, or has possessed belief and lost it is not important. The important point is that this person's agnosticism is not the result of complacency or indifference, but the inability to affirm or deny with certitude the foundational articles of traditional orthodox faith. As far as the creeds are concerned, this person's credo ends where that of the faithful begins. Yet this person might still feel a genuine longing for a substantive spirituality that captures the better and more humane aspects of authentic Christianity, and therefore remains open to the possibility of the transcendent, despite the fact that daily life must be lived here and now in the realm of the imminent.

The term "agnostic" derives from the combination of the Greek "ginosko" (I know) with the privative prefix "a." Thus, the agnostic is one who "does not know." The epistemic state of the agnostic is one of acknowledged ignorance regarding divine things. The Latinized equivalent

[2] Both the Apostle's Creed and the Nicene Creed open with affirming in the first person ("Credo") the belief in God the Father Almighty. This is an affirmation that God exists, and it is a mark of belonging to the faith community that one affirms it.

of the term might be found in our less than flattering English word, "ignoramus." So be it. But avowed ignorance is not in itself enough to recognize the kind of agnostic on whose behalf I am writing. Concern for matters of faith is requisite as well.

Socratic Agnosticism in a Poker-Faced Universe

All agnostics are skeptics of some order. Socrates was famous for his skepticism, but he is more properly identified as an open agnostic. Unlike many of his skeptical interlocutors, Socrates was not hostile to philosophical inquiry, nor eager to throw in the towel when he found answers to difficult questions elusive. Though he maintains he has no knowledge of ultimate reality, he never ceases to insist that the pursuit of truth is not a fool's errand. Unlike the skepticism of his Sophistic counterparts, Socrates' agnosticism patiently persists in the midst of doubt and uncertainty. For Socrates, the telos of philosophical inquiry is truth; for the Sophists, it is confusion or mere persuasion of another for some immediate purpose of gain. For Socrates, doubt was energizing and invigorating. It inspired him to press forward in the pursuit of truth. But for many of his skeptical interlocutors, doubt was enervating, leading them to conclude that either there was no hope of attaining truth, or worse, there was no truth to be attained. The agnostics on behalf of whom I write are those who live in the Socratic spirit. Though puzzled, they press forward amidst the dogmatists on either side who surround them, seeking a certainty that eludes them without losing heart or hope that their pressing forward is worthwhile.

The agnostic is readily distinguished from the theist, who holds with some considerable level of confidence the positive belief that God exists, as well as the atheist, who maintains with some considerable level of confidence the antithesis of that thesis. This distinction is important not only epistemically, but also dispositionally. For the confident theist and the atheist alike, the matter is settled. They have answered the question of God for themselves and are free to organize their life's practical orientation around the verdicts they have issued. Unlike the agnostic, the theist and the atheist are free to engage in divisive apologetics. The theist can do so by defending the transcendent framework that he or she already confidently affirms; the atheist can do so by defending the "good news" that all questions of a spiritual nature derive from delusion, psychological immaturity, superstition, or some form of pernicious fantasy. The agnostic finds herself at home with the confidence of neither. She remains genuinely (and often painfully) open to the possibility of God, but unable to render a confident verdict in either direction.

Unlike the confident atheist, the agnostic is free to remain open to the possibility of there being a transcendent Good behind the veil of reality, but (and this is important) he or she does not orient the whole of his or her life according to a fideism that insists it be so. As such, he or she feels the pull toward the need of constructing an imminent framework within which to edify his or her spiritual longings, all the while leaving open the possibility that a transcendent Good exists behind the veil of reality. Though this imminent framework need not shut out the possibility of the transcendent or God's actually existing, it does not require that the question of God's existence be settled in order to find meaningful expression.

The Socratic sort of agnostic with whom I am concerned does not find himself agnostic due to complacency or indifference toward sacred or divine matters. Indeed, nothing I have to say in this essay will give comfort to the spiritually complacent. There are many reasons that believers lose faith or unbelievers fail to attain faith. And contrary to many believers, not all of those reasons are due to having lost heart or hope, let alone having "hardened" one's heart. Sometimes they are due to one's genuinely not being confident enough to render a verdict on the matter. The problem of divine silence and hiddenness leaves many people in just this sort of position.

Some believers suggest that if we only seek the Lord sincerely enough, open our hearts, and attend to the evidence, it will become indubitably obvious (or at least obvious beyond all reasonable doubt) that God exists. Evangelical Christians frequently proof-text Jeremiah 29:13 as evidence for this point: "You will seek me and find me when you seek me with all your heart."[3] If this text is time indexed to the moment of seeking, it is demonstrably false. God does not always show up and reveal Himself in undeniably recognizable ways when sought with the most sincere attitude and maximal effort. The number of suicides that have occurred in the midst of final fervent prayers that God intervene and reveal Himself is evidence enough for this claim.

Just as there are believers who abuse those who seek and find not, so also there are unbelievers who abuse those who claim to have sought and found God. These unbelievers argue that if we would but put away our fantasies and attend to the evidence before us, we would see that there is no

[3] The Holy Bible, New International Version.

reasonable room for belief in God. I believe that both the believer and the unbeliever, when they operate in this fashion, are mistaken. And this is a point with deep ramifications.

Cardinal Newman famously denied that there is any certain proof for the existence of God. He was intellectually honest enough to admit that there is nothing rationally inconsistent about atheism, and that its explanatory power rivals theism in many respects. He was at times given to expressing his own struggles with doubt:

> REV. J. H. NEWMAN TO MISS H.
>
> *Oriel College*: 1840.
>
> Be assured that I have my doubts and difficulties as other people. Perhaps the more we examine and investigate, the more we have to perplex us. It is the lot of man: the human mind in its present state is unequal to its own powers of apprehension; it embraces more than it can master. I think we ought all to set out on our inquiries, I am sure we shall end them, with this conviction. Absolute certainty, then, cannot be attained here; we must resign ourselves to doubt as the *trial under* which it is God's will we should do our duty and prepare ourselves for His presence. Our sole question must be, *what* does a merciful God, who knows whereof we are made, wish *us to do under* our existing ignorance and doubt?[4]

Despite his ignorance and doubts, Newman remained a man of faith. But his was not a faith that (as C. S. Lewis seems to suggest of his own) was the result of coercive evidence (whether internal or external) for theism. One reason for Newman's continually held faith seems to be located in where his nonnegotiable affections were invested and what he found to be the most meaningful and beautiful way to understand the world, and more importantly, himself in the world. I think it is true that there is some volitional element in faith. Choice becomes involved at some point. I address this point in more detail when I later distinguish belief from faith. For now, I simply acknowledge the intellectual honesty of Newman when it comes to the real problem of divine hiddenness. His attitude toward the question of God's existence leaves room in the fold for the doubting Thomas, the disciple who finds himself with the quandary of the inability to believe, yet finds his breast bursting with hope that God does indeed exist and is the savior of not only himself but of mankind.

Whether we like it or not, and whether we acknowledge it or not, the universe is, as John Cottingham has recently observed, "poker-faced."[5] Try

[4] See: http://newmanreader.org/biography/mozley/volume2/file11.html.

[5] J. Cottingham, "Confronting the Cosmos: Scientific Rationality and Human Understanding," *Proceedings of the American Catholic Philosophical Association*, 85 (2011), 29.

as we might to peer over the wall into eternity, we cannot. So we are left to deal with what we have as best we can, and to try to make sense of our lives and our world while wandering (at least to some extent) in darkness. This means, among other things, that we have to figure out what role if any faith might have in our lives in the absence of belief.

The overall evidence for or against God is coercive in neither direction. Despite many elegant and powerful arguments in both directions, the evidence that lies before us doesn't yield anything that rises to the order of "proof" that God does or does not exist. Newman acknowledged this; so should we. When people claim they've "proven" God exists or that God does not exist, I usually tend to grab my wallet and start slowly backing for the door. I do think that, due to their life history and psychological makeup, it is impossible for some people not to believe in God. Yet I also acknowledge the converse, viz., that there are some people for whom – given their life history and the suffering they have endured – it is equally psychologically impossible to believe in God. Notice that this is not a consequence of the "overall available evidence" calmly evaluated from a distance, but a result of an individual's cumulative painful personal experiences in the absence of a recognizable loving God. Such is the consequence of severe suffering in many people's lives, and we do violence to our humanity and that of others if we refuse to acknowledge this.

Some less reflective laity suggest that God demands of each of us that we "believe," and that absent such belief He abandons us to the flames. I say such people cannot truly say of God that He is good. And if they attempt to do so, then either whatever they mean by "good" is not what I mean by "good," or whatever they mean by "God" is not what I mean by "God," *by God!* Infinite punishment of a finite creature for such an epistemic offense in a poker-faced universe is malicious and perverse. As for those who believe that God operates in this manner, I suppose, as George MacDonald might say, their punishment for believing it lies in the fact that they are able to believe it. There are agnostics who want to believe, but for whom an active hope is all that is possible. But active hope is no small thing. And while one can certainly remain within her intellectual, epistemic, and rational rights to maintain that hope, this hope is not merely the result of one's rational resources evaluating evidence and formulating syllogisms. It's deeper than that. Much deeper.

As for whether a person will be inclined to desire the life of faith, much hangs on whether that person experiences the world as personal, or as a hostile, alien, and indifferent place. While one might believe that the mechanisms and laws according to which our world moves forward are indifferent to our temporary well-being, there is no logical entailment from that honest observation to the claim that ultimate reality is ultimately impersonal. That claim is simply beyond our ken. Nietzsche seems to regard ultimate reality as an impersonal abyss, whereas Walt Whitman declares that whatever will be will be well. What say you? Here we are left with a pragmatic question: Given that I don't *know* the world to be way X, how can I best make sense of the world and my place in it? This question doesn't merely consult the available evidence; it also requires an "internal turn." One must venture into the interior castle of one's soul and see what one finds. Sometimes this internal turn requires no small amount of doing battle with oneself. But what must finally be searched out and dealt with is this question: Do I really believe that I could ever be totally and absolutely alone? The atheist answers this in the affirmative. That is something that some agnostics cannot do. Though I won't be so bold as to declare him an agnostic, I believe that Cardinal Newman was a man of this sort: "Whether I rise on the wings of the dawn, or settle on the far side of the sea, still He is there" (Psalm 139:9–10).[6] Unlike dyed-in-the-wool believers, the agnostic does not find himself firmly seated in the place of confident belief that God exists. He or she might experience murmurs, whispers, and seemings, but nothing that enables the tall epistemic order of belief, as some hopeful agnostics' attempts at belief are vulnerable and sometimes crushed by the facts of suffering and divine hiddenness in the world. Yet despite all of this, I will argue that an open agnostic can cultivate a disposition that results in a practical life-orientation that affirms faith. To explain this point, I will turn to William James. But first I offer a meditation on a classic example of faith without belief in the scriptures.

The Faith and Hope of Saint Peter, Sans Belief

Before he was a saint, Peter was just a common fisherman of Galilee who had befriended an odd man whose identity he knew not.[7] Peer in with me on a story of one of the more peculiar nights of Peter's career as a fisherman:

> But the ship was now in the midst of the sea, tossed with waves: for the wind was contrary. And in the fourth watch of the night Jesus went unto them, walking on the sea. And when the disciples saw him walking on the sea, they were troubled, saying, It is a spirit; and they cried out for fear. But straightway Jesus spake unto them, saying, Be of good cheer; it is I; be not afraid. And Peter

[6] The Holy Bible, New International Version, paraphrased.

[7] My reflections here are on Matthew 14. Yet it was not until Matthew 16 that Peter properly identified who Jesus was, viz. the Christ, the Son of the living God.

> answered him and said, Lord, if it be thou, bid me come unto thee on the water. And he said, Come. And when Peter was come down out of the ship, he walked on the water, to go to Jesus. But when he saw the wind boisterous, he was afraid; and beginning to sink, he cried, saying, Lord, save me. And immediately Jesus stretched forth his hand, and caught him, and said unto him, O thou of little faith, wherefore didst thou doubt?[8]

If we wish to understand the life of faith, we must come to terms with this story. Its historical veracity is irrelevant, as is its departure from Mark and Luke's account. What is relevant is that it presents us with an act of faith and a loss of faith. Philosophers interested in faith should therefore reflect deeply on Matthew's account of Peter walking on the water, trying as carefully as possible to identify the conditions of Peter's faith and its loss.

My own conviction is that we cannot understand this story properly without understanding who Peter is and what the sea represents. Peter is a person of faith. But his faith did not consist in his doxastic assent to a system of theology; nor is there any evidence that Jesus had the slightest interest in giving him such a thing. On the contrary, Peter's faith consisted in his fidelity to the cause of Jesus – the coming of the kingdom of God, the triumph of justice over wickedness, and the defeat of the powers of darkness. If we are to locate Peter's faith in this story, therefore, we must identify how Peter was faithful to the cause of the kingdom amidst the boisterous waves.

No less important than understanding Peter is understanding the imagery of the sea. In the world of the Bible, the sea often represents chaos and the powers of darkness: it is the sea that rises and drowns the world in the deluge of the Noahic flood; it is the sea that prevents Moses from leading the Israelites to the promised land and that must be parted for their benefit before swallowing the chariots of Pharaoh's army; it is the sea from which the demonic monsters in the books of Daniel and Revelation arise; it is the sea to which Jonah runs when defying the will of God; and it is the sea that, according to Revelation, will be abolished when the kingdom arrives.

What we are to understand, then, is that Peter and the disciples find themselves overwhelmed and helpless amidst the forces of darkness that oppose the kingdom of God. In the midst of their despair, they see a ghostly figure and cry out in terror. The figure is Jesus, who represents the coming of the kingdom of God in the midst of the world's darkness. Of course, Peter does not know that the figure is Jesus; it is hard to see why Peter would even *believe* it was Jesus. Everything Peter does indicates that

[8] Matthew 14:24–31, The Holy Bible, King James Version.

he cannot tell if the figure is Jesus. He tells the figure, "If you are Jesus, command me to walk on the water." But the issuing of the command does nothing to prove it is Jesus; a ghost could just as easily have issued the command. Peter does not know it is Jesus, but steps out anyway. Why? Because Peter is surrounded by the forces of darkness, and the figure is the only thing in Peter's world that *has a chance* of defeating them. To understand Peter, we needn't think of him as believing that the figure is Jesus; it is far from clear that he did. Instead, we need only think of Peter as believing that *there is a chance* that the figure is Jesus. In his loyalty to the desire to see the kingdom of God realized, Peter risks his life and walks toward the only thing that has a chance of ushering in that kingdom. Peter acts in faith, that is, in *faithfulness* to the kingdom agenda. But Peter despairs; he is overwhelmed by the forces of darkness and begins to sink. We are to understand that his sinking is *his own fault.* How could it be his fault that he is overcome by the forces of darkness? Peter's failure was that he gave up hope – he lost his courageous hope in the kingdom agenda, and began to sink. Peter lost his faith.

So what are we philosophers to think of Peter's faith? In what did it consist? It seems clear that Peter is acting in faith when he steps out; but it is equally clear that his faith did not consist in belief. He did not believe the figure was Jesus; his act would have been less impressive if he had. But he did believe there was a chance it was Jesus, and out of loyalty to the kingdom agenda, Peter walked toward the only thing that had a chance of defeating the powers of darkness. Peter's faith in the ghostly figure, then, did not require him to believe of the figure that it is Jesus. It required only that he believed there is a chance that it is Jesus, that he *hoped* that it is Jesus, and that out of loyalty to see the kingdom of God realized, he risked his life by *acting on the assumption* that the figure is Jesus. But Peter despaired and lost his hope, and thereby lost his faith.[9]

So what would it be to have faith – Peter's faith – that God exists amidst the horrors of this world? Such faith does not require one to believe that God exists; it doesn't even require one to believe it is likely that God exists. It requires only that one think there is a chance that God exists, that one hope that God exists, and that one live on the assumption that God exists. All of these conditions are consistent with what I described previously as the disposition of the open agnostic, the person whose faith is a form of

[9] See Joshua Golding's "Toward a Pragmatic Conception of Religious Faith," *Faith and Philosophy*, 7 (1990), 486–503, for a defense of faith as a form of pragmatic commitment that does not require belief.

trust amidst doubt. One loses such a faith by losing *hope*. For Peter, faith is intimately connected with hope and impossible to achieve without it. Like Peter, one loses faith in God by despairing amidst the wickedness of the world, losing hope that God exists, relinquishing the commitment to live as if God exists, and sinking into the waves. The enemy of true faith is not the belief that God's existence is unlikely; rather, it is the loss of hope. Thus this story illustrates hope and faith are intimately linked.

William James: Faith without Belief

I now turn to William James for another substantive distinction between faith and belief. In his well-known essay "The Will to Believe," William James defends the right to believe things that the evidence does not demonstrate are true. But it is not at all clear that belief is the epistemic attitude James should have been discussing. Belief – unlike acceptance or perhaps even faith – is not a directly volitional epistemic attitude. Thus, the notion that one can simply "decide" what to believe seems confused. I can no more decide to believe that I am not sitting here writing this sentence than I can decide to believe I am a turnip. Much of what James says is more plausible under the aspect of faith.

Whatever else faith is, it seems at least to require three things: (1) you cannot be certain of the truth of the object of your faith; (2) you must be inclined to see what you have faith in as good and important, something that, if it were to fail to be true, would be regrettable; and (3) you must be willing to act as though the object of your faith is secure or true, at least with respect to some range of actions.[10] Perhaps a mundane example will illuminate this. Suppose that my favorite basketball team is currently 25–0. If I have faith that my team will go 40–0 this year, then I cannot be certain that they will go 40–0; it must matter a great deal to me that they go 40–0; and there must be some action I am willing to perform – one that would constitute a risk on my part – that would count as me acting as though they will go 40–0 (e.g., planning an elaborate celebration party a week in advance). Unlike believing they will go 40–0, whether I have faith that my team will go 40–0 is largely up to me, since it is up to me whether, given my uncertainty and its importance to me, I am willing to perform actions that would count as me living as though they will go 40–0. Notice that

[10] For an account of faith along similar lines, see L. Buchak, "Can It Be Rational to Have Faith?," in J. Chandler and V. S. Harrison (eds.), *Probability in the Philosophy of Religion* (Oxford University Press, 2012), 225–47.

nothing about this requires that I *believe* my team will go 40–0. I might think it no more likely than not that they will go 40–0, but nevertheless have faith that they will and manifest this faith by planning an elaborate celebration.

What then would James's views look like if we interpreted them as a defense of faith, as opposed to belief? It would be this:

> James's Faith Principle: You are within your epistemic rights to live in faith that *p* if and only if:
>
> (i) The truth status of *p* cannot be determined on the basis of the evidence.
> (ii) *p* is something that you reasonably judge might be true.
> (iii) Living in faith that *p* provides you with goods of great importance.
> (iv) There is no other way to obtain those goods other than living in faith that *p*.

Construed in terms of faith instead of belief, James's Faith Principle is immune from the evidentialist objection that we ought only to believe in accordance with the evidence, always suspending judgment and maintaining epistemic abstinence when the evidence is not coercive. The reason is obvious: James's Faith Principle is not – at least as I have construed it – about belief, but is instead about faith; and it's far from obvious that faith requires belief. Someone with Jamesian faith might neither believe nor disbelieve that God exists, but still decide that with respect to a range of actions – prayer, practices of charity, and participation in a faith community, perhaps – he is going to live as though God does exist for the sake of the goods such a life extends to him here and now. These goods might include hope for life beyond the grave; a hope that ultimate reality is on the side of the good; knowing that one is living receptively to the divine (if there be such a reality); and closer fellowship with faith communities, etc. This seems a sensible appropriation of James's "The Will to Believe," even if it is not what James himself intended. For this way of construing the essay provides the distinct advantage of surmounting the evidentialist challenge by rendering it irrelevant.

Furthermore, this way of reading James has the advantage of rendering his argument more plausible than it is when applied to belief. Of course, more conditions need to be added to James's Faith Principle – e.g., that living in faith that *p* is consistent with your moral duties – but the salient point is that James's "The Will to Believe" is not only more interesting, but more philosophically sensible if regarded as a defense of faith, as opposed to belief. And insofar as one interprets the essay in this fashion, it opens up possibilities of engaging in faith practices within a faith community while wholly circumventing irrelevant evidentialist objections to doing so.

Conclusion

The open agnostic might experience to the point of nausea and vertigo the unhappy thought that God does not exist and that the universe is ultimately a hostile, indifferent, impersonal place. But what upholds him in the midst of this is not belief in the contrary, but faith. Faith is an attitude of assent and hope related to a practical life-orientation that affirms that for which there is no definitive proof in either direction. It appropriates goods of great importance that cannot be appropriated in any other manner than by stepping out and aligning oneself with the hope that the world is not ultimately impersonal, and that God exists and cares for human beings. It does this not by rising to the level of belief, but through a person's living and acting in the hope that there is more than a nonnegligible chance that this is so. Faith can affirm a hidden God that cannot be reached through belief.

The open agnostic is one who, like Socrates, remains keen in the search for the hidden God in the face of evil in this world. He sees and acknowledges evil and divine hiddenness as heaven remains silent in the face of human anguish. Silent, yes. Indifferent? That he is not ready to believe. And to that charge he responds with the Scottish verdict, "Not proven."[11]

[11] I would like to thank Joshua Watson for discussions that helped to shape my thinking in regard to this essay.

Select Bibliography

Adams, R. M., *Finite and Infinite Goods: A Framework for Ethics* (Oxford University Press, 1999).

Anderson, P. S., "A Turn to Spiritual Virtues in Philosophy of Religion: 'The Thoughtful Love of Life,'" in J. Cornwell and M. McGhee (eds.), *Philosophers and God: At the Frontiers of Faith and Reason* (New York: Continuum, 2009).

Annas, J., "Happiness, Virtue and Religious Commitments," in H. Ramsay (ed.), *Truth and Faith in Ethics* (Charlottesville, VA: Imprint Academic, 2011).

Antonaccio, M., "Spirituality and the 'Humane Turn,'" in D. Jaser, D. Wright, M. Antonaccio, and W. Schweiker (eds.), *Theological Reflection and the Pursuit of Ideals: Theology, Human Flourishing and Freedom* (Burlington, VT: Ashgate, 2013).

Bellah, R. N., *Religion in Human Evolution: From the Paleolithic to the Axial Age* (Cambridge, MA: The Belknap Press of Harvard University Press, 2011).

Bellah, R. N. and H. Joas (eds.), *The Axial Age and Its Consequences* (Cambridge, MA: The Belknap Press of Harvard University Press, 2012).

Benatar, D., "What's God Got to Do with It? Atheism and Religious Practice," *Ratio*, 19 (2006), 383–400.

Berger, P., *The Sacred Canopy: Elements of a Sociological Theory of Religion* (Garden City, NY: Doubleday, 1967).

Carlisle, C., *On Habit* (New York: Routledge, 2014).

Carr, D., "Three Conceptions of Spirituality for Spiritual Education," in D. Carr and J. Haldane (eds.), *Spirituality, Philosophy and Education* (New York: Routledge, 2003).

Carr, D. and J. Haldane (eds.), *Spirituality, Philosophy and Education* (New York: Routledge, 2003).

Chase, M., S. R. L. Clark, and M. McGhee (eds.), *Philosophy as a Way of Life: Ancients and Moderns – Essays in Honor of Pierre Hadot* (Malden, MA: Blackwell Publishing, 2013).

Comte-Sponville, A., *The Little Book of Atheist Spirituality*, trans. N. Huston (New York: Penguin Books, 2006).

Cooper, D. E., *The Measure of Things: Humanism, Humility, and Mystery* (Oxford University Press, 2002).

Cornwell, J. and M. McGhee (eds.), *Philosophers and God: At the Frontiers of Faith and Reason* (New York: Continuum, 2009).

Cottingham, J., *On the Meaning of Life* (New York: Routledge, 2003).
Cottingham, J., "Spirituality, Science and Morality," in D. Carr and J. Haldane (eds.), *Spirituality, Philosophy and Education* (New York: Routledge, 2003).
Cottingham, J., *The Spiritual Dimension: Religion, Philosophy and Human Value* (Cambridge University Press, 2005).
Cottingham, J., "What Difference Does It Make? The Nature and Significance of Theistic Belief," *Ratio*, 19 (2006), 401–20.
Cottingham, J., "Human Nature and the Transcendent," in C. Sandis and M. J. Cain (eds.), *Human Nature*, Royal Institute of Philosophy Supplement 70 (Cambridge University Press, 2012).
Cottingham, J., "Philosophy, Spirituality, and the Good Life: An Interview with John Cottingham" (by D. McPherson), *Philosophy & Theology*, 24 (2012), 85–111.
Cottingham, J., "Spirituality," in C. Taliaferro, V. S. Harrison, and S. Goetz (eds.), *The Routledge Companion to Theism* (New York: Routledge, 2013).
Cottingham, J., *Philosophy of Religion: Towards a More Humane Approach* (Cambridge University Press, 2014).
Cottingham, J., *How to Believe* (London: Bloomsbury, 2015).
Cottingham, J. (ed.), *The Meaning of Theism* (Malden, MA: Blackwell Publishing, 2007).
De Botton, A., *Religion for Atheists: A Non-believer's Guide to the Uses of Religion* (New York: Vintage, 2012).
Dennett, D. C., *Breaking the Spell: Religion as a Natural Phenomenon* (New York: Viking, 2006).
Douglas, M., *Purity and Danger* (New York: Routledge Classics, [1966] 2002).
Dreyfus, H. and S. D. Kelly, *All Things Shining: Reading the Western Classics to Find Meaning in a Secular Age* (New York: Free Press, 2011).
Dunne, J., "After Philosophy and Religion: Spirituality and Its Counterfeits," in D. Carr and J. Haldane (eds.), *Spirituality, Philosophy and Education* (New York: Routledge, 2003).
Durkheim, E., *The Elementary Forms of Religious Life*, trans. C. Cosman (Oxford University Press, [1912] 2001).
Dworkin, R., *Religion without God* (Cambridge, MA: Harvard University Press, 2013).
Eliade, M., *The Sacred and the Profane: The Nature of Religion*, trans. W. R. Trask (New York: Harcourt, 1959).
Ellis, F., *God, Value, and Nature* (Oxford University Press, 2014).
Ferry, L., *Man Made God: The Meaning of Life*, trans. D. Pellauer (University of Chicago Press, 2002.
Flanagan, O., *The Bodhisattva's Brain: Buddhism Naturalized* (Boston: MIT Press, 2011).
Fleischacker, S., *Divine Teaching and the Way of the World: A Defense of Revealed Religion* (Oxford University Press, 2011).
Freud, S., *The Future of an Illusion*, trans. J. Strachey (W. W. Norton & Co., [1927] 1989).

Girard, R., *Violence and the Sacred*, trans. P. Gregory (Baltimore, MD: John Hopkins University Press, 1977).

Goodenough, U. and T. W. Deacon, "The Sacred Emergence of Nature," in P. Clayton (ed.), *The Oxford Handbook of Religion and Science* (Oxford University Press, 2006).

Graham, G., *The Re-enchantment of the World: Art versus Religion* (Oxford University Press, 2007).

Hadot, P., *Philosophy as a Way of Life: Spiritual Exercises from Socrates to Foucault*, ed. A. Davidson, trans. M. Chase (Malden, MA: Blackwell Publishing, 1995).

Haldane, J., "De Consolatione Philosophiae," in M. McGhee (ed.), *Philosophy, Religion, and the Spiritual Life* (Cambridge University Press, 1992).

Haldane, J., "On the Very Idea of Spiritual Values," in D. Carr and J. Haldane (eds.), *Spirituality, Philosophy and Education* (New York: Routledge, 2003).

Haldane, J., "Philosophy, the Restless Heart and the Meaning of Theism," *Ratio*, 19 (2006), 421–40.

Hampson, D., "Searching for God?," in J. Cornwell and M. McGhee (eds.), *Philosophers and God: At the Frontiers of Faith and Reason* (New York: Continuum, 2009).

Harris, S., *Waking Up: A Guide to Spirituality without Religion* (New York: Simon and Schuster, 2014).

Hume, D., *Dialogues Concerning Natural Religion [1779], in Principal Writings of Religion*, ed. J. C. A. Gaskin (Oxford University Press, 1993).

Hume, D., *The Natural History of Religion [1757], in Principal Writings of Religion*, ed. J. C. A. Gaskin (Oxford University Press, 1993).

Ignatius of Loyola, St., *Spiritual Exercises*, trans. J. Munitz and P. Endean (Harmondsworth: Penguin, [ca. 1525] 1996).

Jacobs, J., "Spirituality and Virtue," in D. Carr and J. Haldane (eds.), *Spirituality, Philosophy and Education* (New York: Routledge, 2003).

James, W., *The Will to Believe and Other Essays in Popular Philosophy and Human Immortality* (New York: Dover, [1897] 1956).

James, W., *The Varieties of Religious Experience: A Study in Human Nature* (New York: Barnes & Noble Classics, [1902] 2004).

Joas, H., *Do We Need Religion? On the Experience of Self-Transcendence*, trans. A. Skinner (Boulder, CO: Paradigm Publishers, 2008).

Johnston, M., *Saving God: Religion after Idolatry* (Princeton University Press, 2009).

Jung, C., *Modern Man in Search of a Soul*, trans. C. F. Baynes (New York: Harcourt, 1933).

Kenny, A., *The Unknown God* (New York: Continuum, 2004).

Kenny, A., "Worshipping an Unknown God," *Ratio*, 19 (2006), 441–53.

Kenny, A., "Agnosticism and Atheism," in J. Cornwell and M. McGhee (eds.), *Philosophers and God: At the Frontiers of Faith and Reason* (New York: Continuum, 2009).

Kerr, F., *Immortal Longings: Versions of Transcending Humanity* (University of Notre Dame Press, 2007).

Lash, N., "Thinking, Attending, Praying," in J. Cornwell and M. McGhee (eds.), *Philosophers and God: At the Frontiers of Faith and Reason* (New York: Continuum, 2009).

Maslow, A., *Religions, Values, and Peak-Experiences* (New York: Penguin, 1964).

McGhee, M., "Facing Truths: Ethics and the Spiritual Life," in M. McGhee (ed.), *Philosophy, Religion, and the Spiritual Life* (Cambridge University Press, 1992).

McGhee, M., *Transformations of Mind: Philosophy as Spiritual Practice* (Cambridge University Press, 2000).

McGhee, M., "Making Spirits Attentive: Moral-and-Spiritual Development," in D. Carr and J. Haldane (eds.), *Spirituality, Philosophy and Education* (New York: Routledge, 2003).

McGhee, M., "'Seeke True Religion. Oh, Where?,'" *Ratio*, 19 (2006), 454–73.

McGhee, M., "Humanism and Spirituality: Or How to Be a Good Atheist," in J. Cornwell and M. McGhee (eds.), *Philosophers and God: At the Frontiers of Faith and Reason* (New York: Continuum, 2009).

McGhee, M., "Spirituality for the Godless," *Royal Institute of Philosophy Supplement*, 68 (2011): 227–44.

McGhee, M. (ed.), *Philosophy, Religion, and the Spiritual Life* (Cambridge University Press, 1992).

McPherson, D., "Cosmic Outlooks and Neo-Aristotelian Virtue Ethics," *International Philosophical Quarterly*, 55 (2015), 197–215.

Midgley, M., "Concluding Reflections: Dover Beach Revisited," in P. Clayton (ed.), *The Oxford Handbook of Religion and Science* (Oxford University Press, 2006).

Midgley, M., "Darwinism, Purpose and Meaning," *Royal Institute of Philosophy Supplements*, 68 (2011), 193–201.

Midgley, M., "Why the Idea of Purpose Won't Go Away," *Philosophy*, 86 (2011), 545–61.

Miller, L. J. (ed.), *The Oxford Handbook of Psychology and Spirituality* (Oxford University Press, 2012).

Murdoch, I., *Existentialists and Mystics: Writings on Philosophy and Literature*, ed. Peter Conradi (New York: Penguin Books, 1997).

Murray, M. J. and J. Schloss (eds.), *The Believing Primate: Scientific, Philosophical, and Theological Reflection on the Origin of Religion* (Oxford University Press, 2009).

Nagel, T., *Secular Philosophy and the Religion Temperament: Essays 2002–2008* (Oxford University Press, 2010).

Norman, R., "The Varieties of Non-religious Experience," *Ratio*, 19 (2006), 474–94.

Nussbaum, M. C., "Transcending Humanity," in *Love's Knowledge: Essays on Philosophy and Literature* (Oxford University Press, 1990).

Nussbaum, M. C., "Transcendence and Human Values [a review of Robert Merrihew Adams's *Finite and Infinite Goods*]," *Philosophy and Phenomenological Research*, 64 (2002), 445–52.

Nussbaum, M. C., "Judaism and the Love of Reason," in R. E. Groenhout and M. Bower (eds.), *Philosophy, Feminism, and Faith* (Bloomington: Indiana University Press, 2003).

Otto, R. *The Idea of the Holy*, trans. J. W. Harvey (Oxford University Press, 1923).

Putnam, H., *Jewish Philosophy as a Guide to Life: Rosenzweig, Buber, Levinas, Wittgenstein* (Bloomington: Indiana University Press, 2008).

Rachels, J., "God and Human Attitudes," *Religious Studies*, 7 (1971), 325–37.

Roberts, R. C., *Spiritual Emotions: A Psychology of Christian Virtues* (Grand Rapids, MI: Wm. B. Eerdmans Publishing Co, 2007).

Sacks, J., *The Great Partnership: God, Science and the Search for Meaning* (London: Hodder & Stoughton, 2011).

Sandel, M., "Mastery and Hubris in Judaism: What's Wrong with Playing God?," in *Public Philosophy: Essays on Morality and Politics* (Cambridge, MA: Harvard University Press, 2006).

Schleiermacher, F., *On Religion: Speeches to Its Cultured Despisers*, trans. R. Crouter (Cambridge University Press, [1799] 1988).

Scruton, R., "Piety, Purity and the Sacred," in H. A. Harris (ed.), *God, Goodness and Philosophy* (Burlington, VT: Ashgate, 2011).

Scruton, R., *The Face of God: The Gifford Lectures* (New York: Continuum, 2012).

Scruton, R., *The Soul of the World* (Princeton University Press, 2014).

Smith, C., *Moral, Believing Animals: Human Personhood and Culture* (Oxford University Press, 2003).

Solomon, R. C., *Spirituality for Skeptics: The Thoughtful Love of Life* (Oxford University Press, 2002).

Soskice, J. M., "Love and Attention," in M. McGhee (ed.), *Philosophy, Religion, and the Spiritual Life* (Cambridge University Press, 1992).

Stump, E., *Wandering in the Darkness: Narrative and the Problem of Suffering* (Oxford University Press, 2010).

Taylor, C., *Sources of the Self: The Making of Modern Identity* (Cambridge, MA: Harvard University Press, 1989).

Taylor, C., "A Catholic Modernity?," in *A Catholic Modernity?: Charles Taylor's Marianist Award Lecture*, ed. James L. Heft, S.M. (Oxford University Press, 1999).

Taylor, C., *Varieties of Religion Today: William James Revisited* (Cambridge, MA: Harvard University Press, 2002).

Taylor, C., *A Secular Age* (Cambridge, MA: The Belknap Press of Harvard University Press, 2007).

Taylor, C., "Recovering the Sacred," *Inquiry*, 54 (2011), 113–25.

Taylor, C., "Re-enchanting the World: An Interview with Charles Taylor" (by D. McPherson), *Philosophy & Theology*, 24 (2012), 275–94.

Tillich, P., *Dynamics of Faith* (New York: Harper & Row, 1957).

Turner, V. *The Ritual Process: Structure and Anti-structure* (New Brunswick, NJ: Transaction, 1969).

Weber, M., *The Sociology of Religion*, trans. E. Fischoff (Boston, MA: Beacon Press, [1922] 1964).

White, R., *The Heart of Wisdom: A Philosophy of Spiritual Life* (Lanham, MD: Rowman & Littlefield, 2013).
Wielenberg, E. J., *Value and Virtue in a Godless Universe* (Cambridge University Press, 2005).
Woodruff, P., *Reverence: Renewing a Forgotten Virtue*, 2nd ed. (Oxford University Press, [2001] 2014).
Wynn, M. R., *Emotional Experience and Religious Understanding: Integrating Perception, Conception and Feeling* (Cambridge University Press, 2005).
Wynn, M. R., *Faith and Place: An Essay in Embodied Religious Epistemology* (Oxford University Press, 2009).
Wynn, M. R., *Renewing the Senses: A Study of the Philosophy and Theology of the Spiritual Life* (Oxford University Press, 2013).
Zagzebski, L., *Divine Motivation Theory* (Cambridge University Press, 2004).
Zagzebski, L., *Exemplarist Moral Theory* (Oxford University Press, 2017).

Index

Lightning Source UK Ltd.
Milton Keynes UK
UKHW021833080821
388117UK00016B/166

9 781107 589681